MW01243362

Inside Herman's World

The Kenny Wallace Story

by Kenny Wallace
with Joyce Standridge

COASTAL 181
PUBLISHER

CREDITS

Book Design   *Sandra Rigney Design*
Cover Design   *Joyce Cosentino Wells*
Front Cover Photo   *Joyce Standridge*
Back Cover Photo   *ASP, INC/Walter Arce*

Every reasonable effort was made to locate and credit the original copyright holders and photographers of the photos included in this book. If your photo appears in this book and you are not properly credited, please contact the publisher.

ISBN 10: 0-9789261-2-9

ISBN 13: 978-0-9789261-2-0

For additional information or copies of this book, contact:

Coastal 181
29 Water Street
Newburyport, MA 01950
877-907-8181, 978-462-2436
www.coastal181.com

First printing May 2007

Printed in the United States of America

Contents

Acknowledgements

So, I was riding down a highway in North Carolina and the phone rang. It wasn't my phone or my truck, but the call led directly to this book. I was shotgun for Kenny Schrader, on the way to his television show during the time we worked on his autobiography, *Gotta Race!* The caller was Kenny "Herman" Wallace and he ended up on speaker phone for a group conversation.

Joyce Standridge

When Schrader hung up, I made an off-the-cuff observation that Herm was possibly the only other NASCAR Nextel Cup driver that I really wanted to do a book with.

"Well, it wouldn't be what you'd expect. Everybody thinks they know him from watching him on the TV shows. But what he's never shown is that he's been shit on in his life," Schrader said to my surprise. "People in racing he thought he could trust have hurt him. He's got up in the morning and found himself unemployed when he didn't expect it. But he's always bounced back and he's never given up."

And there's your book in a paragraph. Kenny Schrader is one of Kenny Wallace's closest friends—they even call each other "brother"—so he knows what he is talking about.

Somehow, even though we're all St. Louis-region people, I didn't know Herman except in passing, in spite of knowing the Wallaces forever. My husband took delivery of the very first Poor Boy Chassis built by Rusty Wallace, way-way back in the 1970s. We've been ships in the night ever since. Rick also raced with other brother Mike for many years at most of the Missouri-Illinois short tracks, but somehow, even though Herman is the friendliest, most outgoing guy to come out of our area, we just never hung out.

So, unlike the Schrader book, which was completed with a wonderful, long-time friend, I went into this project with a relative stranger. And while I—like everybody who sees Herman on television—thought I knew him, that Schrader observation piqued my interest and was in the back of my mind.

As a result, I shouldn't have been surprised by Kenny's life story. I gotta tell you, though, it was so cool—every single conversation we had, he stunned me. In 30 years of interviewing people, I've never encountered anyone so open and honest. "Let the chips fall where they may," he said.

Wading through the chips, we clicked. It's as simple as that. The comfort level from the very first conversation was exceptional and I totally "got" Herman, got why Kenny Schrader views him as a brother. And I wasn't alone.

A book is a major project that takes huge chunks of time over an extended period, and in my case involves about a half dozen people who are transcribing tapes and reading the first draft as we go along. All these individuals became very fond of Herman as the book progressed (so, he now has a bunch of would-be sisters), and, as a wonderful and unexpected bonus, all came to admire and love his wife Kim, too. Auto racing has probably never had a more inspiring story of two high-school sweethearts who remain devoted to each other through a long, good marriage.

And now I need to acknowledge those people who worked behind the scenes to make this book happen.

As with every project I've ever been involved in, my husband Rick has been my anchor and guide. When Herm told me what racing means to him, I could understand why he would choose the uncertainty of a race car ride over a large, six-figure television contract because I've lived for 34 years with a man who would do exactly the same thing. And, at the end of the day when I shut down the computer, everything in life looks better when you love and can share with someone you trust completely, as I do Rick.

My sister Kathy and daughter-in-law Dawn spent countless hours transcribing tapes for me. Herm and I like to talk (that's an understatement), so it really was a lot to wade through, especially since the St. Louis Cardinals play-offs and World Series wins came during this period, and we both are life-long fans. Beyond the endless chatter, Herm really affected them. One night, Dawn called and said, "I've got tears running down my face. Didn't you just want to reach through the phone and hug him? Tell him everything's going to be okay?"

Yes, I did.

I also wanted to hug all the good folks at Coastal 181 for their continued support and encouragement throughout this project, especially Lew Boyd, MaryRose Moskell and Jim Rigney. Our conversations and e-mails meant more than I can express, especially when I fussed about getting Herm's story right. Sandra Rigney's book design was right on, and Joyce Wells got another cover exactly perfect. And Mud Slide Slim—like Herman—reminded me that life doesn't always turn out exactly the way we dreamed, but it's what we've got and it's up to us how we interpret it. But most of all, I don't know how we would have succeeded in pulling this all together without the oversight of our production manager Cary Stratton, who brought her heart as much as her mind to the project.

As always, thanks to Mom, Kathy, Chris, Alicia, Richie, Dawn, Kyle,

Bryan, Shelbi, Shawna and Cully the Wonder Dog for distracting me at those key times when I needed a break. To other family and friends, I want you to know that my life would be terrific without the books because you make it so, but thanks for the encouragement along the way.

Special thanks to Kenny Schrader, Mark Martin and Dale Earnhardt Jr. for taking time out of very hectic schedules to add their thoughts. Most people who meet Herman end up liking him, but your insights added significantly to making this life story special.

I can't begin to calculate what a difference the photos meant in pulling the whole story together, so many thanks to Judy Wallace, Kenny's mom, for spending so many hours going through her collection and supplying us with some unique and meaningful shots. While I hesitate to single out anyone, it would be remiss if I didn't note the considerable effort of Jim Compton, another St. Louisan who has been taking pictures of the Wallace family for many years. When we asked for something specific as we went along, Jim went through thousands of images to try to find just what we needed. Others who went the extra mile included LaDon George, Phil Cavali, the good guys at *Speedway Illustrated,* Bruce Bennett, Steve Rose, Don Thies and Bob Fairman, among others. In fact, to all the photographers who allowed us to use their work, a great big thank-you from all of us working on this book.

It's impossible to document what Kim Wallace meant to the book's progress as she spent many hours tracking down and securing photos for us. This was in addition to reading and correcting text. Beyond that, it's just fun to spend time talking with Kim. Everybody knows how social Herman is, but while his lovely lady is happier in the background, she is no less enjoyable. I also came to appreciate what she means to his life. After so many years of being dragged down the road chasing NASCAR, Kim has allowed herself to be pulled into the world of short-track dirt racing with astonishing good grace. Herman says it's because she loves meeting people and talking with fans, but I think it's because she loves him to distraction.

Thank you, Kim. I hope you feel the hours Herman and I spent talking and working on this book—which came out of your time with him rather than racing's—were worth it.

And, Herm—what can I say? I found out why our mutual pal, Mr. Schrader, has become so fond of you. I've met a lot of good people in racing, but few such good souls. You wouldn't brag on yourself as we worked on the book, but there are a few things I want the readers to know that you are too modest to say:

That when you talk about your love for your wife and daughters, it's not because some public relations person told you to say these words.

That even though your birth family is not the Waltons—y'all are far more interesting, as far as I'm concerned—your love for your parents and brothers is the real deal.

That you are as committed to working for charity as you are for keeping car owners happy.

That Kim is right—you don't know how to say "no" to friends and family.

That you go the extra mile when you know that there is some way you can make a fan's life a little more special.

That you have impacted all who worked on this project—we are better people for having come to know you.

We talked at times about how life can be strange, and how the best-laid plans don't always work out. So, I'd like to conclude by telling you that the life you've led is not just a matter of happenstance but one that probably ends up being more moving and motivating than if you'd just run off a string of race wins. While many race fans are interested in the big winners, some of those guys become insulated and so single-minded that their entire lives become almost solely about the racing. They also become afraid to share intimate details because they feel they've become public property. By living the life you have, you are accessible and readers are going to identify with your experiences because, really, most of us are far more familiar with disappointment, struggle and striving for the brass ring than actually grabbing it.

Thanks for the laughter, the tears, and the honesty. I've never had more fun "working" on a project.

JOYCE STANDRIDGE

Foreword
Dale Earnhardt Jr.

I MET KENNY WALLACE through my dad's and Rusty's friendship. We became instant friends because we both seemed to be in the same place at the time. Kenny, as I did, felt the need to prove himself. That was a daily chore with my father and me, and Kenny was no different with his brother, Rusty. Kenny often saw the frustration I had with my father, involving racing and other things. It was Kenny who could easily explain the situation to me. We might not have found a solution, but he understood.

Dale Earnardt Jr.

Kenny spoke my language. I ask him for advice quite often, not because he is all-knowing or any crap like that. He just shoots straight. When you talk to Kenny, he is thinking, listening, and sincere with his response. Even more impressive is having him seek advice from me. That's the most sincere form of respect. I've spent my entire life being told what I want to hear, or told nothing at all. Kenny is the opposite of that. Rare, indeed.

Kenny's path through racing has been full of highs and lows. I remember watching him in the Cox Treated Lumber Pontiac back in his early Busch series days. He ran head-to-head with them all. He built up a good reputation, and I kept thinking he was one to keep an eye on.

His years in the Cup series, as you will read, were not what anyone would have expected. Mediocre equipment and hand-shake deals were often his only choice. There were some high spots, some good runs with good teams. Ultimately though, he will admit he never, or for that matter we never, got to see his real potential.

I could care less about his track record, myself. What he gave this sport isn't measurable with statistics and trophies. This sport can be shallow; it can be deceitful.

Kenny is a silver coin in a pile of coal, with a face full of expressions as easily read as the morning paper. Most notable is his distinct laughter. If Kenny is in the building, you know it.

He has been a great father and husband to his wonderful family. He's a man with his priorities in order. This book is a great account of the person Kenny is, and I'm very proud to be a part of it.

Thanks, Kenny.

Foreword

Mark Martin

Mark Martin

THERE'S NO SHORTAGE of smart, brave people in NASCAR racing, but when I think of people who have extraordinary strength of character there are three who come to mind with no effort: Kyle Petty, who overcame the shattering loss of his son to build a lasting legacy to Adam's memory; Dale Earnhardt Jr., who not only had to deal with the loss of his father in a public way but also has wrestled with unrealistic expectations from too many people; and Kenny Wallace.

You might wonder why I place Kenny in that category, especially since he's had neither the high profile of an Earnhardt or a terrible loss like the Pettys, but there's much that goes on behind the scenes in racing that the general public doesn't see. And in that regard, Kenny's life and career have been challenged like few other people.

In this book, you'll read about the disappointments—and frankly, he's been very kind to others in writing about many of those instances—but when you're done you'll have some sense of what those of us in his life have long considered to be too many heartaches. But Kenny has a real strong sense of himself, and he doesn't let his expectations or his ego get in the way of pursuing his dreams—and maybe more importantly, being happy. He could have let the disappointments in his career really mess up all the good he's experienced, but I think he's the person he is because Kenny's a giver. He's not a huge taker—you just look at how he helped Rusty's career, and all he's given to his fans and the other competitors and you realize that.

I don't even remember first meeting Kenny, but it was when he was crewing for his brother. I was trying to get my racing career going when I met Rusty Wallace, who was doing the same. We were both in our late teens at the time, and we raced at the Springfield, Missouri, state fairgrounds regularly. I was going up there from our garage in Arkansas, with my dad and car builder Larry Shaw, who were helping me, so ours was a stricter, more regimented group compared to Rusty's Evil Gang. Considering that Rusty was the senior guy on the team, it was a wild and crazy, unsupervised outing every weekend for them. It stayed that way, too. Those guys were a very fun-loving bunch, and I envied them in some ways because it was a very different environment from what I was experiencing. I was always with the grown-ups, so it was fun for me to get in that circle from St. Louis and run with them. We were kind of exercising our newborn freedom.

On the track, Rusty and I battled for the same little piece of real estate, because in short-track racing there's room for only one big dog. We fought for that spot, but we never had a problem—neither the drivers, nor the crews.

One thing that always got on my nerves, though, was that Rusty was late every single time he came to Springfield. And I'm very punctual, so eventually I just asked him, "Rusty, why are you always so late getting here?"

"Man, I gotta wait for Herman to get out of school."

That speaks volumes. That just always stuck in my mind of exactly how valuable Rusty's little brother was to his team, because Rusty flirted with missing hot laps and qualifying to wait for Kenny to get out of school.

I didn't even know Kenny was only 14 years old at the time, but it didn't matter anyway. When you're 18 or 20 years old, you're not quite an adult yourself, but Kenny was just one of a bunch of kids. I respected what he could do at the track, but, to be honest, he was just one of the gang after the checkered flag. I never gave a serious thought to him having dreams and aspirations of his own.

And then one day, I turned around and there he was, driving a race car in ASA. He knew all about the cars. He knew how to work on them, he knew how to set them up, he just knew everything except the part behind the wheel. But, that's really only a very small piece of the equation, and since he had mastered all the rest, it didn't come as a surprise when he moved up very quickly to NASCAR.

What happened then is just a matter of circumstance. When Kenny says that he's a racer, he's not exaggerating. He truly is. I think he's done a wonderful job with every situation he's been presented with, and this is what you need to take from his experiences behind the wheel: Winning in NASCAR is not just about the driver. It takes the entire team, and that's not just something we say on-camera. It's totally true.

Take for example, the fact that Kenny has decided to take on dirt-track racing. I'm not surprised at all because it's clear that what he does today in NASCAR is just not enough for a racer like him. Like Ken Schrader or Tony Stewart, Herman has to fill a void that demands he be a complete racer. He's challenging himself and meeting a need at the same time. Winning at Eldora was probably one of the biggest thrills of his life, and it should be. I would assume that it ranks as big as anything he has ever done because it showed what a complete package he is. He had the right opportunity there and he did that mostly by his own hand.

He can't make a Nextel Cup win happen with his own hands. Kenny, like all Cup drivers, is at the mercy of other people for that. On dirt, he has help from others, but he doesn't have to depend on a 30-man team to make him successful. I think the learning and winning have been good for his self-confidence, too.

I also like that he's found his own unique niche in the racing world, and he's at peace with what he's done in his career. Not everybody will recognize what a good driver he really is, but even the winningest drivers run into that, too. Because Kenny loves racing so much, beyond driving cars he's learned how to share that love with other people who feel the same way. Through his television career he's become very popular with NASCAR fans, and I'm happy to see that. He's a natural because he doesn't have to put on an act. That guy you see on the screen isn't self-conscious—that's really Herman, although there's many other facets to his personality, and you'll find out more about that in these pages.

Kenny has had an impact on my life, too. I find it funny that he thinks I helped him years ago put things into perspective because the roles have been reversed in recent times. A couple of years ago on the television show, Kenny called me a pessimist.

It was like a slap on the face.

Coming from somebody else, it might have offended me, but by this time Kenny and I had a good history. And I knew he was just trying to hold up a mirror for me to see how I was perceived by others, rather than as a harsh criticism.

Well, it worked. I'm not a pessimist, but obviously I must have been giving off that impression, and that meant I had some work to do. It changed me—it changed my attitude, because I didn't want to give off that impression to people. I think I've improved how I express things in public, and I believe that has also changed the way a lot of people see me, too, so thank you, Kenny.

People who fall short of their dreams sometimes let that tear them apart. But Kenny Wallace is not one of those people. And that brings me back to my original observation about him: He is one of the strongest people I know.

Yes, some people's words still have the power to hurt him, lack of results at the race track can depress him, and knowing that lots of career wins are probably beyond his reach, could have made him a bitter, reclusive man. Instead, all that's happened to him—the good and the bad—have molded him into a human just about everybody in the NASCAR pit area thoroughly enjoys being around. It's deservedly won him a lot of fans, and a great outlook on life has earned him a private life to envy.

Our friendship has evolved over more than 20 years time. It's hard to remember that at one point I just viewed him as my friend's kid brother instead of a person in his own right, with a lot going on inside that head of his. This much I have also learned about Kenny: If our lives had turned out differently, I don't think our friendship would have. It's not the careers that have brought us closer through the years. If anything, what has happened could have been a wedge. But when we talk, the on-track business doesn't matter. I know that Kenny truly cares about the man inside me, and that feeling will only grow over time. I know that, because I feel the same way about him.

Enjoy his story, and you can count on never looking at him quite the same way again by the time you're finished. It's a journey well-worth taking.

Foreword
Ken Schrader

Ken Schrader

THE RACE DRIVERS AT THE TABLE were Russ Wallace and Bill Schrader— and maybe a few of their pals. It was a common sight on Sunday nights in the late 1960s and early 1970s following the races at Lake Hill Speedway near St. Louis. It was real important to the kids allowed at the table to be taken seriously. Mostly, we nodded our heads and acted like we knew what our dads were talking about, whether we did or not. And occasionally Rusty, Mike or I would get brave and throw in a comment or two of our own—kind of like pulling the pin on a hand grenade and lobbing it—and then hoping that none of the adults would look at us like the dumb kids we were and throw the comment right back. There was just no way we wanted to be viewed as anything but equals to those men we looked up to.

And while this rite of passage was going on, there was this incredibly hyper little guy in our orbit, who couldn't sit still, couldn't be quiet, couldn't leave us more mature types alone. We would offer to give Kenny "Herman" Wallace $2 if he would just shut up for five minutes. And as bad as he wanted the money, he just couldn't do it. On those rare occasions when he actually tried, he couldn't make it two-and-a-half minutes before he would be sound asleep.

Little did any of us dream we were watching the birth of a future television commentator who probably has no peer. As his brothers Rusty and Mike have learned, and as I've found out in doing some ARCA broadcasts and *Inside Nextel Cup* for SPEED, television wants . . . no, demands . . . energy. For all of us and everybody else we know in the industry, it's a conscious effort. For Herman, it's the most natural element of all. If anything, he has to take it down a notch or two.

But, if you've ever seen Herm in action, you probably figured that much out for yourself. What I'm here to do is tell you a little bit that you might not know. Like how he got his "driving" career started.

He will tell you that the first time he was behind the wheel, he sat on my lap at my parents' farm, but I don't think that was actually the first. And in this book, he will tell you about getting behind the wheel of the cars on Bob Mueller's car lot and pretending to race, but I don't think that was the first time either. No, I believe the first time was back when Jerry Sifford—a real good race driver and everybody's pal—borrowed Daddy's school-bus camper to haul a car to Florida. When he got back, for some reason, it was parked at Russ's house for a while. And Kenny, unknown to anybody else—that boy needed a keeper—got behind the wheel and knocked it out of gear. Well, it rolled down the hill and into a tree.

The tree fared better than the bus.

In those years, Rusty and I were close buddies, being just a year apart in age. The younger boys were around a lot, too, at the race track, and we didn't mind. A lot of teenagers wouldn't want the little ones there, but it never bothered us because Mike and Kenny were just as devoted to racing as we were. Mike's not a lot younger, but Kenny is eight years younger than I am—something that is meaningless today, but was pretty significant back then. And yet, he wasn't a bother because he could keep himself busy. At a really young age he was able to focus that incredible energy so it was a real force on the race cars—especially Rusty's, as that career got started. Rusty had the talent and determination that he was going to make it in racing no matter what, but I believe Kenny's efforts helped speed up the process. There's no question that Rusty was a winner early and often in his career because of having a good crew, and Kenny was a very valuable part of that.

And then we all kind of went in different directions for a while. Rusty went asphalt racing and I went dirt. One day, out of the blue I heard that Kenny had won a major street stock race at the Illinois State Fairgrounds. Not too much longer, I heard he was going ASA racing. I thought, hell, I've missed something here.

I promised that I would tell you something you probably don't know about him, and it's this: There's probably nobody in a race car anywhere in the country who's more serious about racing than Kenny Wallace.

That fact gets lost in his out-there personality. Everybody loves him—I mean, that's easy—but an awful lot of people don't bother getting below the surface. He doesn't try to be funny like comedians who sit around thinking up jokes or something. Kenny is just naturally quick, and he picks up on how silly things can be, much faster than most folks—and then, he doesn't censor that sense of fun. So, people—sometimes people he would have liked to have take him serious—don't.

There's been some things happen in his career that were just screwed up. Just when it seemed like he was about to break out and prove to everyone what a genuinely talented driver he is, stuff happened. Every time he's been in something solid, he has done real well, but like most of us in racing, we wind up in a couple of deals that aren't really what you want—but you take the best deal that is available at the time.

When I first went to Charlotte to drive for Elmo Langley in 1984, I would go out to eat with Kenny and his wife Kim, at first because they were the only people I knew in Charlotte. That's when he was a crew chief. But they went back to St. Louis for a few years, and it was really when he returned as a driver that we started hanging out at the track and away from it.

We didn't just decide one day that we were "brothers." I mean, we both have brothers and good relationships with them, so it wasn't like we were starved for more relatives. But my brother is a generation older than I am and lives back in the St. Louis area. Herman's brothers are competitors, and even though I don't think there's anything in the world he wouldn't do for either one of them, they're three people with really different personalities.

So, sometimes—especially on a Sunday night when your race has sucked big time—it's nice to have somebody to call who totally understands. We found that out, and right up to today, one will call the other and remind him that you were doing your job. Whatever screwed up that day wasn't because you didn't try to make good things happen.

That's what a *chosen* brother is for.

And, then we started sharing some goals, too. Kenny and Kim are going to end up back in St. Louis when their girls are grown, and I expect that one of these days before too many more years, Ann and I will, too. It's not that we don't appreciate the Charlotte area or have any dissatisfaction with the hub of NASCAR racing. It's just that somewhere along the way, we all realized that we missed our old hometown and the down-to-earth people who live there. Seems like a good place to retire, although neither he nor I will be there a lot.

We're going dirt racing 'til all the dirt blows away or we die. That's always been my plan. Sort of surprised me a couple of years ago when Herman decided that he needed dirt track racing, too.

For a while, I just let it rattle around, waiting to see if it was just wishful thinking or a wild hare or whatever. But he didn't let the idea go. And when we first fixed him up with a dirt deal, we sort of had to wonder. He was a wild man for a while there, but you know, he's got all that talent and basic car knowledge, so it really didn't take him very long to figure out dirt. I'm as proud as any brother could be of the job he's doing in mastering it. He's reached the point now where he's confident, doing well, and he's really having fun. I've always figured that if you're having fun doing something, you're a winner by any definition, but he's picked up some legitimate race wins in pretty short order, too.

Because he's so special, I wish he could have had more stability in his Cup racing career, just because it's what he wanted. Way too many fans place value on winning or being champion, when really it's just an objective. It isn't who you are, and it doesn't define the quality of spirit a person has. It's a whole lot more important to look in a mirror and know that you gave your all than that you got lucky at the checkered flag.

A book about Kenny Wallace's life is sure to be fun, but I think you're going to be surprised, too, at the depth of thought. He doesn't often get to express the serious side of his nature, so in that regard, this book is going to be a very interesting ride through the world of auto racing. I think when you get done, you're going to like and respect Kenny even more. You're going to realize that there's a lot to him that doesn't usually show to the world.

But, if you've got one, I still wouldn't let him borrow the camper.

Introduction

I WANT TO BE REMEMBERED as more than just the guy with the machine-gun laugh. The laugh is my signature. It makes me stand out, but it is sometimes the curse of my existence, even though it is part of the reason you may have heard my name beyond being in a race line-up.

But you need to know this about me, above and beyond everything else: **I am a racer.**

(Kenny Wallace Collection)

I am also a husband, father, son, friend, diehard fan of the St. Louis Cardinals, pretty decent mechanic, Cracker Barrel regular, rock 'n roll air-guitarist, charity fundraiser, seeker of Truth, Justice and the American Way, and a racing fan of what other drivers do, too. But everything in my life—*absolutely everything*—is somehow shaped by my passion to go racing.

I can't help myself.

I would be just as narrowly focused if I was running the local Street Stock division, because I am totally eaten up by the need to compete. It's important to me that people recall what I do on the race track more than whatever I say behind a microphone, and while I realize that people will think what they will and believe what they will, I like the idea of having the opportunity to tell you what it's been like walking in these racer's boots. I also found it appealing to take you behind the scenes in this crazy world of auto racing, at least as seen through my eyes.

Beyond saving stories for a longer period than just over a post-race beer in the pits, there's a need in me to preserve at least one story about a guy who was lucky enough to be born into an interesting family, marry the girl of his dreams, raise three beautiful girls, and, not-so-incidentally, spend his whole life in the vicinity of race cars.

I think I'm a pretty average Joe living a distinctly non-average life. If I hadn't won that race at the Springfield mile, if I hadn't been a Winston Cup crew chief at 20 years old, if my brother hadn't believed in me enough to put me in good equipment, if Dale Earnhardt hadn't given me a chance in a Busch ride . . .

. . . *if, if, if* . . .

I guess all our lives are a series of "ifs." Mine have just been the stuff that a lot of people dream of happening. Even if nothing else ever happens again to advance my career, I know that already I've accomplished enough to meet my Maker with a smile on my face. He will probably ask me to hold the laugh, though.

I have been so lucky. I have lived a life that I would envy if I'd heard it happened to somebody else. Along the way, I've had one hell of a good time, and there are some stories you just have to hear. I mean, from Little Kenny getting run over on Main Street to the Hermanator trying to move a concrete wall with his helmet, there's stuff that you just flat aren't going to believe, but I promise, it's all true.

It's 100 percent, to-the-bone, for-real, and it all begins in 1963, in Rolla, Missouri.

1

Do I Look Like Road Kill To You?

I HAD A DEER-IN-THE-HEADLIGHTS moment before I can ever remember seeing a deer. In fact, while my story starts in the middle 1960s, it darn-near ended then, too.

I blame an ice cream cone.

To set the stage, let's go back to the very beginning. I am a native St. Louisan, but only just. Mom and Dad moved our family about 80 miles southwest to Rolla when I was three months old, and I'm not sure why. Probably staying a step ahead of the bill collector, or chasing rainbows, or trying to scrape together enough money to keep my dad's race car going. I don't know because what mattered to me back then and still does to this day is that Rolla was a truly great place for a little kid to live.

As long as I stayed out of traffic.

This is the house my family lived in when I was born. It's located in the Spanish Lake area on the north side of St. Louis. *(Judy Wallace Collection)*

I'm not positive how old I was, but it was old enough to toddle along behind my older brother Mike. One of the great things about maneuvering on my own was that I didn't get left behind when he went to the ice cream shop that was a couple of blocks from the race car garage. If you've ever endured a mid-summer day in the Ozarks, you'll understand why, at a very tender age, it was a treat you didn't want to miss.

After paying for the order on that particular day, Mike headed back to the shop, telling me, "C'mon, Kenny, let's go."

I guess I was preoccupied with my double scoop or something because I sort of lagged behind, and Mike wasn't old enough to be especially good at herding me. Anyway, he got across the street, and I hadn't. And a college kid, minding his own business driving along one of Rolla's main drags, apparently didn't see this little squirt standing in the middle of the street.

Thank God, cars had more clearance in those days. Wish they'd had better brakes, too, but somehow or other, he just sailed over me. My mom—who had been watching us from the family's taxi-cab office nearby—didn't faint, my brother didn't cry, the kid didn't have a heart attack, and I . . . well, I came up on my feet with the ice cream cone still intact.

I believe I finished it off while everybody else engaged in a freak-out.

And, that's how I nearly came to being finished off, too, which would make for a much shorter book, but hang in there with me. I'm really glad to have survived being mowed down in the street without so much as a scratch because I would hate to have missed all the great stuff that came afterward.

Early childhood started in Green Acres.

You read that right. We lived in the Green Acres subdivision of Rolla.

We lived in several houses in Rolla, but this is the one I remember best. And because it was pretty good sized, we often rented out rooms to students from the university. This is one of them standing in the yard with Mike and Rusty after a snow fall.
(Judy Wallace Collection)

However, there were no displaced lawyers or socialites like the television show, no climbing the telephone pole to make calls, and no Mr. Haney taking us for our last dime, although there was a Christmas we woke up cold because the heat bill hadn't been paid.

Coupled with having also lived many years in Arnold, Missouri, I have never been able to get out of my head the whole Green Acres and Arnold the Pig connection. No, we didn't have critters living in the house and sleeping in the bed, although Mom probably would tell you that she wondered if pigs were sleeping between the sheets considering the state they were in when they got put in the laundry.

We always had German Shepherds when I was growing up. I don't think these were two that washed up in the great Rolla flood.
(Judy Wallace Collection)

In fact, our Green Acres didn't look anything like the television show. It was better. This will confirm it for you as it did for me: It was a place where a big rain made the creek behind the house swell up one day and then, there they were—about ten German Shepherd puppies washed up in our yard. It was the wrong time of year, but I thought Christmas had been rescheduled!

I don't remember Mom being as excited, but I can still hear the giggles as those puppies squirmed all over us kids while we rolled around the wet yard with them.

If the Spoons Were Silver, It Was a Spray-Paint Job

There's a misconception among some racing fans that the Wallace family was wealthy, and that we were born with silver spoons or something. And, I suppose today that if three brothers tried to get all the way to NASCAR Nextel Cup racing, somebody in the family would have to possess a bulging wallet right from the get-go.

Even back in the era before anybody had heard of Rusty, Mike or me, there were people who assumed we were rolling in dough because our dad Russ won so darned many races that there just couldn't be any other explanation.

They couldn't be more wrong.

I was an adult before I realized that while we were very, very lucky people, it had nothing to do with the almighty dollar. We moved several times when I was a kid because my mom and dad struggled to make a better life for us. But, you know what? I thought we were about as "rich" as anybody could be, and here's why: In my young eyes, we had it all, because we had each other, we had fun at the races and at home, and I never knew what part money—or lack of it—played in any of the great things that happened to us.

Look at how lucky we were: We had a house where the basement flooded only occasionally—not deep enough to swim in, but enough to stomp the puddles and get each other wet and filthy, which was great for little kids. There was also a radiator shop near our cab office that was the neatest, most mysterious place imaginable for a pre-schooler. I mean, they used to dip radiators and stuff down in these tanks, and it smelled so weird, and you figured, in your five-year-old mind, monsters must live in the bottom of the tank. There was grease a quarter-inch thick on the floor—deep enough you could draw pictures in the goo if they didn't chase you away first.

I also remember that there were loads of soda machines around town where Mike and Rusty would urge me on because my hand and arm were so small that I could get up inside the machines and get us free Cokes. And, maybe most importantly, there was also the little

I can't remember a time when we didn't go racing, but why not? My dad was one of the winningest drivers ever in the St. Louis region. Here he's racing with Fred Tiede, another of the great local stars, at our home track of Lake Hill Speedway. *(Rocky Rhodes Photo; Kenny Wallace Collection)*

rented garage where my dad kept his race car, which was just a wonderland to me.

Until they burned it down.

I thought the fire engines were cool. The chaos was better than H.R. Puffenstuff on Saturday morning television, too, but it was a few years before I understood that the circus had not come to town.

See, Dad couldn't afford much of a place. It was adequate and that was all. "Crowded" would be a kind term, so when he and fellow racer Larry Phillips worked on the race car—especially if they were working on different things at the same time—it could get a little crazy. Not too many years later, I came to understand that Larry was one of the greatest short-track racers ever, but at that time, he was just the other big guy in the garage, and they didn't have their best day, as the fire engines proved. They were using a cutting torch on something and it sparked some gas tank fumes. The next thing I knew, the kids I'd been playing with outside on the street were asking if they could have a ride on the fire engine.

I don't want you to think, from this story, that my dad was some kind of a goof. On the contrary, he was just about the hardest-working person I ever knew. There wasn't a lazy bone in his body or my mom's,

In addition to my dad (left), my uncle Gary Wallace was another important influence in my life. He is the level-headed member of our family, and he always gave us jobs when the rent was due. Thanks, Uncle Gary. *(Kenny Wallace Collection)*

which is why eventually they clawed their way up out of flirting with poverty to become a lot more comfortable in recent years. You see, they got married without two nickels to rub together.

My dad's brother Gary hit the ground running, working hard and setting a good example for everybody with a maturity that we should envy. I often think that my brother Mike got Uncle Gary's work ethic, in fact. Make some money, they understood, and, in turn, make a better life.

It took Dad a little longer to accumulate some money because in his youth he was a rebel—right down to the Harley, and we're talking an age when it wasn't middle-aged doctors and lawyers riding them. And that fabulous-looking, bottle-redhead on the back of Dad's bike was my mom.

She'd gotten off to a tough start, too. Judith Grace Buckles and her sister grew up over a tavern in Baltimore, so they learned at a very young age how to take care of themselves. Mom wasn't ever somebody to mess with. Just ask any of the men in the Lake Hill Speedway grandstand when Mom and her friend Sue Sifford beat them with umbrellas if they said anything bad about Dad or Sue's husband Jerry.

Many years later, I was reflecting back on the time we really came up in the world and had an acre-and-a-half, with a three-bedroom house, a garage for the race car, and a yard littered with stripped vehicles (for race car parts). "Gosh, Mom, were we really the Rednecks of Jefferson County?"

And she smiled and said, "Yes, honey, I'm afraid we were."

Lifestyles of the Poor and Unknown

It wasn't exactly Ozzie and Harriet around our house, but it wasn't Ozzie Osbourne either. My dad was stern enough I could believe that he was capable of biting the head off a bat, but there were never any drugs, recreational or otherwise, and not a lot of alcohol either. Every dime that wasn't needed to pay a bill went into the race car, and I've always thought that was one of the great things about racing. It'll eat into your wallet about as deep as you'll let it, but it keeps families together and there's nothing left over for temptation.

Dad worked damned hard, getting up at three in the morning to deliver the St. Louis newspaper, both when we lived in Rolla and then later in Arnold. He put in a full day at King Dodge in south St. Louis, working as a passenger car mechanic. Dad used to tell me, "Son, there's parts replacers and then there's people who fix things. We fix stuff, because we don't have money to waste."

I was a little bit afraid of my dad when I was a kid. I understand better as an adult that he was always worrying about bills, and the race car, and the responsibilities he had. I think he always felt a little in his brother's shadow, too, at least the part about being a financially successful adult. But I can remember being afraid to ask for a dollar because Dad

I'm holding on to my Mom and wondering why she is kissing that man—even though it's my dad. This picture probably sums up my early life as well as any that exist because it's after yet another win at Charleah Speedway, around 1970. *(Kenny Wallace Collection)*

would chew my ass, wanting to know what I was going to do with that dollar and whether I was going to waste it.

In spite of that, I love my dad with all my heart and even if I got a do-over and could choose anybody in the world for a father, I'd still go back to Russ Wallace. In most ways, he set a great example for us, and if you want to find out what he's like, watch my oldest brother, Rusty. As a kid, he just lived with Dad and so he's turned out pretty much the same in outlook and personality.

Mike was a pretty classic middle kid, I think. He spent a lot of time with Dad, too, but Mike was awfully good at figuring things out for himself. The person he became was probably influenced by Uncle Gary, as I've already noted, as they have both always had a knack for making—and keeping—money.

And me? You might have guessed by now that I was a classic Mama's Boy. It was partly because of being the youngest, partly because I have always had a happy-go-lucky personality that didn't always mesh as well as I would have liked with the other males in the household, and partly because my mom is just about the coolest woman I know. I mean, running around with her was always a laugh, always fun, always some new adventure. And she tolerated my inquisitive nature with a patience nobody else had.

The other strong female example in my life was my paternal grandmother. The other three grandparents had already passed away by the time I came along, so MawMaw was really special. She spoiled me, but really, she spoiled the whole family by making holidays so great that I stubbornly continue to try to make them as good as the ones she put together.

This is my grandmother, Marie "MawMaw" Wallace, Easter 1980, the only grandparent I knew. (Judy Wallace Collection)

The Boogie Man

Our subdivision in Rolla was on the outskirts of town so we traveled a semi-rural road to go into town. One night when I wasn't even school-age yet, I was riding in my mom's car along that road, which had a pretty deep ditch beside it.

All of a sudden, this THING popped up out of the weeds in the ditch. I don't remember if Mom and I screamed when we saw it, but almost forty years later I still remember like it happened last night so I'd guess we probably hollered pretty good.

I don't know what Mom thought she was seeing, but I was pretty sure it was the Boogie Man. My brothers had tried to scare the crap out of me with tales of the Boogie Man, but they never really said where he lived. From that night on, I knew.

I figured out later that it was one of the town drunks. Apparently, he had fallen and cut his forehead somewhere along the way, so he had these rivulets of blood running down his face, and, of course, he was very unsteady on his feet, which added to the scare factor.

My dad ran a taxi-cab service at the time and we think this guy had called for a cab but didn't wait for it before starting out for wherever he was going. When he heard us coming, it must have awakened him from the stupor in the weeds so he got up thinking his cab had come for him.

Instead, if he had been able to look through the headlight beams, he would have seen a freaked-out young woman and her equally terrified kid, who still sees that guy in nightmares.

Let's just say that all Samaritan thoughts fled down the road, and so did Mom and me.

My mother is a winner in every sense of the word, from the days she won Powder Puff races right on up to her 60th birthday, which she celebrated with all of us. And if you know her, you'll find it hard to believe she was afraid of the Boogie Man! (L: Rocky Rhodes Photo; Kenny Wallace Collection; R: Kenny Wallace Collection)

There's no reason to feel sorry for Little Kenny hanging with the gals, not that I figure you were inclined. But, spending so much time with females turned out to be a good thing because I ended up with a great marriage and three beautiful daughters, and I don't know that I could have been a good husband and father without understanding the influence that the women early in my life had on me.

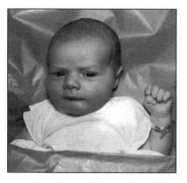

The very first photo ever taken of me, shortly after I was born in St. Louis. Note that already I am working on my steering-wheel grip. *(Kenny Wallace Collection)*

Sit Up and Pay Attention, Kenny

Even though I was born at Lutheran Medical Center on the south side of St. Louis, I've always felt like Rolla was our hometown. Here's the deal, though: If you live within about a hundred miles of St. Louis, you feel like you're part of a single community. I know there are parts of the country where people get offended if you say they're from the biggest city in the region—there's some real divisions there. But out in our part of the world, we're comfortable being identified with St. Louis, because we figure we're all in it together, whatever "it" may be.

The thing of it is, St. Louis has terrible weather, but that binds us. It's sort of like, you have to be tough to live there so we get a little smug that the wimps have all gone to Florida or wherever. It's a sauna in the summer, and in the winter there's nothing to stop the cold wind coming out of Canada except a barbed wire fence in North Dakota, and it's not stopping much.

That's the downside. The upside is that you'll meet the best people imaginable. A snob doesn't have a chance there because, well, we don't have a lot to be snobby about. And, personally, I think that's a good thing. It's a big part of the reason why I believe that my wife Kim and I will end up back there when our girls have graduated from high school. One of the girls is already living in St. Louis and going to a professional school there. I wouldn't be surprised if the other girls go back, too, because that's where a lot of our family is, and where you don't have to be anything or anybody but who you are.

That's the future—it's also the past.

When we left Rolla, Mom and Dad took us to the Jefferson Barracks apartments on the far south side of St. Louis, a kind of low-rent area, and I went to Beasley Elementary School for kindergarten. Within a year, though, they found that little acre-and-a-half in Arnold, and we were

We lived in Rolla until I was six, and most of the rest of my childhood was spent in Arnold, but we have always considered ourselves St. Louisans because there's such a great sense of community here. It's small town feel with big town fun. *(Joyce Standridge Photo)*

School Daze

I was probably about 10 or 11 years old and we were at a restaurant after the Sunday night races at Lake Hill Speedway. The school year started the following day, and in spite of being too old to throw a fit, I threw a fit.

My dad finally banged his hands on the table and said, "Dammit, Kenny, you're going to school."

I was crushed.

I was so eaten alive with racing that I viewed going to school as punishment. In the summertime, it was okay if I wasn't in the garage 24/7 because I could always get off my bike, or leave the kickball game and go back to the garage whenever I wanted. But when I went to school, I felt estranged from the family racing. And I hated that. And I hated everybody who kept me from the racing, at least until the bell rang.

Here's how obsessed I was with racing: Seated in the classroom, I would position myself so I thought my body was closer to a race track. So, if I'm in this room and I know that I-55 Raceway is south of the room, I would actually twist myself so that I was leaning that way as much as I could be without the teacher yelling at me.

Pretty screwed up, huh? Well, it got me through the day.

You know why I'm grinning? Because I have my body turned in the direction of the nearest race track! (Kenny Wallace Collection)

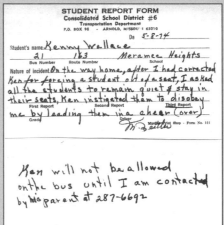

More proof of how rambunctious I was as a kid. I wonder why Mom saved this. (Judy Wallace Collection)

settled for the long run. I went the rest of the way through school in the C-6 District, from Meramec Heights Elementary to Seckman Middle School and then to Fox Senior High School. I dwell on these details only because it was the hardest progression in St. Louis region history since Lewis and Clark set out to explore the Louisiana Purchase. Took them only a couple of years. Took only four years to build the Gateway Arch that commemorates their trek, too. Took me, my folks and my teachers 12 hard years, and nobody's planning any monuments to the job. More likely, people are trying to forget.

You see, I had a little trouble with my attention span.

And I was a little disruptive. Like if I found that my chair had a squeak, I would make it squeak over and over and over, until the teacher was ready to put a Smith & Wesson to her head. Or, maybe my head.

Anyway, at the school's recommendation my parents got me tested, and the determination was ADD, Attention Deficit Disorder. Pretty common diagnosis for a squirmy kid like me—maybe too much so. They also said I had a sibling rivalry, which is true on the race track where I want to beat them the same as everybody else, but anybody who's ever known me is well aware that my brothers are two of the most important people in my life and I've never wanted more than to be like them.

They put me on Ritalin, and I went from 100 miles per hour to 20 miles per hour. I mean, like somebody had wrapped a chain around me and dropped the anchor overboard. After a short time, my mom said, "What happened to my Kenny?"

And I said, "Mom, the answer is right there in that bottle."

She didn't hesitate. She took the prescription container and threw it in the trash can right that minute, right in front of me. She said, "I want my Kenny back."

So, folks, because of my mother throwing the Ritalin away, I am what the world has now! *Blame Mom!*

Seriously, I'm glad she did that. I fully realize that there are kids out there who respond very well to Ritalin, and who have no hope of a normal childhood without it or one of the other drugs they've come out with to deal with the disorder. But, it wasn't right for me. It turned me into a zombie. So, I'm glad that through some pretty difficult events involving school, Mom and Dad stood firm and didn't let them drug me up. I hope I didn't hurt anybody else's education by my antics, but I wasn't mean, I wasn't a bully, I never hurt anybody, so I really don't see why it was necessary to make my life a step away from *One Flew Over the Cuckoo's Nest*.

Looking back, it's unfortunate, but I didn't go to school to learn. I went to school because some stupid law said I had to, and Mom would do about anything for me but she wasn't serving time in jail because I didn't want to go to school.

She didn't go so far as hanging over my shoulder, pounding learning into my hard head or making me do three hours of homework every night. In fact, Mom and Dad were pretty laid back about the whole thing. I was either in the garage or running the streets until pretty late at night, instead. I mean, it would be 10 or 10:30 at night and Mom would come out of the house and start hollering, *"KENNNNNNNY!"*

It wasn't to come in and go to bed, though. From a young age, I was allowed to set my own bedtime, and frankly, that led to a recurring memory more special to me now than any I can remember from a classroom. My mom would be sitting on the couch and I would stretch out with my head in her lap. She would stroke my hair until I fell asleep, while we watched Johnny Carson together.

This is the home in Arnold where we moved when I was in first grade. We lived here until I was grown, and that garage was where I spent most of my time, along with Dad and my brothers. *(Kenny Wallace Collection)*

Sounds slightly sissy-boy, I know, but I never felt safer or more loved in my childhood than during those times. I've always needed—still need—reassurance, affection, and a sense of being loved for myself. In a simple act that I don't think she even really thought much about, Mom gave me all that I needed.

And before you go into diabetic shock from how sweet it was, let me tell you another unintended result of that freedom and comfort. It meant that I didn't always get a shower that night. And since I'd been up late at night, there were many mornings that I had to settle for a quick wash of my face and hands.

So, one day in sixth grade, Miss Grab took me aside and told me, "Kenny . . . ummm . . . honey . . . *you smell.*"

Now, Miss Grab had a relative who raced, so it wasn't like she was unfamiliar with the odors that come from a race shop, but she was just trying to protect me from my peers, who weren't going to be so kind.

At that young age, though, I was pretty devastated. From that point on I made it a point to carve out the time for proper grooming. I still don't mind being around people who smell of honest, hard work, but I know that not everybody sees it that way. And, whether I like it or not, I represent the Wallace clan, my race team, and anybody who wants to be a fan, so I try to make sure the Right Guard hasn't worn off.

My poor kids have never been allowed to get dirty and stay that way. I mean, I'm like, "Get your ass in that shower!" and while I may be a

I showed you how nice the house and yard, and even the garage, looked at times. Now this is what the driveway tended to look like. As Mom confirmed, we were the Rednecks of Jefferson County, Missouri. *(Judy Wallace Collection)*

pushover at some things, ain't no give-and-take on that, thanks to Miss Grab's little comment.

I'll bet the original Herman the German didn't worry about hygiene, though. Of course, he had to spend his time trying to save an entire country, while I was only concerned about 30 sixth-graders' sensibilities. But his name, if not his goal, was about to become a big part of who I became.

2

Herman the German Is Born

AHUSH FALLS over the crowd.

Anticipation builds until finally the cars take the green and they're off on the first lap. The announcer, as intent on the action as anyone, bellows, "Russ Wallace is off! He jumps into the lead immediately and the rest of the pack scrambles behind him.

"Russ Wallace is in turn one now, and the field continues to trail! Wallace has been winning everything in sight for weeks now—can anybody hope to catch him?

"He's through two and down the backstretch, still in the lead. He sails through three and . . . **into the milk!**"

The "crowd," consisting of my parents and brothers, broke into laughter. Completely consumed by racing, I had been lost in a world of Hot Wheels toy cars on a corner of the breakfast table.

When I wasn't "racing" through the milk on the kitchen table, I was racing my toy cars on the patio. *(Judy Wallace Collection)*

The announcer at Lake Hill Speedway used to let me come up into the booth and spend time while he was announcing. He was a DJ from WIL radio and a pro, but he used to amaze me by putting the microphone to his throat instead of his mouth, and the same sounds came out. Many years later, my mom and dad bought his Lake Hill microphone at an auction and then gave it to me. I have it in a glass case in my home.
(Judy Wallace Collection)

One might observe that I was practicing for a future as a television commentator, but I could not have cared less about such stuff back then. Auto racing—NASCAR Grand National, which became Winston Cup and then evolved into Nextel Cup—was just an occasional 15-minute highlight on ABC's *Wide World of Sports* then, and Chris Economaki, with his wonderful nasal, New Jersey accent was the brain, while regular sports broadcaster Jim McKay usually offered the play-by-play. Not that there was a lot to talk about when 500 laps were reduced to the 25 or so actually shown, unlike the hours and hours we fill today.

This was a very common sight at Lake Hill Speedway in the early 1970s—Russ Wallace with the checkered flag.
(Rocky Rhodes Photo; Kenny Wallace Collection)

No, on that long-ago, 1960s morning I was echoing what I heard at the race track because it gave my little Hot Wheels events realism. At least up to that last part.

Dad didn't run through milk very often, even on the table. He did run through the field to win about as often as he did in my fantasy races. Seriously. Dad won something like 500 races in his career, which, even though it spanned a couple of decades, meant he won a lot. I mean, *a lot*.

In fact, we went to the race track expecting to win every time. It wasn't like we had massive egos and flaunted our superiority. Or even that he always won, because it was a time period when there were some really great drivers in eastern Missouri and southern Illinois. Dad had to go up against guys like Wib Spalding, C.C. Corbin, Kenny Schrum, Fred Tiede and Dandy Don Klein, among others. If you don't know who these guys are, I can sum it up by telling you that you cinched up your belts a little tighter when you were racing against them because they were going to make you run a little harder, a little tougher, and a little faster if you were going to win than you had to if they weren't there.

But even against the great drivers of that era, we still expected to win. And when we didn't, the drive home would be really quiet. We weren't miserable, and we didn't bad-mouth the guy who did win or anything like that. It's just that not winning meant we hadn't gotten the job done.

This goes all the way back to Rolla. Dad drove at a little bitty quarter-mile track called Charleah Speedway. Like many little hometown tracks of the mid-twentieth century, it's long gone. I think the Chamber of Commerce office sits now where the track was, but it was a neat place with a pretty lake just off the second turn. And it was from that time that I got the inspiration for my current UMP Modified dirt car number. Dad drove the dark brown Blades Shoe Shack #36. I chose the number 36 in honor of

Dad in action at Ft. Leonard Wood Speedway in 1967 or 1968. This is the race car I try to honor by carrying #36 on my own cars today. *(Judy Wallace Collection)*

Go-Karts As Alarm Clocks

I think my dad was involved in a "thrash."

That's where you bend up a race car pretty good at the track and then bring it home to work on it all night so you can take it to another race track the following night and probably bend it up again.

I did my chores on the car, but I didn't want to be banished to the house. I'm sure I was mostly in the way, and I'm sure they told me that, but there's an electricity in the air when a thrash is happening, and no way does a kid want to miss out.

Since I knew Dad would take only so much interference before he would boot me out, I figured out that there was enough stuff in the garage that I could build my own go-kart over on the side.

The basic frame was already there, but I

wanted it to be more like a *real* race car. So, I took a lawn chair and "engineered" it. The legs and seat ended up being my roll cage and I think I did some chopping on the chair back because a race car, after all, needs to be aerodynamic. Didn't want that back creating any wind resistance.

Well, along about 6:30 A.M., I fired 'er up and I set a new track record down Vogel Road in Arnold. In looking back, I hope it was a work day (I can't really remember that part) so the neighbors were getting up anyway.

And since they probably couldn't have seen me tucked under the chair legs, I hope they'd already had that first cup of coffee before they pulled back the curtains to see half of a lawn chair roaring down the street.

May 1979: It's my go-kart, but I can't believe no one took a photo of the kart with the lawn-chair roll cage! (Kenny Wallace Collection)

the car I remember so fondly from my childhood, but I passed on the color. It's true that at some tracks you get so much mud all over the car that you'd mistake it for brown, but my Modified is associated with the St. Louis Cardinals, not to be confused with the old St. Louis *Browns*.

If Dad had never run anywhere but Charleah Speedway in Rolla, probably nobody would have ever heard of the Wallaces. It would have been a whole lot more difficult for us boys to have gained name recognition, that's for sure. But Dad hooked up with a guy by the name of Lee

Lutz, and burning down the garage became a footnote. Winning came to the forefront.

Dad was just a terror in our area, from paved tracks like the half-mile Ozark Empire State Fairgrounds in Springfield, Missouri, to the quarter-mile Lake Hill Speedway in Valley Park, Missouri. From dirt tracks like the half-mile Tri-City Speedway in Granite City, Illinois, to the State Fairgrounds mile at Springfield, Illinois. It didn't matter where or when—if there was a race within driving distance, we showed up and we were competitive.

That's not the royal "we," either. We weren't taking credit just by virtue of being related to a winner. From diapers on, the Wallace boys were in the garage learning to be fixers instead of parts changers. We all had jobs to do, and by the time I was in grade school, in addition to household chores through the week, my job was to switch the quick-change gears for the track we were going to, and keep up on the brake maintenance.

Today, we have really good disc-brake systems, even on support-division short-track cars, but back then Dad and his contemporaries were running drum brakes. I would have to take the brakes off and wire brush the pads. Then I would have to blow the brakes and the suspension area with an air hose. I don't even want to think about how much asbestos we probably breathed in those days.

And finally, I would change the tires. Bear in mind that at the time we had a total of eight tires—a set we put on the car for early on when the track was likely to be tacky, and another set that went on after the track dried out.

In spite of this lack of sophistication compared to today—which

I've been asked where Rusty gets his incredible intensity and drive. Since Dad won 500 races, that's a clue, but I want you to look at my mother's face (left) when she was racing, and then the shot of Rusty winning his first ever race at Lake Hill Speedway in 1972. *(L: Rocky Rhodes Photo; Kenny Wallace Collection; R: Kenny Wallace Collection)*

isn't so much figuring out which tires to run as how deep to go into the wallet buying new ones—I'm convinced that Dad won a lot of races by being really smart with his tire stagger. There were a lot of guys who ran tons of stagger all night long, but when the track dried Dad really reduced the amount he had, and it made the car more responsive on the straightaways and tighter in the turns.

So, if you want to beat Russ Wallace today in an Oldtimers race, you better check out his tire set-up.

Winning Can Be Like a Hot Poker in the Eye

All my heroes ran race cars, and they all conducted themselves as class individuals. If they spun somebody out, it was an accident and they apologized. I remember that my dad was always humble and never cocky about winning either—and the guys he raced against were the same way. They were mostly quiet people off the track and they had supportive families, too. In turn, we became like one big, extended clan. When we broke something at the track or needed something through the week, we knew we could borrow from a competitor. Nobody ever thought, "Well, hell, if I don't loan that trailer ramp to Russ he won't be able to make it to the race track, and I'll get the win."

Guys back then always, *but always,* wanted to win on the track. If you won on a night when Russ, or Wib, or C.C. wasn't there, it kind of tarnished the win. You still took the trophy and the money, but it just didn't mean as much.

To this day, I consider all those great drivers, their wives and their kids, part of the extended Wallace clan, whether they want to be or not. And sometimes, they didn't.

Like any family, we had our dysfunctional moments. Within the racing community, there was a bit of a clique that consisted of Jerry Sifford's family, Tom Hannick's family, Bill Schrader's family, which included future NASCAR driver Kenny, and the Wallaces. But for a brief period of time, the unbreakable bond between the Siffords and the Wallaces got stretched. Real bad.

It was probably worse for the Hannicks and Schraders because they didn't want to take sides. And you know what, I honestly don't remember what happened that caused the ruckus in the first place. I think it was something bad my dad was supposed to have said about Jerry. Like a lot of stupid crap, it didn't matter, but the strain on the friendship did.

About a month later, it was all cleared up when it came out that a kid who hung around on the fringes of our group had told Jerry some nonsense that he attributed to Dad. The kid broke down in tears and admitted that he'd made it all up. He just wanted to be big time—feel a part of that winner's circle and he thought by telling this tale it would make him Jerry's best friend because he was supposedly looking out for Jerry's interests.

Well, it didn't really change anything. Even when Jerry was mad at Dad. And seeing two such great friends at odds over something completely false finally got through to the kid's conscience. We all made up and everything went back to normal pretty quick after that.

And it was real important to have your friends within the racing circle because sometimes it could be hard to find them in the grandstand. People have always had trouble with the idea of somebody winning too much. Just ask Jeff Gordon. Even as he wins less often, he's never been forgiven by some for all those victories and championships earlier.

It was that way for my dad, and it hit home with stun-gun reality one night when I was still pretty small.

Dad won again. I was in the grandstand with my mom, like always, wishing I could be in the pits with Dad. Even more so after a so-called racing fan turned to my mom—as God is my witness—and said in front of me, *I hope your husband burns to death.*

Up to that point, I'd never understood how much people who don't even know you could hate you. I guess I still don't understand it, but I've known for too many years that it happens. And I know that you can't let it stop you. Whether it's fueled by loyalty to somebody else, or jealousy of what you have, or some genetic defect within them, there are people walking around out there that just apparently don't let a little thing like human decency get in the way of a case of hatemongering.

I hope the "fan" slept that night. Because I sure didn't. It was an awful young age to learn how frustrating it can be when you're too little

It's important to include this photo because this is Dad winning in Ed Hall's car at Lake Hill Speedway. Ed's daughter Patti married my brother Rusty. *(Kenny Wallace Collection)*

to think of any kind of response, mostly because you never dreamed that someone could be that cruel.

Start Your Engine, Herman!

My dad held a series of jobs when he was a younger man, always looking for something better to make a more comfortable life for us and to help pay those race car bills. Most of his work was hard, and I can recall when he was a mechanic that a spring broke out of a car he was working on and hit him in the eye. He thinks that started the eventual trouble with his vision that he has today, and I expect he's probably right.

Some time after we moved to Arnold, Uncle Gary brought Dad into his business, O.K. Vacuum and Industrial Supplies. All of us worked there at some time or other, too. Because it was a family-owned business—and a successful one, at that—I think that's where people got the idea that the Wallaces had money.

Uncle Gary had money. Dad had a job. A good one, and eventually he became a partner, but there's no way Uncle Gary would have allowed anybody to funnel a lot of profit into race cars.

Dad ran the residential side of the business, selling and servicing the household vacuum cleaners, but it was the commercial side that really made the company's name, with accounts like Anheuser-Busch, Monsanto, McDonnell-Douglas and other major St. Louis companies.

This was on top of his delivering newspapers for many years, and always—*but always*—spending seven days and nights in the garage. And in spite of that incredible work ethic, Dad found time to meet friends at a local café for coffee almost every day. He also liked to go around to pals' garages or businesses, mostly to talk racing.

We took my show car to Uncle Gary's O.K. Vacuum some years ago. He and Dad retired in 1994 and sold the business. Unfortunately, the purchasers didn't take care of things with the attention to detail and customers that Gary had, so the company no longer exists. *(Kenny Wallace Collection)*

Everybody in our family has won races, including Uncle Gary (center). That young, solemn kid on the left is my brother Mike. *(Rocky Rhodes Photo; Kenny Wallace Collection)*

One of those people was Bob Mueller. Bob was a big ol' guy with a crew cut in the age of shaggy hair in the eyes, and I guess he was a pretty tough dude. Had to be, running the Central Auto Racing Division and promoting Lake Hill Speedway, but he was always really nice to me. I think he got a kick out of my inability to sit still.

Bob also had a used car lot—real small, maybe 10 or 12 cars at most—and Dad went down to visit him there a few times. While they jawed about racing, I *went* "racing."

I got in every one of those cars, perched myself behind the wheel on my knees so I could see over (or sometimes through) the steering wheel. And I would just wear those cars out! I mean, I did 500 laps, making an engine noise through my lips that left them numb, and about the time I took the checkered flag in one car, I'd hop out and move on to the next car.

The man who gave me the nickname of Herman the German: Bob Mueller. He ran the local racing sanctioning group, but he also knew how to win races himself. *(Nancy Slover Collection, Courtesy Nancy Slover)*

I don't think Bob gave it any real thought, but one night he dubbed me "Herman the German," which I thought was pretty cool, and everybody else thought was funny enough that it got repeated.

And repeated, and repeated, until everybody but my mom was calling me that or "Herm." I was told that Herman the German was a cartoon of a funny little guy who moved in warp speed and never settled down. *(Sound familiar?)* I found out years later that there never was such a cartoon, but by then the nickname—and the description—was permanent.

Memories to Last a Lifetime

I might have mentioned that my dad was strict.

When we got home from school, we all had jobs to do, and in looking back, there was nothing wrong with Mom and Dad, who both worked full-time jobs, expecting us boys to help around the house.

We'd get off the bus at four o'clock, and while the rest of the

The REAL Herman(s)

I'm not the only Herman the German. Apparently, there have been, at the least: A great soldier, a great engineer, a great piece of equipment, a not-so-great music album, and a really . . . um . . . interesting musician, all known as Herman the German.

When he laid the nickname on me, I'd like to believe that Bob Mueller was inspired by the great general. He was known as Arminius in his time, but his brilliant strategy defeated one-tenth of the Imperial Roman Army. There's a statue in his honor, the third-largest copper statue in America, in the Minnesota town of New Ulm. Settled by Germans, the residents had the figure installed in 1890, but it had to be taken down and fixed a few years ago. Seems some bored locals had been shooting at it, so water got inside and corroded it.

Sure hope nobody gets any ideas out of that. I don't think I'd corrode, but I sure would leak.

Gerhard Neumann was one of the German engineers who emigrated to America after World War II. His book, titled *Herman the German*, tells how he developed gas-turbine engines for General Electric. Don't feel bad if you haven't read it. The book was written in 1984 and still hasn't made the New York Times Bestseller List. But then, I'm not likely to, either.

Then, there's a spoils-of-war naval crane capable of lifting 400 tons. It once lifted the famous wooden airplane "Spruce Goose" and sailors fondly called it Herman the German until it was decommissioned in 1994.

Herman ze German was a 1985 album by Scorpions drummer Herman Rarebell.

Yeah, I never bought it, either.

And, finally, there is a German-born guitarist living in Austin, Texas, playing Jewish music and recording for a Finnish record label called Texicali.

Hmmm.

I gotta meet this guy.

One of my fans sent me a bobblehead of Hermann the German and the story of how he got his nickname. (Kim Wallace Photo)

neighborhood kids would get the kickball or flag football games going, the Wallace boys were doing chores. My tasks were to do the dishes and clean up the kitchen, then vacuum the living room. By the time I got done, there usually wasn't a lot of light left outside, but there was no bargaining to put off the work until later. It damned well better be done by the time Dad came home. I don't know which was worse, the ass-chewing or being banished from the garage.

Mike sometimes tried to wrestle me into doing his chores, too, which really stunk because my own took long enough to do, as far as I was concerned.

This is how much I hated chores: One year for Christmas, my folks asked what I wanted, and I told them—with total and complete honesty—that I wanted a dishwasher.

And I got it.

This was key to getting outside sooner and playing with my friends. There were several really good friends back in that old Arnold neighborhood, but mostly Bobby Mahoney, Monty Kincaid and I were the Three Musketeers. And Monty was the best friend a guy could ever have.

When we moved to Arnold I noticed a tractor (as in big truck, not farm equipment) at a house in the next subdivision. It turned out that Monty's dad was an over-the-road driver, so they didn't have tons of money either. We met as pretty much equals.

In the summer, Monty and I would gather soda pop bottles and cash them in at the 7-11 for our running-around money. We were the guys you didn't want to see in your neighborhood, at least if you left your soda pop on the back porch! Let's just say that if it was a slow day for gathering empties we weren't all that hesitant to help ourselves out, and we weren't particular about brands because we emptied them so we could redeem the bottle deposit.

Then, we'd go to the A&W Root Beer Stand and get us a hamburger, fries and a root beer, and think we were living high. After that, we'd ride our bikes all over Jefferson County. I mean, *all over!* We didn't think anything of going 10-15 miles from home, sometimes to places that would have made our dads' hair stand on end—if we'd bothered to tell them. We weren't intimidated by traffic, so we'd ride up to South County, which was the southern edge of St. Louis. It didn't matter. We were curious, and I think our folks quit asking what we were up to because grounding the bikes didn't cure us once we got them back.

When we got about halfway through high school, our lives changed. Literally.

I hit the road with Rusty as he started to expand his racing career, which I'll tell you more about in a little bit. Monty, on the other hand, went with his family back to Pocahontas, Arkansas. His daddy was from there originally, and they went back to a really nice little place there.

In the 1970s, everybody was Kung Fu fighting—including my gang. Here I land a good one on Bobby Mahoney. We're still close friends, and that's another pal Loren Wright, me and Bobby at a function in late 2006. *(L: Bobby & Kellie Mahoney Collection; R: Joyce Standridge Photo)*

In 1978, Monty Kincaid and I paused in the pursuit of soda pop bottle deposits to pose for a photo. Many years later we were still pals, but less than a couple years after the adult picture was taken, Monty was dead. *(Both photos: Kenny Wallace Collection)*

But after the bright lights of Arnold (which would be a laughable thought if you'd ever spent any time there), Pocahontas turned out to be a hard fit for Monty. When he got out of school, he became a trucker like his dad. It was pretty cool for quite a while that we'd be off racing somewhere—say, Phoenix—and I'd get a phone call from him that our paths were crossing.

And it meant the world to me that after I buckled myself into the race car, Monty would be the one guy who would lean in, look me square in the eye and say, "Hey, Herm, now be careful." I knew he didn't care whether I won or not. He just wanted me to come back off the track in one piece.

Several years ago, Monty and Bobby met up with me at Gateway International Raceway outside St. Louis after a Busch race there. We settled in and shared stories and laughs like always, but I noticed that Monty had these real big dark circles under his eyes and he was sucking down beer at a rate beyond anything I'd ever known him to do.

"You doin' okay, Buddy?" I asked him, and he said, "Yeah. Everything's fine."

But he didn't look me in the eye.

Several months later, out of the blue, Monty called and he was talking real fast. If you know me or have heard me during broadcasts, you have to know that what I consider fast is flat dizzy for most people.

"Monty," I said, "what's wrong with you? You don't sound like yourself."

There was a painful pause and then he admitted, "Herm, I've got myself hooked up with the wrong crowd." I could hear him kind of choke up. "I got on some drugs."

It was a kick in the gut for me, but he's not the first, nor probably the last, person I've known whose gotten into this kind of trouble. I thought it took guts for him to admit it, and that made me want to help him out.

"Look, I'm going to be in Memphis next week for the Busch race," I told him. "It's only a couple hours from Pocahontas—can you meet me there?"

He agreed.

But the race came and went.

No Monty.

The next phone call came from Bobby. He could hardly get the words around the tears choking him up. "Monty's been killed."

The wind went out of me. I felt like the whole world had tilted, and maybe I shouldn't have been surprised because bad things always seem to happen when you bring illegal drugs into the mix. But, we were *so close* to helping Monty. You see, if he'd met me at Memphis, I was going to bring him back to St. Louis, get him an apartment and Bobby was going to help with a job. We had a plan. We had a way for Monty to get back to being the guy we'd grown up with and loved.

No matter what, we still loved him, but now it was a memory we loved. None of us were ready for that.

Rusty was kind enough to loan me his plane to fly down to Arkansas for the funeral. There, Monty's dad Bill told me what happened.

Monty had been making and dealing in crystal meth, the scourge of the rural Midwest. If you're not careful, if you need money because jobs are so hard to come by, if you crave a little excitement in the quiet backwoods, it's just too damned easy to fall into that trap. Especially if you hook with the wrong people, and Monty's ex-brother-in-law served that purpose for him.

Monty heard over the scanner that the police had a warrant and were coming out to the travel trailer where he was living at the time. Monty and the other guy took off on those winding back roads. I don't know if they were strung out or not, but they got into a police pursuit and then wrecked.

Bad.

Monty, who was a passenger, was thrown out and died at the scene.

I felt so awful I still can't describe that sick-in-the-pit-of-my-stomach feeling I had. It's back just telling you about this.

I asked Bill if I'd failed Monty; if there was something I could have done to prevent this tragedy. I knew the contrast between the ways our lives had turned out was pretty stark and I thought maybe I should have offered a hand sooner. Maybe I should have recognized that pride was keeping Monty from asking for help.

But Bill shook his head. "Nobody could reach him anymore, Kenny. The meth had him and nobody could get through anymore. He was so strung out that he was rebelling against everything he'd ever known."

This is Monty's son Dustin, and I feel it's very important that he know how much I loved his dad and miss him still. *(Kenny Wallace Collection)*

Bill's words helped. But I guess I'll go to my own grave wondering if it had to be this way for the best friend any kid ever had.

And I'll hold on to the sound of his laughter echoing in my mind as the replays run there of sheer joy, of young boys wildly pedaling bikes, without a care in the world and nothing but happy dreams of a long future sharing adventures.

And I'll always wonder why it couldn't turn out that way.

3

The Evil Gang Rides

TRUTH IS, there's a lot of bologna-and-cheese circulating in my system. Somebody at the Wallace household would usually throw together some macaroni and cheese, too, so we managed most nights to include the four major food groups: fat, sugar, soda pop, and cheese. Gotta have cheese.

It wasn't that Mom wouldn't cook. It's that we wouldn't come out of the garage to sit down at the table after we got going out there.

A lot of things in the Wallace household remained constant, so there was a feeling of having your feet on the ground. Even as Mom and Dad became more solidly middle class, life at home didn't really change. We boys still had our after-school chores, but we never had a Walton-style, sit-down dinner either. I know there's people who will be horrified at that, but I thought it was special. And considering how many hours we spent together in the garage, it's not like we scattered to the four winds after dinner.

It was an evolution, not a revolution, what happened at our shop as we moved into the 1970s. It's not like I remember walking out into the garage one night and Rusty was building the short-block instead of Dad. But it happened. Slowly but surely, Dad was getting tired of the countless hours busting knuckles putting those damned race cars together. And if you win 500 races, how many more are enough? It's not like he was going to hit the road and chase NASCAR. I mean, NASCAR wasn't even a destination in those days.

But Rusty was ready to chase the brass ring, wherever it was.

It didn't start out that way. In the beginning, he just wanted to race at Lake Hill Speedway, our home track. I was only nine years old when he went to court and got legal permission that first season. I was already working in the garage, but it's not like I was dropping in pistons or mounting springs. Not yet.

The thing of it was that Rusty showed signs right from the very start of being every bit as talented as Dad was. That creates pressure, stress,

When you grow up in a family where your mom and dad are both into the same thing, you'll end up spending a lot of time together. Add to that parents who are winners at racing, and, well, you probably won't end up in competitive fishing tournaments. *(Rocky Rhodes Photo; Kenny Wallace Collection)*

and work. Loads of work, especially during those early days when there were two race cars to prepare. Over time, Dad spent more and more time helping Rusty and less time working on his own car.

I remember the night Dad announced he wasn't going to race the next night. You could have heard a pin drop in that garage. I mean, if there was a race in our two-state area, dirt or pavement, regular show or extra laps, Russ Wallace was there.

At this point, we were looking at a race car that wasn't wrecked. In fact, a few more hours of work (nothing abnormal), and it would be as competitive as anything on the track.

Dad wasn't sick.

Mom wasn't having a baby.

The Russians weren't launching missiles at us.

What the hell was going on here?

I busted into tears. But that had no more effect on my dad than the older boys' haranguing questions. And you know what? Dad didn't give in. He didn't stop racing altogether, mind you. Nothing quite that earth-shattering, but it was the beginning of a very, very long process of passing the torch to the next generation. Slowly but surely we were shifting our attention to Rusty's racing as Dad's became secondary. He still raced, but only when Rusty was totally ready to go, and only when Dad felt like it.

During those years of two race cars (and Mike chomping at the bit to get old enough to drive, too), nobody was throwing the snot-nosed

Even before we'd succeeded in establishing Rusty's career, Mike teamed up with a local car owner and began racing, too. And as you can see from the four-wide racing, it was a hell of a lot of fun. *(Rocky Rhodes Photo; Kenny Wallace Collection)*

kid *(that's me)* out. We had some other help, but generally it was just the four of us working long hours every night. It's not such a big secret, but I wouldn't take a billion dollars for those years, not even when Rusty would yell at me, *"Herm, what the hell are you doing now?"*

I was Inside Herman's World.

It was a really cool place to be, as far as I was concerned. You see, I liked to do the things that challenged me or scared me a little bit.

Like learning the welder. Or the grinder. Those things could also make you a hero. *(Hey, remember I was only about nine years old when they started depending on me to help out instead of just putting up with me being underfoot.)*

Seriously. If you could master the big tools in the garage you could make some real progress on the race car, so when I had my tasks completed (mostly cleaning and straightening up, and believe me, I got those things done first because I didn't want to get hollered at), I would go off in the corner with the welder and some metal.

That's what would get Rusty's attention. And because we were pinching pennies pretty good on the race car, he didn't want me wasting precious resources playing around. But I was careful about it and just messed with scrap.

(Unless there wasn't any scrap, but don't tell Rusty that.)

The Honestly Named Poor Boy Chassis Company

We had places to go and races to win. It was clear from the start that Rusty had extraordinary talent, and we were all committed to helping him out. I mean, racing was like a "religion" to us.

This is how our racing eventually changed—that's Rusty in the #66 and Dad in the #6. And you can see Mom's changing priorities, too, in the Union Jack sponsorship on Rusty's car instead of Dad's. *(Don Figler Photo; Judy Wallace Collection)*

Please don't be offended by that observation. We don't place racing ahead of God or anything stupid like that, but an alternative definition of the word in Webster's is *"something a person believes in and follows devotedly."*

Slam dunk. That's what racing is to the Wallaces.

Even Mom. I can remember her going all over the area, trying to get sponsorship for Rusty. Wasn't any way in the world we could keep that car competitive without some help. She managed to ram-rod a couple of deals from Union Jack (a local retail store that specialized in jeans) and CMC Stereos. She worked so, so hard to get that.

I guess I understand the lack of overall response. St. Louis is a baseball town. Just ask the football Rams or the hockey Blues. Even with three Wallace brothers and Kenny Schrader in NASCAR through the '80s,

Even as a kid racing at the Springfield, Missouri, fairgrounds in 1977, Rusty recognized the need for a sharp-looking car that sponsors would be attracted to. *(Kenny Wallace Collection)*

Rusty the Protector

For some reason, it was just us three brothers working on Dad's race car down at the shop. I think it was 1969 or 1970, so I was about seven years old and Mike was 11. Rusty was just 14, but he was the senior mechanic that day when suddenly there were tornado warnings. Too quick for Dad or Mom to get to us, and as anybody from the St. Louis area can tell you, storms pop up quick, and they pop up bad.

Rusty's always been smarter than the average person, and he figured out that if he put helmets on Mike and me, and then put us inside the race car we would be protected by the roll cage, too.

Shit is blowing around outside like crazy, and we don't know what's going to happen, but even though there wasn't room for all three of us in the race car, Rusty never hesitated to protect the little brothers.

We didn't take a direct hit from that storm, but I have never doubted for one minute from that day forward exactly where we stood in Rusty's heart.

From a very early age—in this case 1978— this is how it's been, big brother (and hero) Rusty taking care of Kenny. (Kenny Wallace Collection)

'90s, and '00s, getting attention has been really hard in local media, so it follows that sponsorship was precious to come by back then. She's still pretty bitter about the lack of support Rusty got in the area. I suppose that if I'd worked as hard as Mom did, I'd be pissed, too, if there hadn't been more help.

Even before Rusty had any kind of success to back up Mom's efforts, we were all working, earning money, to keep those two race cars going for Dad and Rusty. You may recall me telling you that Dad had a second job delivering newspapers back in our Rolla days. Well, he never gave it up. And sometimes, especially after we got old enough for driver's licenses, we boys got drafted to do the delivery. Even when we were young we often rode along and pitched papers so the driver could concentrate on the road and keep us moving. That meant the job would be done sooner.

During the Arnold years, we would head up I-270 to Des Peres Road and deliver the Community Press for miles around the suburban area. And in one of the driveways there was always parked a Penske-Sears van.

We'd already heard of Roger Penske. We knew he was on a tear, winning Indy 500s, and as an outstanding businessman, race-car finances weren't a worry like they were to us. So, here's a driveway with a Penske-

Sears van, and we figure there's this really long shot that maybe the homeowners are interested in racing?

Man, we're desperate. You look at a racing tire bill these days and freak out, but back then in the age of no tire rules you couldn't build enough racks on your trailer to hold all that you needed, because you needed several sets *for every track*, and you needed different sets *for every track*. It's awful now—it was worse then.

So, one day we stopped at that house. I don't remember who got up the courage, but I'm sure it was one of us desperate people who was too aware of a threatening bill collector.

Turned out the homeowner was a guy by the name of Charlie Chase. And Charlie, who was the local fire battalion chief, was a friend of Don Miller. If you haven't followed Rusty's career close enough, Don was a major player in Penske-Sears tools in those days, hence the van in the drive. And best of all, Charlie and Don were huge racing fans.

I'm telling you this, and you can take it to the bank: Every good thing in life is a matter of timing and luck. I know there are literally thousands of capable race drivers across the country, and hundreds who probably ought to be competing for a Cup ride, but it always—but always—turns out that you were in the right place at the right time and met the right person.

Meeting Charlie started it for Rusty, and inadvertently, for me, later on, because Rusty's good luck led to mine.

We needed more than a newspaper delivery route to pay the race car bills. I was only in junior high school, but I knew that much. I certainly heard it often enough at the shop and at the track.

Here's the deal: Rusty was going racing for a living.

Small problem: We didn't make enough money at racing to call it a living.

So, we started Poor Boy Chassis, but there wasn't room in our home garage for it, so Charlie rented the space in a shop on St. Louis Road in Valley Park, Missouri, not far from Lake Hill Speedway. It wasn't a showplace, by any means, because Charlie wasn't rich. He had a real good job and he was well-off, at least by Wallace standards, but he wasn't going to make the Forbes list.

What the shop lacked in new bells and whistles it more than made up for in cleanliness. I know this because Rusty was always cracking the whip to make sure it was clean. He had previously worked in an engine shop and he knew how critical it was to have a surgical kind of cleanliness building engines. He just figured that ought to extend to building race cars, too. And why not? He had Herman.

You could not wear me out. I was hyper, I was off the Ritalin, and I lived and breathed racing. So, I kept the shop, the tow truck and the trailer almost spotless. If I missed a spot, Rusty didn't, and he pointed it out.

About this time, a bunch of really good things started happening for us. And I want to start by saying that none of it happened by plan. We

When Poor Boy Chassis started up, Rusty knew we needed to get attention beyond our area, so they were also marketed as a Gator Chassis through our friends Mike and Dorothy Allgaier's speed shop in Springfield, Illinois. *(Kenny Wallace Collection)*

didn't sit down one day and say, "Y'know, we're gonna go ASA, and then USAC, and then NASCAR."

Shit, we weren't capable of thinking past the next race.

But we got some really good people into our lives about that time. Dad certainly gave Rusty the start he needed to get attention, but after we brought Charlie, John Childs and Don Kirn into our circle, things changed. Big time.

Those are the three key people who got Rusty out and away from Lake Hill, Tri-City, and the other area tracks to go regional racing. We were going to the American Speed Association (ASA) and it was because John gave us the money we needed to travel, Charlie picked up all kinds of bills for us, and Don built us engines and then didn't charge anything like he could have.

That last one was critical. When we met Don, I couldn't believe—flat *could not* believe—that people were paying $20,000 for an engine! I mean, that's more money than our house had cost!

Well, we didn't pay that. We paid for parts and some up-front costs, and then we gave Don one-third of what we made. It was a good deal all the way around because we could almost afford that, and we won enough that Don wasn't getting the shaft.

Here's another deal you need to know about that time: We'd go to Milwaukee or Winchester and win a big, big show—and we were broke before Rusty got off the stage with the trophy.

Seriously. There were so many bills stacked on the desk at Poor Boy that the winner's check was spent before we got back home. We **HAD** to win. If we hadn't won all those races—and if we hadn't also been stacking chassis three-high on the open trailer, to sell at any price we could get at Dave Dayton's Thanksgiving auction for racers in Indianapolis—we'd all be doing time in debtor's prison.

Talk about living on the edge. We begged, borrowed and stole.

And I ain't talkin' about the "stole."

"I Can't Take the Ticket"

There were more people coming into our lives very quickly. Knowing Charlie meant getting to know Don Miller, and that was critical to the contacts that Rusty eventually made. Paul Andrews worked at O.K. Vacuum—until Rusty corrupted him by convincing him to come work at Poor Boy. Fortunately, it worked out really good for Paul—who also helped me—as he's become one of the most sought-after crew chiefs in NASCAR.

But back in the late 1970s, Paul was just one of a motley crew around Rusty, including me. We were always clean and neat, but we were a bunch of crazy kids. Rusty had a big Afro, me with my big Afro, the rest of the crew looking wild, too, so we got attention whether we wanted it or not. I'm thinkin' there was a lot of testosterone in that truck, too, so we might have wanted it.

In fact, Bobby Allison crossed our paths pretty frequently back then at short-track races because he was the ultimate racer who wasn't afraid to go anywhere and race anybody, and he just shook his head at us one night. "Boy, what an *Evil Gang* that is."

Bingo. We not only had a "style," if you can call white-boy Afros a style, but we had a gang name, too. We didn't know that we were a decade ahead of the urban culture. We even ended up with Don Miller getting us patches—a logo of the Missouri state outline with the words "Evil Gang" in the center—for our little clique.

Now, most big brothers are trying to shoo away little brothers, but not Rusty. Mike, on the other hand, was pretty much doing his own thing, having hooked up with a guy by the name of Bob Quinn. They were on their way to being the toughest team on St. Louis-area dirt tracks.

I mean, this sounds less than humble, but I'd turned into one hell of a good mechanic. Rusty knew that, and he wanted me with him. Over time, I got to be a good fabricator, and a minor legend as a tire changer, too, but from the earliest days with Rusty's career, I kept everything clean and neat. And, as soon as we hit the road with ASA, I drove the hauler.

Did I mention that I was 14 years old?

That was illegal as hell, for sure, but it's got to be told.

The thing of it was that all the guys with Rusty worked their asses off and when it came time to get on the road, one of them would drive the hauler through the heavy traffic in the 'burbs and across the Poplar Street Bridge in St. Louis. We'd get onto the Illinois interstate highway and they'd pull over.

And then Herman the German got behind the wheel.

Herman drove like he did everything else. Which means 100 miles per hour, so it came as no surprise, I suppose, that one morning in the wee hours as the sun was trying to come up just outside Chicago, I looked in the mirror—and saw the bubble gum machines going off on top of a cop car.

Although Dog Wirz is missing from this photo, this is the genesis of the Evil Gang—from left, brother Mike, Jeff Thousand, Rusty, Paul Andrews (yes, the guy who became a Cup crew chief), and me. I think I was about 15 years old at the time. *(Kenny Wallace Collection)*

"Crap, crap, crap!" I screamed bloody murder. (It might have been a stronger term than that, but I'll give myself the benefit of the doubt since I wasn't even old enough to shave.)

People were crashed out, sound asleep throughout the hauler, but that got them waking up.

"Rusty, Rusty—there's a cop! There's a cop on my tail!"

It's interesting that nobody asked if I was speeding. The assumption had already been made that I was. The question was whether the cop would take them to jail for contributing to the delinquency of a minor. Or worse. I'm pretty sure there was a cooler in there somewhere, and no-body was over 21.

Well, Rusty had been ticketed in just about every state we'd ever been in. If he climbed over into the seat, he would, for sure, be going to jail. So, he told crew member Dave Wirz, "Dog, you gotta take this ticket. *You gotta take this ticket!"*

Our hauler at the time was a modified St. Louis newspaper delivery truck—a sort of box truck so it was open inside, all the way back. That meant that Dog came up, crawled over me and got out the driver's door. He walked back to the cop, and he was back there for like 30 minutes. I mean, we were sweating bullets and trying not to crap our pants.

Pretty soon, Dog came back to the truck. We're like, "What'd he say, Dog? *What'd he say?"*

Dog told us the cop had asked, "Do you know how fast you were going?"

And Dog had replied, "No, I was sleeping."

He still took the ticket.

Slavedriver, Thy Name Is Rusty

If you've followed racing to any degree you've heard of my brother, Rusty Wallace. And if you've followed racing pretty closely, you are aware that

Two guys I owe a great deal to and for very different reasons: Dave "Dog" Wirz took a ticket for me (and then came back several years later to crew for me when I drove in ASA) and John Childs, who was responsible for launching both Rusty and me as regional drivers in ASA. *(Kenny Wallace Collection)*

he has always had his shit together. He met good people willing to help him out, but there was no red carpet laid down and nobody was sitting in Daytona Beach going, "Gee, we'll be glad when that Rusty Wallace kid gets old enough and good enough to come grace our little racing series."

Rusty owes some people like those I've mentioned, and some I'm going to mention farther along, but basically Rusty happened because Rusty made Rusty happen. And the deal was, if you were going racing with him, you had to take it every bit as seriously as he did. It had to be Priority #1 in your life. That began with the Sunday-night 25-lappers at Lake Hill and extended all the way into his NASCAR career.

Show you what I mean.

Over time, I gained more jobs at the shop, including, in time, being the guy making the tire choice.

But, first I had to prove myself to the real Boss.

I'm the tire guy. Big deal. Rusty tells me I have to get him 1-1/2" stagger on the rear.

If you don't know all that much about racing tires (and if you do, bear with us for a second), we used to run usually two inches of stagger on the front, meaning two inches less circumference on the left front than the right front. The back had some kind of stagger, too, but that often differed, depending on the track you were running. You had a bit

Rusty is always so neat about himself and his car so it's rare to find a photo where he's not clean. It was worth it, though, as he'd just won at DuQuoin (IL) State Fairgrounds in the early 1980s. That's me on the left, John Childs, the trophy queen and Rusty being interviewed. *(Kenny Wallace Collection)*

Changing Gears

Talk to anybody who's crewed on a short-track race car, and they'll probably tell you that the worst job at the race track is changing gears.

For more than a quarter century now, short-track cars have been equipped with lightweight rear ends that have a back cover on them. Remove several bolts, and the cover comes off, exposing the rear end gears. Since these are still rear-drive cars, unlike today's street vehicles, the two gears that fit inside determine how much torque—or bite—gets from the engine's horsepower output to the track surface.

Your thought might be that it would be desirable to get all the horsepower the engine can produce, but the truth is that it's an art more than a science because too much and you'll break the tires loose. Never get the traction you need. Too little, and everybody else on the track is gonna go sailing by you like you've got an anchor.

So, it's not at all unusual for teams, especially when they're running dirt or when they've gone to a strange track, to change gears, sometimes even between races at a single event.

And here's the catch—it's the messiest, yuckiest job on the race car. Because when you remove the cover, the rear end grease, which is sort of the color and consistency of motor oil, runs out. You have a catch can under it but I don't know anybody who's ever changed gears and not ended up with some of it on them. And since you're laying down on the ground, hopefully on a tarp or piece of plastic (but not always, especially if you're in a hurry) you can multiply your opportunities to get filthy. So, trust me on this, if nothing else—everybody hates to change rear-end gears.

We were at an ARTGO race in Rockford, Illinois. ARTGO shows were pretty exciting and carried some prestige to winning, but there wasn't anything particularly special about this show. It was just another race that summer.

Among my jobs on Rusty's crew was gluing lug nuts to make pit stops easier. (Kenny Wallace Collection)

The third time Rusty made me get under the car and change the gears, I got mad. I looked at him and I said in my best smart-ass manner, "How many more damned times do you want me to change gears?"

He looked me square in the face and he said, "Do you want to win?"

I said, "Yes, of course."

"Then change the gears."

That stuck with me through the years. If you're lazy, if you're afraid of getting a little grease under your nails, you don't belong in racing. Besides, the grease washes off. The trophy just might shine forever.

of a handful on the straightaways if you had a lot of stagger, because stagger makes the car still want to turn, no matter where you are. But all racing set-ups are a matter of compromise—sometimes, a really fine line of compromise.

So, at this particular event Rusty wanted 1-1/2" more in the right rear circumference than the left, and I had been sweating like it's a sauna

One of the very few photos of the entire Evil Gang together, and you can see that we were just a tiny bit full of ourselves. But we were basically harmless. *(Judy Wallace Collection)*

(which our delivery truck was during the summer, I think), and I told him, "All I can get is 1-5/8" stagger."

The taskmaster was unimpressed.

One-hundred-forty degrees in the truck? Tires literally melting in the heat? There are only forty tires in there and you don't have a vulcanizer to build me a new one?

Well, get this, kid—there's no money to go buy more tires, so you get back in there and find me 1-1/2" of stagger. Not one-eighth of an inch more or less. **Got that?"**

Yessir.

So, I would drag my 155-pound, scrawny carcass (down from 157 before we got to the track) back to the truck, tail between my legs, and I would start measuring tires again.

I found Rusty his 1-1/2" stagger somehow, but I think the tires were just scared of him. If they didn't bend to his will they were doomed, and I think they knew that.

You might not be surprised to hear this: I still hate tires. Because this scene was replayed dozens of times. And I sometimes thought those damned tires shrunk just so they could laugh at my sorry ass dragging over in their general direction.

4

I Didn't Drop the Trophy on the Highway

MY JUNIOR YEAR of high school I missed 36 days. Not all at once, of course, but there might have appeared to be a suspicious pattern to it—like, lots of Mondays and Fridays. Regardless, the school district had a rule that if you missed a certain amount of days—and I think it was substantially lower than my record—you were held back a grade.

I did not get an automatic pass. Wallace was not a name to get a good restaurant seat, much less ignore school district rules. I was called before the school board, principal and superintendent to explain myself, and at 17 years old, I stood before a table full of adults ready to doom me to repeating 11th grade. This experience was so unnerving that it made holding a microphone and talking to millions of people across the country on television later seem like a snap. You can't reach through the set and squeeze the old *cojones,* but the school board could have reached right out and put the hurt on.

I can't believe that the school district allowed me time off to go to Florida with Rusty's race team. Wait a minute. I don't think they did. Maybe that's why I almost didn't pass my junior year! From left, on the beach at Daytona, John Childs, me, Rusty, Patti, another guy from home, and Steve Shear.
(Kenny Wallace Collection)

Somehow, I found the courage to address them, and this is what I told them:

"All my family are auto racers. It's more than a hobby for us—it's a way of life. When I'm done with school I'm going to make a living from racing somehow. Right now, I'm traveling with my older brother, working as a mechanic on his crew. We go all over the Midwest with an association called the American Speed Association, and we race with other groups, too. Rusty is successful at this and he's building toward a big career, so we're not just messing around.

"I promise you that I don't smoke dope, I'm not out partying or doing anything illegal. We just go all over and sometimes we have to leave on Friday, or we are still on the road on Monday."

They didn't give me an answer that afternoon.

Maybe they figured I needed to sweat a little more. Yeah, like the buckets dripping all over the floor hadn't been enough.

Here's the deal: Rusty had gone before a judge at age 16 to get a court order allowing him to race at Lake Hill Speedway. (Our pal, Kenny Schrader, had set the precedent a year earlier.) By Rusty's senior year at Fox High, he was gone all the time racing, and he already was working any and all available hours to support his racing. Considering how smart he is and how much he absorbed growing up, passing a G.E.D.-type exam was a snap, so he was free to pursue his calling. The way things have turned out for him, it appears to have been the right decision.

In the years when the Evil Gang was getting perms and going blond, so was our lifelong friend, Ken Schrader. *(Kenny Wallace Collection)*

Mike, on the other hand, was a walking brain at school and he was really serious about it. He took all kinds of extra-credit classes and he was done early. He graduated, but in a non-traditional way.

So, here I am, recipient of a checkered legacy. I mean, Rusty and Mike were never trouble at school, either, so that wasn't an issue. But the school board might have figured out that secondary education wasn't the highest priority at the Wallace household, and I'm their last chance to get it right.

A few anxious days later I got the verdict: I was going to be a senior after all! They totally believed I was straight with them and that the absences were racing-related. I guess they sort of believed that I was getting a kind of advanced education, too, traveling and meeting people. Seeing so many different things. Even back then, it didn't take a rocket scientist—or school board member—to figure out that racing ate up every dime and every minute of time, and that if you had the passion for racing, there was no room for a life of drugs, sex and rock 'n roll.

Well, at least the first one.

I've always liked rock better than country. And when it comes to females, we weren't a race team of monks.

The memories of my school years must have faded, as in 2005 I was inducted into the Fox High School Sports Hall of Fame. It's mostly baseball, basketball and football players, but they found room for a racer, too, so I loaned them a trophy from Rockingham, which was something they couldn't get from the ball players. *(Kenny Wallace Collection)*

Homecoming

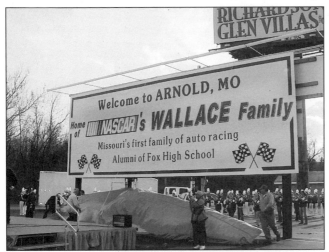

Rusty used to get in trouble for pulling up at Fox High School with the tow rig, waiting for me to get out of school. But in 2006, I was invited to bring my Modified and park it in front of the auditorium as the city and school honored the Wallaces. How times have changed. We received keys to the city, got serenaded by the school band, and had a billboard unveiled next to Interstate 55. *(All photos: Joyce Standridge Photos)*

One of my all-time favorite teachers was Mr. Kasey. I actually (almost) paid attention in science class because he made it interesting and he forgave my antics, too. More than 20 years later, our reunion was a genuinely happy one.

A.J. Foyt

Rusty thought the sun rose and set on Bobby Allison. I felt the same way about A.J. Foyt. I mean, I would run around as a hyperactive kid telling people, "I'm A.J. Foyt. Four-time Indy 500 winner."

So, imagine my sweaty palms when I actually got to meet him. We raced with A.J. in the twilight of his career in the late 1970s. We actually finished ahead of him sometimes, which, I think, is the reason we came to his attention. If it had been earlier, during the years he was almost unbeatable, we would have been just a bunch of punk kids underfoot, but we were the *Evil Gang* and legends in our own minds.

Meeting him was cool. Having him say, "Hi, how ya doin', Kenny?" in that Texas drawl, well, let's just say I understood the concept of swooning after that.

But no matter how many times we spoke, and believe me, I would look for opportunities to cross paths, it never, ever got old. It doesn't even today. A.J. is still one of the handful of idols I hold in high esteem.

So, here's a somewhat related tale for you.

In 2006, I raced a Busch show at Kentucky Motor Speedway and then flew up to Michigan International Speedway for a Cup race the following day. I hitched a ride with Kevin and DeLana Harvick on their plane, so it was only fair that I drive the rental car to the track.

When we got there, it was about two o'clock in the morning, and I'll blame that. We also didn't have any credentials with us (dumb move), so I roared up to the guard shack by the motorhome compound in our super-impressive rental Hyundai and chirped, "Hi! I'm A.J. Foyt. Four-time Indy 500 champ!"

And the guard said, "Yessir," and waved us on through!

The name still gets the job done. The name still impresses the hell out of people, even when it's a lie.

I don't think I look like A.J. I don't think I ever looked like A.J. and my posse definitely didn't look like Texans.

Especially when DeLana got out of the car and kissed the ground.

Did I mention I drove about 95 miles per hour from the airport to the track? Talking all the while to my spotter, who was shotgun?

And I have to look at people when I'm talking to them.

There's nobody in racing I respect more than A.J. Foyt, so imagine the thrill of not only getting to know him, but having him recognize me by name! (Bruce Bennett Photo)

Look Out, Raquel

On the first day of school my senior year I arrived a boy. And I left for home a man.

Okay, not really a "man," but seriously wanting to be. You see, in

The lovely Miss Kim Poole. *(Kenny Wallace Collection)*

photography class, these two sisters walked in about three or four minutes late, so right off the bat you couldn't ignore them. Add to that, the Poole girls were knock-outs, especially Kim.

I mean, *one look.*

Up to this time, I had been consumed with racing. I had noticed girls, especially some of the pretty ones who walked up to introduce themselves to our team's handsome race driver after the races, but they weren't about to notice the teenage pit-crewman covered in rear-end grease and tire dust. And, I hadn't really cared.

But, Kim Poole walked in wearing a gray vest over a white blouse that did nothing but accent the best assets any girl ever had. I mean, Raquel Welch had been my ideal of what the perfect woman should look like, but in walks Kim with that same tanned skin, shiny dark hair, and a body to keep a teenage boy awake and sweaty all night long.

Holy crap.

This girl is beautiful. *And Kenny's hormones have kicked into overdrive. It's photography class, and I intend to make use of the dark room! Yessss!*

So much for intentions.

And, frankly, that's about how smooth my technique was, so you'll not be surprised to learn that, initially, at least, the biggest dork at Fox High did not sweep the most beautiful girl he'd ever seen off her feet. I could change a rear-end gear in Rusty's race car with my eyes closed, but my experience in charming the ladies was limited to what I saw on television and in the movies, pretty much. The problem was that when the words came out of my mouth, it sounded less like James Bond and more like a Stooge. I even had a curly-haired perm at the time, so it would be Larry if you are choosing a Stooge to relate to.

What I lacked in being suave, I more than made up for with persistence. I just continued to flirt with Kim and tell her how pretty she was. I even badgered her for a kiss, which she finally relented and gave me. It was a chaste peck on the cheek, but I thought I was going to die.

Baby steps, Kenny, baby steps. And for me, where Kim was concerned, very little encouragement was needed to keep panting after her.

Over time, though, she wore me down. Even though we found out that her parents knew Jerry Sifford, and therefore, knew a little about racing, and even though she seemed kind of interested in all the traveling (and missing school—I hadn't turned over a new leaf), by the time the class ended, I was totally and thoroughly sure that I'd blown any chance of attracting the lovely Miss Poole.

We were into the second term a bit, photography class just a memory and I wasn't seeing Kim every day. But one day I got a message on the school bus by way of mutual friend Regina Sullinger. She said, "Kim Poole said she wants to go out with you."

And I replied, "Well, you tell Kim Poole she's nothing but a big tease."

(Yeah, you're right. I was demonstrating how to be a jerk, but it comes so

High School sweethearts. *(Judy Wallace Collection)*

natural when your hormones are raging. Guys will understand, girls will wonder why the story doesn't end there.)

A little later, the phone rang at Poor Boy Chassis, and I answered it.

"Kenny Wallace?"

"Yeah, this is Kenny."

"Well, this is Kim Poole, and I want to know if it's a crime to want to go out with you?"

I can only guess that the guys in the rest of Kim's classes were stupid, blind or not as pushy as I'd been, but I kind of think that she missed being told she was beautiful.

Or maybe she likes dorks.

I never asked.

It's got to be the latter because our "date" consisted of waiting until her folks went to the wrestling matches in downtown St. Louis one night, and I went over to her house to prove what a catch I am. Meaning, I didn't spend any money on her, I didn't take her someplace nice, and I tried to put the moves on her!

I don't know what she saw in me then—or even now—but the good Lord was watching over me, because that was the start to the best, most enduring relationship of my life, even though I don't suppose I ever improved my technique significantly.

Dammit, I Want to Drive a Race Car

I felt like I got lost in the shuffle.

There's a lot of reasons why that happened. It's nothing so straightforward like nobody was going to invest in a kid who was hopelessly in

Getting It Wrong

I am so glad to be getting older. I am now way past that crap of thinking I have to be cool, because that's a trap that can make otherwise decent people do really stupid things. I have succeeded in being a jackass on a number of occasions in my life, but never quite so bad as the night I graduated from high school.

I was the third Wallace boy to graduate from Fox Senior High School, but the first to actually go to the graduation ceremony at the football field and throw my cap in the air. It was a big deal, even to a kid trying to act cool, but I was going through a bad phase when I didn't want my racing buddies to know I had a girlfriend.

In spite of that, Kim made a card for me, dressed up in a pretty skirt and high heels, and then walked the three miles—in those damned heels—to the football field because she didn't have a car and her idiot boyfriend didn't offer a ride.

After the ceremony, she came up and handed me the card. And because my family and pals were standing around and I just couldn't bear the thought of the teasing I would get, I took the card, maybe mumbled a "thank you," and then turned my back on her.

The gang went on to Rich and Charlie's restaurant in South County, but maybe there's the tiniest bit of redemption for my soul because I was absolutely miserable. I didn't enjoy my big night

at all because I realized I'd been so awful to the sweetest girl I've ever known.

I have no idea of why she forgave me. I can't even bring myself to ask her how she felt, because I'm afraid the answer would be devastating even after all these years. But, I've done my penance. I have admitted to my children what a jerk I was, and how that whole deal still bothers me to this day. Every so often, I give Kim a big hug like I should have that night, and I'll whisper, "I'm so sorry."

I truly believe that Kim deserves a medal.

She has always just wanted to be a wife and mother, and for some reason that makes no good sense, she wanted to share her life with me. You'll never see Kim Wallace strutting down through the pits at a NASCAR event. She never wanted any of the so-called lifestyle—she just wanted to be with me.

So, when I see these dudes toss aside the first girlfriend or first wife when they arrive in the big time, I just want to shake them. If the girl was good enough when you were nobody, why would that change when you're "somebody?"

In our case, at least, the wife is the better partner, and I'm smart enough to recognize that. She tolerates my racing, she makes it better by being a part of my life, and she's forgiven me for so much.

That's why I love her even more today than I did over 20 years ago.

Proof that I walked the stage when I graduated. The other photo was taken later at Rich & Charlie's restaurant where friends and family went to celebrate. But you'll notice the smile isn't as big as usual, and that's due to Kim's absence—which was my own fault. (Both photos: Judy Wallace Collection)

love. Kim and I had our act together, and she so totally believed in me that if I wanted to go racing, she not only wanted me to race, she was indignant that the rest of the world didn't feel the same way.

I guess looking back, it was, once again, a matter of timing. Rusty came along in the age of cheap gasoline. We could put a car together for him in those early days for like $1,000. Mike got some family attention, too, but he was real quick about finding outside help.

And I realize that my dad was getting just real tired of working on race cars. He'd been spending seven days a week on the damned things for 25-30 years by the time I was old enough to drive one. Mom had flat worn out potential sponsors. So, the options were less by then, too.

A lot of people thought that because of the extra effort I put into Rusty's career—short-changing school, practicing pit stops, working countless hours in preparation, traveling everywhere, not giving Kim as much attention as she deserved—and being so thrilled when things went well for Rusty, that what I wanted was to be Super Crew Man. Or maybe people just thought that's what I *SHOULD* want.

Well, if you read the Introduction, you are aware that I am a racer. I done told you so. And it's not like I, or any other racer, has a choice. Maybe if my dad had been a fisherman, Rusty, Mike and I would have been tussling with Bassmaster Jimmy Houston instead of Busch driver Tommy Houston. I mean, part of being a racer is that it's what my father did and I never really knew anything else.

But, it was a lot more than that. Racing has always spoken to my soul. I can't control how I feel about it, and while I have compromised with aspects of it, I was always willing to do whatever I had to. That feeling goes all the way back to Hot Wheels in the milk.

So, by the time I was 18 years old—a significantly retarded age for a Wallace to *not* be behind the wheel—I was unbelievably frustrated that all these really smart people in my life had not recognized what a hell I was living in.

And then one of them noticed.

The Legendary Springfield Mile Is Conquered, Thank You Very Much

My brother Mike called Pat Walsh. It was late summer 1982 and the Illinois Street Stock Championship race was scheduled for the one-mile dirt track at the Springfield Mile. *Let Kenny drive your car at the race,* Mike told Pat.

Today, Pat is married to Kenny Schrader's sister, Sherry, and his son Joey is an exceptionally good crew chief on Kenny's dirt operation, but back in 1982 Pat Walsh was Da Man. A good race car driver in his own right, so if he had told Mike, *no way, man,* I don't think anybody would have been surprised or particularly upset (except me). I mean, there wasn't this huge groundswell of support that was ready to scream at Pat,

Mike talked our friend Pat Walsh (left) into letting me drive at the 1982 Illinois State Fairgrounds Street Stock Nationals. Pat is now Kenny Schrader's brother-in-law, but was then a good driver in his own right. *(Kenny Wallace Collection)*

you're denying a brilliant talent! There shoulda been, but there wouldn't have been. (I'm just kidding, of course.)

Anyway, Pat, being the astute judge of talent (kidding once more), and a really, really good guy (not kidding at all), agreed.

Wow.

Now, it's not like I'm a total novice at driving. I mean, Kenny Schrader took me down to his parents' farm in Licking, Missouri, when I was still not much more than a grade-school student, sat me on his lap behind the steering wheel of an old truck and worked the accelerator and brake while I steered. We flat wore out that old field and even though Kenny had the patience of a saint, I could have done that just about forever. Who needs reading, writing and arithmetic when you've got shifting, turning and sliding?

Plus, we've already documented that I had about 300,000 miles on the highway before I had a legal mile with a driver's license. So, let's say that I wasn't exactly a novice when I went to Springfield that day. But even doing a helmet-less 100 mph on I-55 isn't the same as getting behind the wheel of a race car with the full race gear (which makes you feel different anyway) and racing with a whole pack of experienced drivers. Because, make no mistake—they may have been "street stock" race cars but anytime cars go on the Mile track, there's no shortage of experienced, capable drivers who want to run on the longer oval. Like 80-100 of them dudes, all wanting to win as much as I did.

Well, I did it.

I was just incredibly lucky. Everything fell into place exactly like in a fairy tale, plus Pat had a wonderful car under me. What I hadn't ex-

This is it—my very first time ever in a competitive race, driving Pat's car—and we won! (Kenny Wallace Collection)

pected, however, as I stood on the Fairgrounds stage with pretty girls, the promoter and a bad-ass trophy for the Victory photos, was the sense of relief that washed over me.

Let's face it—I had a hell of a legacy to live up to: Russ, Rusty and Mike Wallace. Mom had won Powder Puff races, and even Uncle Gary had won Hobby stock races. Man, to call yourself a race driver and a Wallace, you just had to prove that the genes hadn't bypassed you.

After the race, in one of those quirky moments life sometimes throws, we had just gotten out on I-55, headed back home, when along comes Rusty and the rest of the crew. What timing, huh? They'd been up at Grundy County Speedway near Chicago for an ARTGO race and were headed home, too.

When I saw Rusty, I was just euphoric. I rolled down the window on Pat's truck, grabbed the trophy and, running at least 55 miles per hour—

I appear to be in shock during the post-race interview after the win on the Springfield Mile. (Kenny Wallace Collection)

Mom made the sash for Kim, and then posed us with the trophy and the $863 that was my share of the winnings. *(Judy Wallace Photo; Kenny Wallace Collection)*

but probably faster, considering the people involved—leaned out and stuck that damned thing out there, shaking it and hollering at Rusty and the crew. I was like, *"Look at this! Look at this! Woooo—hoooo!"*

So, you're thinking what a great launch to a racing career, and you'd be right. And you might also be thinking this opened the door and Kenny rushed through to go racing.

Well, I woulda liked to.

Unfortunately, in spite of the win, nobody—I mean, absolutely nobody, including family members—was waiting on the other side of the door. I didn't guess Junior Johnson or Cliff Stewart would be throwing guys out of their rides and calling me to pack my bags for NASCAR Land, but really, I sort of hoped I'd proven a point.

The truth is that my on-track abilities, showcased just once, continued to be overshadowed by my off-track abilities, demonstrated every week. I had screwed myself out of launching a driving career by being a good crew man. I mean, hell, Rusty wasn't about to put me in a car. I was too valuable in the pits. Mike was involved in getting his own career launched.

Dad was tired.

Mom was tired.

So, I went back to the garage. Maybe I should have worked the whole angle a lot more or from a different attack, but I was an 18-year-old kid and not a particularly sophisticated one. And, at that point I went back to making tires stretch and shrink to Rusty's specifications.

I ain't whining. Yes, I wanted to drive race cars, but if I couldn't, I

This is an important memory because we'd thrashed to take Rusty's pavement car and get it ready for Mike to race on dirt. As you can see, he won. Paul Andrews is fourth from left, then Mike and the trophy girl, and our engine builder Don Kirn next. Rusty holds the checkered flag, I'm next to him and on the end is my pal Monty Kincaid. *(Terry Young Photo; Kenny Wallace Collection)*

still managed to have a life that other guys could envy. I would be an idiot to complain, but it's been alleged . . .

And Then We Went to McDonald's One Morning

We were on our way to a show in Jefferson, Georgia. Nice little track down there, and I can't even remember how we eventually did with the race. We were eating breakfast that morning at McDonald's so I'll hazard a guess that we were close to being broke.

Remember back in the last chapter when I said that timing is everything? You have to meet up with the right people in the right place at the right time? Who could have thought that a McDonald's four states away from home would change my life? I mean, what if we'd had more money and went to Shoney's instead?

We crossed paths that morning with Joe Ruttman. Man, talk about somebody on a roll. I'll talk about him more a little later, but at that point we were all just in awe of him. He was a great driver who challenged us as few racers did at the time. We'd raced with him and he'd been one of the guys who could run with or ahead of us on the track, but—being a lower-buck operation—was getting left in the dust on pit stops.

Well, he'd also been watching what went on in the pits, too. He

Getting It Right

Kim had left her family and her All-American life to follow me to NASCAR Land, without any real promise of what the future would hold. For a hard-working girl who had always played by the rules, it was pretty daring stuff to cast her lot with a racer whose future was uncertain at best. I mean, we were living in a Wal-Mart-decorated apartment and driving a truck so awful you'd pull into the gas station and say, "Check the gas and fill up the oil." Really.

I wasn't the happiest guy because I wasn't racing like I wanted to be, and I was being driven by a terrible fear that I would eventually end up so poor that I'd have to live in a cardboard box under an overpass. And that's why I had hesitated—because I didn't want to drag Kim down with me.

But we'd come back to St. Louis on a visit, and we went on a double date with Carol and Jimmy Eames.

And Carol and Jimmy knew it was going to be special.

During this double date we went to the famous Gateway Arch, too, where by pre-arrangement, Carol and Jimmy kind of ambled away from us, while Kim and I sat down on a bench right under the Arch. I looked into her beautiful eyes, and instead of over-talking, as I've been known to do on many occasions, I simply pulled out a ring and asked, "Kim, will you marry me?"

I think I shocked her.

In fact, I'd say that was a safe bet.

This is it—the bench where I proposed to Kim. (Joyce Standridge Photo)

knew that Rusty was on his way to NASCAR, which was going to leave the rest of us at loose ends. So, on that morning, Joe Ruttman offered me a job working for his Levi-Garrett Winston Cup team.

Wow, you're saying! What incredible luck, Kenny! Did you grin like an idiot when you said, "yes?"

No, I didn't.

Mostly because I mumbled, *"no, thank you."*

Okay, I believe I mentioned a few paragraphs back that I wasn't a particularly worldly kid. Yes, I'd traveled all over the country with my big brother, but very much under his wing and that of his crew.

The prospect of becoming a Winston Cup crew man while still a teenager just flat overwhelmed—and scared—me. I was Arnold, Missouri, through and through. I couldn't imagine getting up in the morning and not seeing Dad, Mom, Mike and Kim sometime almost every day.

So, I went home. And the next day, I drove over to Manchester Road in Des Peres to O.K. Vacuum because it was safe. I think I might have gotten through about half the work day before it occurred to me—like a ton of bricks, you'll be justified in thinking—that I'd been monumentally stupid. I thought to myself, "Oh my God! What did I just do?"

I dropped my screwdriver on the table. I might have gone pale. I certainly went sweaty when I realized what I'd turned down the day before.

And I snuck off into one of the salesmen's offices to find a phone. With far more luck than I could possibly deserve, I'd been given Joe's phone number and told to call him if I changed my mind.

I'd changed my mind.

Now, Mom and Dad were resigned to "losing" Rusty, but it came like a lightning bolt that the baby of the family was headed for North Carolina, too. They hadn't seen that one coming, and frankly, my tougher-than-nails dad actually shed a few tears when I told him that I was going away. But even as he and Mom had concentrated on trying to help Rusty propel his career, they'd never NOT wanted me to chase dreams, too. So, they sent us off with waves, smiles—and a few more tears.

And, scaredy-cat Kenny found it all a whole lot more tolerable because the lovely Miss Kim Poole was willing to throw her lot in with me. (I always thought she went because she thought it would be a fun adventure, but 22 years later she finally admitted that she was afraid of losing me if she didn't go, too.)

Rusty and Patti filled up their car, and Kim and I filled up ours. We

When this photo was taken, Kim and I had already decided we were a couple for life.
(Kenny Wallace Collection)

headed out on the highway one beautiful morning, full of hope and excitement, running down the road to who-knows-what.

I don't know if you've ever been on I-40 east of Knoxville, Tennessee, but if you ever get the chance, make that drive. It's unbelievably beautiful as you go through the Appalachian mountain range, a symbolic dividing line as much as a real one. And after you wind through hills and get out on the piedmont of central North Carolina, you come to a fork in the road—literally.

Rusty and Patti were headed on to Greensboro where he was going to drive the legendary Cliff Stewart-owned Gatorade car. And Kim and I were headed to Charlotte to Joe Ruttman's garage.

So, we came to the I-40/I-77 split. And we honked horns like lunatics, waved, shouted and carried on like it was the biggest deal imaginable.

Well, it was. At least it was for me. My last tie to childhood was a fading speck on the horizon, and I was headed south to a completely unknown and unpredictable future.

I reached over and squeezed Kim's hand.

5

"The Next Time You See Me, I'll Have a Helmet in My Hand"

IT'S HARD FOR PEOPLE TODAY, even long-time fans, to recall that 25 years ago NASCAR wasn't that big a deal. In the stock car world it was growing, but still it was primarily a regional racing group. You could see that the France family was putting everything in place to grow it past the Indy cars in terms of appeal, but it was entirely possible to be a diehard driver or racing fan and not view NASCAR as your destination.

Count me in that group.

When I headed to Charlotte to work on the famed Levi-Garrett team, the only NASCAR racing I had ever seen up to that point was at Daytona. Period. There wasn't time for me to read *National Speed Sport News* or the racing magazines or anything much at all, for that matter, because I was

In February, 1976, at the Sears store across the street from the Daytona International Speedway, I got my picture taken with Bobby Allison. I hadn't even started to dream yet, but one day I would get to count him as a good friend and we would even do a (memorable to me) television commercial together. *(Kenny Wallace Collection)*

too busy working on the race cars. Here's how naïve I was: I figured Lake Hill Speedway had to be about as famous as any track in the country because that was the center of our universe.

Even self-centered short-trackers had heard of the incredible Daytona track, though, and curiosity took us down there when I was still just a kid. In fact, Dad bought a big, ol' yellow Lincoln to make the trip. Dad and Mom rode up front, Rusty and Mike in the back seat—and Herman was in the back window. Seriously.

When we got there, we bought tickets just like any other fans, and my very first impression was a permanent one: We entered through the pedestrian gate into the grandstand and walked right under the flagman's stand—just as a car went by.

What an assault on the senses! It was loud, it was unbelievably fast, it made the ground shake, and there was little Herman the German, wearing his red NASCAR jacket with the Winston cigarette logo, standing below the flagman—and his mouth hanging open! *Holy Moley!*

Turns out the car was just about the slowest one there that year, and he definitely wasn't going the 300 mph I thought he was, but, man, I was hooked! Even cooler was that Rusty would sneak into the pits with Mom's 35mm camera and come back with lots of great snapshots we could all savor, along with eyewitness tales. Like how Richard Petty would change out of a dirty uniform into a clean one each time he went out on the track. How the cars were waxed underneath before qualifying to increase aerodynamics even more. How you could walk through the pits and actually brush shoulders with people like Bobby Allison and A.J. Foyt.

So, when Rusty decided to go down for Speed Weeks in 1980—when you had to live in the Midwest to even have heard of Rusty Wallace—it

It's 1980, our first trip to Daytona as competitors, and Rusty stops to talk with a friend from back home, Rick Standridge. Twenty-five years later, Rick's wife helped me write this book. *(Joyce Standridge Photo)*

During one of the trips to Daytona on Rusty's crew, I wasn't surprised to find Mom and Dad had come down—we were expecting them—but I was shocked at who they brought with them. Without telling me at all, they brought Kim, and you can see that they totally got me! *(Both photos: Judy Wallace Collection)*

didn't take any talking to convince this 16-year-old we should go test ourselves against some really good competition. Besides, it meant taking a couple of weeks off from school, and we all know where I stood on that topic.

In retrospect it's hard to believe but we simply modified our USAC car, which we'd run on both dirt and asphalt, and tried our hand at what was then called the Grand American division. It was NASCAR's brief attempt to race "pony cars," or Mustangs, Camaros and Firebirds. Even with a flat tire toward the end of the race, Rusty still managed to finish in the top five.

Wow! That definitely got him some attention, and even if the phone wasn't ringing off the wall—probably because one race does not make a career—it was a huge boost to our confidence that year.

So, naturally we went back the following February. And this time, we decided to put everything on the line. We went down to run Cup. We put all our money plus a few dollars from Ramada Inn for sponsorship, and went for broke.

Here's the deal about going for broke—sometimes, you end up broke. Literally.

It was the Twin 125 qualifying race on Thursday prior to the 500. Rusty was doing incredibly well—we didn't know how outclassed we were, so he didn't know he wasn't supposed to mash the gas—and run-

In our second trip to Daytona, Mike and I chill before the race, and then Rusty and I looked pretty cool and calm before the race. But as I waited—with my knee pads on—to do a pit stop, the announcement came over the P.A. system that Rusty was in a big wreck on the backstretch. It was bad enough that when I saw him unloaded from the ambulance I thought he was a goner. *(All photos: Kenny Wallace Collection)*

ning like sixth or seventh in the race. But coming off turn two well into the race, Rick Wilson got into Rusty's rear quarter panel.

I was in the pits because I was a tire changer that day, so I didn't see what happened. But I heard over the public address system, *"Rusty Wallace is flipping violently down the backstretch!"*

My heart dropped to my toes.

Later I saw television replays of the wreck, and it would have been a wild one regardless but because of the rain the night before, which made huge mud clods that flew through the air every time the car went over and gouged into the dirt, and because it went over so many times, to this day I wonder how Rusty survived it.

At the time, I just took off running. Aimlessly, as it turned out. First, I went to the garage and hyperventilated, but my brain re-engaged and I realized that they weren't going to bring Rusty back there, only what was left of the car, so I took off running to the Infield Care Center.

At that point, I was the only one from Rusty's team there, and boy, waiting for that ambulance, I'm not sure I've ever felt more alone in my entire life.

We were more than brothers. We were partners with a passion for what we were doing, but don't let anybody kid you about how business goes out the window after a wreck. When a driver is killed or seriously injured, people tend to say, "Well, he was doing what he wanted."

Yeah, but that's no consolation to his family, let me tell you. It won't make you love racing any less if you are truly committed to the sport, but the feeling of helplessness is just freaking overwhelming. And those few minutes of not knowing—not being able to see him or talk to him while they transport him from the scene of the wreck to the care center—are the longest, most awful minutes you can possibly imagine.

Try dealing with that when you're 17 years old.

When the ambulance backed up and they opened the door, I came damned close to passing out. Rusty had a red driving suit on, which was peppered with lots of dark brown splotches.

Blood. I was sure it was blood, and a lot of it.

Turned out it was wet sand, but for a brief time there, I didn't know that. I do know that I aged about 20 years in five seconds.

After we went inside, I calmed down when I realized that we were dealing with more sand than blood. A hell of a lot of sand, in fact. Rusty was just packed with it. I can still remember the nurses trying to dig it out of his nose with Q-tips so he could breathe.

Rusty was in surprisingly good shape considering how bad the wreck was, but they still transferred him over to Halifax Hospital for more care. I went along, and after a while, when we were absolutely sure he was going to be okay, I walked outside the hospital. Didn't make it probably a half dozen steps when I broke down and cried. Big sobs came from my toes all the way up and just shook my scrawny frame.

You know, we all say that we're prepared for the worst if you or a loved one races. And, the vast majority of us are not stupid—we really do know that bad things can happen. But, man, when you go toe-to-toe with a spectacular wreck the reality is going to shake you to the core. Take my word on this.

It didn't stop us. It didn't even slow us down. We took the remains of the car, and the beat-up driver, and went back to St. Louis, but hardly with tails between our legs. Rusty said, very firmly and confidently, that we were going back to ASA, and we did, and he did well, and it went on from there.

But for about 30 seconds, outside Halifax Hospital on a pretty February afternoon, racing had literally scared me sick.

I Was So Prepared—Not

We had crammed a lot of racing—and living—into that time between the 1981 Speed Weeks and the end of the 1983 ASA season, but for all we'd learned, when Rusty and Patti split off for Greensboro, they were abandoning a still-green, still-wet-behind-the-ears couple of kids in Kim and me. I still had never seen a NASCAR race except for those few Daytona races.

It's probably just as well. Had I known what was ahead, I might have thought twice about turning around and fixing vacuums back home.

First, I need to put things into perspective.

The Nextel Cup team today, even a single-car team, has a payroll of

Making It Official

Not only did I work the entire NASCAR Winston Cup season in 1984, but I also managed to get married that summer. You'll not be surprised to learn that Kim did all the preparation.

Rusty and I left the Michigan track in his station wagon and headed on down to St. Louis for the June 23rd ceremony. True to form, I was a real goof-ball during rehearsal. So much so that Rusty, who was my best man, took me aside and said, "Herman, this is serious business."

He was right, but I felt like the stress level was just way-too-high, so my way of dealing with that was to try to loosen everybody else up. Before it was over, everybody was laughing.

Except Rusty, of course.

Our first dance as husband-and-wife, and my feet aren't quite touching the ground because I can't believe she married me! (Kenny Wallace Collection)

dozens. At the big shops, it's hundreds. Everybody is highly specialized and under tremendous daily pressure to perform. Everything is clean, neat and resembles a hospital surgical ward more than a garage. A lot of the shops are even tourist destinations. It's all very impressive.

The Winston Cup team of 1984 might have had a payroll of a half dozen. That's all the Levi-Garrett team had. Everybody was a jack-of-all-trades, and I walked in the door not at all surprised to find that I needed to pack wheel bearings, fabricate bodies, weld chassis, install motors and change the toilet paper in the rest room if it ran out when I was in there. I was also the only guy putting undue pressure on myself. Everybody else seemed to have a pretty good handle on what they were doing and keeping things in perspective, but then they were all a lot older and more mature. As for tourists? You must be kidding. Why would anybody want to watch us change springs?

So, with that in mind, I'll tell you that the Levi-Garrett garage was more impressive than Poor Boy Chassis in St. Louis, but only a distant memory compared to today's Cup shops.

We literally moved in with Joe and Harpo Ruttman for a little while. They lived in a very pleasant, if modest by today's standards, home with their daughters and they didn't find it at all odd to be taking in strays. I'll note that we were treated like family until we could get our own place, and to this day, I love Joe, Harpo and their children because of the wonderful, protective people they were and still are.

At the shop, I was going to work for the legendary crew chief, Suitcase Jake Elder. His wife Debbie met me at the shop the first day and handed me a white alarm clock. She said, "I just wanted you to have this because Jake doesn't like for anybody to be late."

Man, what a great greeting, and I genuinely mean that. I can tell you that today nobody starting fresh in a NASCAR shop is going to get that kind of welcome. If you don't make it on time, collect your paycheck and move on because they're standing 20 deep behind you waiting for your job. But back then, good help was hard to come by, and I guess they thought I was going to be good help.

If my weight loss was anything to go by, I was great help. Or the red, blotchy, allergy-type welts from self-inflicted worry.

I didn't know any different. It never occurred to me that I was doing my work plus somebody else's job or that I maybe was getting into another guy's space. There were only about six of us most of the time, but if something needed doing on the car, hey, I was gonna do it. I remember that finally one day at Atlanta, I needed a spring. And instead of ask-

When we first went to North Carolina, Joe Ruttman's family took pity on me and let me stay with them until Kim and I were able to get an apartment of our own. Here I enjoyed a laugh with Joe and his daughter Carrie. They're just super people. *(Kenny Wallace Collection)*

Joe Ruttman versus Rusty Wallace

When Rusty got to NASCAR, Joe was already fairly well established. He certainly was the Next Big Thing if you paid a lot of attention to the racing media.

But, in retrospect, Joe's career has been a respectable one—he certainly has no reason to apologize to anybody—while one could argue that Rusty, with all his wins and the 1989 Winston Cup championship, had a pretty spectacular one. They are both special people and I'm very proud to have had a hand—however, small—in their careers.

So, what happened after 1984 that affected the overall box score for these two drivers?

In my opinion, it was a matter of adaptability. Both came into NASCAR possessed of intensity and an insatiable desire to succeed. It was easier to work for Joe after having spent several years working for Rusty.

Both were used to running the day-to-day operations of their teams and being the "boss." What happened then was that Joe didn't want to let go of that desire to direct everything that happened. Already in the mid-'80s, it was becoming a more specialized sport with too much detail for any one person to control. Rusty managed to step back and put trust in others, although I don't think he was ever totally successful at that, either.

There were several really good drivers who came along about the same time as Rusty, but I think what propelled his career was his unreal ability to feel out and interpret a chassis. Some guys will tell you they don't know anything about the shocks or springs or set-up—Ricky Rudd told Rusty several years ago that he didn't even know what springs were in his car—and it doesn't keep them from success. Others may know what's in the car but can't communicate back to their crew chiefs what changes need to be made or how changes affect handling. In Rusty's case, however, I think that his understanding and communications are responsible for a fair number of those 55 NASCAR Cup victories and some of the $40-million plus he won.

Joe Ruttman is as dedicated and intense a racer as I've ever known in our sport, and that explains why he's been able to keep on racing for so many years. And it's also why a smile or a laugh from him is something to be treasured. (R.N. Masser Photo)

ing somebody else to go get it, I ran to get it myself. And then one of the crew members pulled me aside and said, "Hey, Kenny, you need to slow down and let us do something."

I had grown up with Rusty, and if Rusty asked for a 9/16-inch wrench, you couldn't walk to the toolbox. You had to run. So, that's what I knew, but I wasn't a one-man band anymore, so there was nothing wrong with asking for a little help.

Even so, I was the team's truck driver, and still without a commercial license, so maybe not the best one in the pits. I pulled that son-of-a-bitch into Martinsville for the spring race and made too sharp a turn. We

This picture not only shows a pit stop on Joe Ruttman's car, but probably sums up my entire time working on the Levi-Garrett team—full-out, non-stop.
(Kenny Wallace Collection)

didn't have the big semis at the time, but it was a large box truck and enclosed trailer. The truck went around the concrete wall, and the trailer didn't. I broke the damned hitch off and backed up progress of other teams trying to come into the pits. Fortunately, I had enough good credit built up with the rest of the teams by then that several guys helped me weld the tongue back on and didn't razz me—too much.

And this was after our crew had shrunk by one.

Suitcase Jake came by his name honestly. Just three months after I started working in Charlotte, they came to me and said that Jake was gone. Moved on to another team. Would I be interested in being the crew chief?

Hell, I barely knew what NASCAR was, and they were asking me to take over responsibility for one of the best drivers and best teams in the business. And you know what? Probably because I was all of 20 years old and didn't know any better, I said yes.

The whole season passed in just one big blur. I was lucky in having good crew members, and I didn't have total responsibility, but here's the difference. When we ran ASA and USAC, the "crew chief" was the driver. He told us what to do. The concept of not being behind the wheel and yet being able to tell the driver what to do was a whole new idea to me. And I had driven in competition exactly once to this point. Yes, I'd won that race, but a street stocker on a one-mile dirt track isn't the same as Daytona. However, I'd also like to point out that there are a considerable number of guys who have crew-chiefed in NASCAR through the years without turning even one competitive lap behind the wheel, so then and now, it's not a requirement.

I didn't have to worry about a budget. Thank God, because here's how really dumb I was. At the end of the first week working in Charlotte, the team bean-counter came around and handed me a piece of paper.

"What's this?" I asked.

"It's your pay check," he looked at me like my head had just exploded from too much helium.

Imagine that. You could actually get paid for working on a race car. What a concept. And I'd never really thought about that before agreeing to go to Charlotte. I don't know what I thought Kim and I were going to live on, but, gosh, it's great to be young and stupid!

Well, anyway, I often found that I depended on the kindness of strangers, to borrow a phrase from Tennessee Williams. Joe was a damned good driver and somehow he did well in spite of his so-called crew chief. I worked my guts out for Joe, and I tried to absorb what was going on around me, too.

Which got me in a little trouble.

I was leaning over Ronnie Bouchard's car one day, eyeballing the front springs, when his crew chief, David Ifft, came up, draped an arm over my shoulder and said, "Boy, you don't need to be spying on my

One of the people who has consistently helped me through the years is David Ifft. When I was early in the learning curve he let me ask a lot of questions. Later, he was even my crew chief. *(Kenny Wallace Collection)*

Being a Crew Chief

I got up at 4:30 in the morning when I was a crew chief. Sleeping in was 5:00 A.M. You worked as late as you could still stand on your feet. For that, I got a weekly pay check, the amount of which I can't remember but was enough to keep Kim and me in a cockroach-free apartment and running down the road in a used pick-up truck.

My driver, Joe Ruttman, finished 29th in points and won $140,150, none of which I got, but I cared about money only as far as eating and taking care of Kim. Couldn't have cared less about points because you couldn't eat points.

Put in perspective, the champion that year was Terry Labonte, who won a little over $400,000 for the entire season. I didn't get any of his money either.

Was it worth it?

Well, at the end of the year, the St. Louis Auto Racing Fan Club, an independent organization that follows all racing instead of just one driver or one type of cars, gave me a large trophy in recognition of the job I'd done. It was the hometown folks, lots of pats on the back, and I'm still very proud that they felt that way about the job I did.

Also, I learned about the intensity and pressure of NASCAR racing, which served me well later even as it kept me from being behind the wheel myself. It's only worse now, so I don't know how Ray Evernham, Robbie Reiser and talented guys like them have done it. I can't believe that anybody can be a crew chief for more than 12 to 15 years without going stark, raving crazy. There's just so much responsibility and hard work that it takes everything out of you.

I always think everything happens for a reason, but really, I sometimes suspect that my year as crew chief—when I lost a lot of weight that I didn't have to spare—was God's experiment to see if I could fall through my ass and hang myself.

We didn't have war wagons in the mid-1980s, but at Martinsville where I was crew chief for Joe Ruttman, I stood up on tires to try to get a better vantage point. (Kenny Wallace Collection)

race car. If you want to know anything, just come up and ask me. You know Joe Ruttman is such a good driver, all you have to do is get him close on set-up and he'll do the rest."

David was right, and he was a man of his word. He will still give me the straight story when I ask, so I have as much respect for him as anybody in our business. And Joe was such a great driver that he overcame my goof-ups.

For a while.

And then he got fired.

I don't think I was responsible. The whole thing went a lot deeper than just the goofy, hyperactive crew chief. I remember Suitcase Jake grabbing me by the collar once and telling me, "Son, you want to learn but you won't listen," but really, I did. I got pretty good at listening and learning as much as a horse—or guy—with blinders on possibly could.

L.D. Ottinger, a fine journeyman driver, was put in the car. But here's the deal. I had come down to Charlotte to work for Joe. And personal loyalty was an obstacle that made it hard for me to retain my enthusiasm for the team.

So, when Harry Hyde approached me about working for him at the brand-new Hendrick Motorsports, I listened. I really seriously considered it, and I was in the process of making it happen when fate intervened.

I've already made the point that everything in life is a matter of timing. In this case, it was a wreck. My brother got together with Geoff Bodine, Harry's driver at the time. It was a big, bad wreck, one that Geoff and Harry blamed on Rusty.

So, the next thing I know, I get a call from Harry telling me, "I'm sorry, but it won't work *because you're Rusty's brother.*"

What? Wait just a cotton-picking minute. Is Harry telling me that I'm not professional enough to divorce my unquestioned love for my brother from the need to put my driver's interests first? Or was he saying that Geoff wasn't professional enough to accept my loyalty to his team?

I don't know the answer to that, but I will tell you it had a profound effect on me.

We Interrupt This NASCAR Career to Go Down a Different Road

I still had a lot of options in NASCAR. Some good ones. I'd earned enough respect that I could probably stay with the team I already worked on. There were other teams, not at all put off by the Hyde debacle, who were putting out feelers. For a young kid, I was in a lot of demand by some of the best racers in the country.

So, it wasn't all that surprising when Eddie Thrapp, who was a Busch spotter at that time, came up to me at the track and asked, "Herm, what are you gonna do next year?"

I looked him in the face, and without thinking about it at all, I said, "Eddie, the next time you see me, I'll have a helmet in my hand."

Huh?

Where the hell did that come from?

I hadn't thought about it at all. Let's face it, if you've been paying attention as we go along, you're well aware that I hadn't been thinking

Although he's a little grayer than he used to be, Uncle Gary Wallace is still a tower of a man in my estimation. Here he is in 2006 with his wife Jane and his grandson Joey. *(Joyce Standridge Photo)*

much of *anything* through. There'd been a lot of knee-jerk reactions through my life to this point, and here came another one.

But, you know what? You can over-think your life, too.

At least, that's what I tell myself.

Anyway, my dad had been telling me how much he missed me and if I would come home he would pay me $20,000 a year to work at the family store. Well, $20,000 at that time was really good money. And for a kid who'd never paid any attention to money anyway (I was the balance for those in the family who paid a lot of attention), it was enough to offset the offers that I was getting in Charlotte.

So I went home. But I really want to emphasize that I went home by choice. No tail between my legs. I was disgusted by the lack of loyalty and trust I'd seen in Charlotte, and I thought I had a better chance of finding those things among the people I knew back home. I also believed that—in time—I had a much better chance of realizing my dream of driving race cars instead of just working on them.

I was playing it safe once again. You may recall how that turned out, and it was no more successful this time. In fact, it was prelude to probably the worst year of my life. I don't know how or why Kim stayed with me through 1985, but I thank God she did because otherwise, it was, in many ways, a truly terrible time.

When I first got back to Missouri, I was riding on a high. Happy to be home, glad to see all my old friends and be with Mom and Dad again. But it didn't last.

By the time the Daytona 500 rolled around, I was seriously questioning what I'd done. On that day, I was sitting at the table in a mechanic's uniform, repairing a vacuum cleaner, with the television turned on. I couldn't quite comprehend in a meaningful way what I was seeing. I mean, they were interviewing guys, and I was painfully aware that last

I had gone from NASCAR crew chief to O.K. Vacuum repairman, but you can see from her smile that it didn't matter to Kim. She's always been in my corner. *(Kenny Wallace Collection)*

year on this date, they were interviewing me. I didn't care that the attention had gone away—I've always been able to deal with that—but it was knowing that I had the knowledge—and I wasn't using it. I could see operations there that I knew I could have run better. And as much as it felt good to be back home, I suspect that day ranks as one of the worst of my life because any happiness in my life at that point had nothing to do with my career. In fact, I had a job—not a career.

Well, I didn't go off to a salesman's office and place a secret call to anybody. With the optimistic resolve that's served me all my life, I decided to build a dirt car for my brother Mike and serve as his crew chief.

I had to include this happy picture because this is another of the very important ladies in my life. Patti Wallace has been married to Rusty for many years, but when I was 10 years old she was my babysitter! And, pssst, don't tell anybody, but she used to dress me up and put make-up on me. But I love her anyway! *(© Steven Rose, MMP Inc.; Kenny Wallace Collection)*

Two years before I'd never even heard of "crew chief," and now I was prepared to bring my newfound knowledge to propel another brother's career. Propel it—hell, we tore through the dirt tracks like a hot knife through butter.

And the more we won, the more miserable I got.

I wasn't delegating work, mostly because there wasn't anybody really to delegate. We'd had a small, full-time crew at Levi-Garrett—now we didn't have *any* full-time help at all. Not even me because I was putting in my days at O.K. Vacuum, and Mike was taking advantage of the situation to spend more time with his wife because they had been through a rough patch with their son's death.

We were winning races, however. My God, we were winning everything in sight it seemed. We went to Jefferson City on Saturday nights and Quincy (IL) Raceways on Sunday night. We usually had a pretty good time at Quincy, but Jeff City was another nightmare. In fact, we were the outsiders who came in and took wins away from their existing local heroes, and it wasn't well-received at all.

One night, Mike got into the back of Ronnie Hoover's car and Ronnie spun out, but did a 360-degree spin and came back. (It's fair to note that while Mike and Ronnie were fierce rivals back then, today Ronnie is a very good fabricator at one of the NASCAR shops—and a good guy, too.)

Trying to catch back up to Mike, Ronnie hit the turn-one wall in one of the worst short-track wrecks I've ever seen. The starter red-flagged the race, so I ran out to Mike's car, leaned in and was talking to him. Next

I don't have photos from the brief time that I crew-chiefed for my brother Mike, except this one and you'll note the winner's trophy on top of the car at Quincy (IL) Raceways. *(Kenny Wallace Collection)*

thing I knew, I looked up and one of Ronnie's crew members walked up. Then he sucker-punched me right in the face.

But, that was not the worst night of that year.

There was a special race scheduled in southwestern Missouri, but it was the same night as my wedding anniversary. I'd been married exactly one year, and my spouse was the picture of long-suffering. Not only did I know that staying home and spending the evening with Kim was the right thing to do, but, *dammit,* Mike, it's what I *WANT* to do!

I begged and begged Mike not to go. And begged some more, but he went anyway. And it says nothing good about me either, because when I found out that the left rear tire fell off during the race, I was happy about it. "Serves you right," is not a mature, thoughtful, adult reaction, but I was 21-freakin'-years-old, and my childhood hadn't been exactly normal, so I assume it was protracted.

This was a turning point for me. I looked in the mirror and I saw a frustrated racer. I came from a family of race drivers, but my one lone race didn't qualify me to call myself a driver. I also realized that no one in my family, save for the one time Mike had asked Pat Walsh to let me drive, understood or made my dreams a priority. Rusty had even flat-out told me some time before that he didn't want me to be a race driver because he needed me working for him.

Oh my God, Herman, I told the face in the mirror. *I NEED to be a race car driver, and I'm not going to be a race car driver if I don't do something! NOW!*

It was time to get on the telephone again.

We had a tough time back in the mid-1980s trying to work as a race team, but there have been far more smiles than frowns where my brother Mike is concerned. Here he puts up with some clowning from Little Bro and Stevie "Wonder" Wallace, Rusty's boy. *(Kenny Wallace Collection)*

6

To Finish First
You Must First Finish

WON'T INSULT YOUR INTELLIGENCE by telling you that the Wallace name was a disadvantage when I decided it was time to jumpstart my driving career. On the contrary, by this time Rusty was making a name for himself on a national stage, and I had earned some credits in ASA regional racing as his crew man. I had been smart enough to collect a lot of names and telephone numbers in the years I went racing with Rusty, and I could pretty much count on my calls being taken by people.

But having access did not mean that people were going to automatically line up to help me. Talk and advice were free, and I'm sure that helped. But assuming that being Rusty's brother greased the skids right into NASCAR would be wrong. It was a different road than a lot of guys took to make it, but it was my road and I had the chance to work with some great people on the way. I was also able to compress the learning curve, where I learned stuff that still helps me to this day cope with whatever life throws at me, and I'm maybe a better person for having a few obstacles tossed in my direction. I know good things that have happened to me, right on up to current times, have helped keep racing in perspective. I value my marriage, my long-time friends, and the success I've enjoyed because nothing came as easily as you might imagine.

And this part of my life started with another secretive telephone call at O.K. Vacuum's office. You'd think Uncle Gary and Dad might have walled off the salesmen's cubicles by now, but I was able to find a vacant phone once again. And my hand maybe shook a little more this time because I was a little older, a bit wiser and considerably more nervous. This wasn't just about working on a race car—it was about *driving* one. That was a hell of a lot more important to me.

This all-important call was to John Childs, who'd helped Rusty launch his regional career. I kind of joked, "I hope Rusty didn't use you up too much."

Brooke

We tried for a year-and-a-half to get pregnant, and just when it got to the point that we were going to get tested, Kim walked into O.K. Vacuum one day with a huge smile and a little stick with a "positive" sign on it.

Kim had some problems with blood pressure and blood sugar during the pregnancy, but she was a real trooper and so happy to be having a baby. She just always wanted to be a wife and mother, and now she was going to realize the second half of that wish.

When the time for delivery came, it was so hard that she was literally breaking tiny blood vessels in her face from the effort to push. In fact, she ended up chewing on a washcloth, and being the idiot I am, I not only thought of Richard Petty—because he used to chew on a rag when he was driving—I told her and the doctors that. The medical staff decided that I was one of the bigger goofballs they'd encountered, but Kim, bless her heart, just rolled her eyes.

And just to prove the staff right, when the nurse said it was time to deliver, I had to run outside into the January night for a cold slap of air to keep from passing out. I can handle blood and gore, all kinds of ugly crap when it happens in the movies, but my Baby giving birth to a baby? Well, I had to gather my wits before I could go back in for the delivery.

I know proud papas always think and say their children are beautiful, but honestly, mine was exceptional. Rusty used to tell me to put Brooke in commercials because she would have made a lot of money for us. She had a lot of dark hair and Kim's beautiful complexion and she got attention wherever she went.

She also became my little darling. Even after I got to racing and worked horrible hours preparing the car, I still came home and washed the worst of the dirt and oil off my hands to fix her baby bottles. Kim did most of the work, by far, but I managed to carve out time to help some, especially since Kim had to work, too. However, it didn't take a whole lot to convince me to spend time with Brooke.

By the time she was a toddler, she was also my pal. Sometimes, we would go to McDonald's and get chicken nuggets. Of course they were too hot to eat right away, so I would either hold the nugget in front of the air-conditioning vent in my truck or out the window as we drove along until it was cool enough to give to her. Pretty soon, she started imitating me, doing the same thing I was doing.

I can't tell you how it made my heart swell with pride to see my little daughter copying me.

Little Miss Go-Go, Brooke tries on safety goggles like we wore in those days, and decides she likes them so well that Mama is not getting them back. She was just over a year old at the time, but with her hands like that can you blame me for hunting for a steering wheel? (Kenny Wallace Collection)

Very quickly, Brooke became the big sister—a very pretty and sensitive sister—and Brandy (left) and Brittany (right) will confirm that. (Kenny Wallace Collection)

John chuckled at that so I went on, "I want to become a race car driver, John, and I wonder if you would consider helping me."

I can't describe the relief I felt when he said, "Well, sure I would."

So, I drove out to one of the tire stores he owns and we sat down to talk about it. John agreed to pick up travel expenses and to buy a car for me, if I would set it up and maintain it.

Would I? I would have done that standing on my head and twirling batons if that's what it took.

This was a bigger decision for John than it might seem. Rusty had a ton of local experience and almost no personal responsibilities when he first hooked up with John, but I came to John with one—count 'em, one—race as a driver under my belt, and I was working full-time at O.K. Vacuum because I had a wife and a daughter to take care of. I don't think John agreed simply because he felt sorry for me, and what he agreed to was a pretty good sum of money even in those days. But he'd seen the intensity and drive I'd had working on Rusty's car and I believe he trusted that I would be just as driven—if not more so—when I got behind the wheel.

I'm glad to report that I managed to repress Herman the German while John and I discussed this deal, and I behaved as maturely as a 22-year-old is capable of doing.

And then, before I pulled out of the parking lot, Herman broke free. **YEAAAAAHHHHHHHH!!!!!!!!! Whoopeee!!!!!!!!! Yippeeee!!!!!!!!! Hurrahhhhhh!!!!!!!!!**

Oh, man, oh, man, this is just too great. And in this decade before cell phones, I tore down the street to the Waffle House where there was a phone booth. With shaking hands I plugged that sucker with a coin and called home. "I'm going to be a race car driver, Kim! *I'm going to be a race car driver!*"

This was only the start, however, and I sobered up on the drive home. I realized that I still had to get a hauler and trailer—and an engine for the race car. You can work a 40-hour job and probably afford all the bolt-on stuff and tires, but it's going to take a lot more than that to afford a competitive engine, especially for regional racing. But once again, an old friend came to the rescue. Don Kirn had made Rusty fast, and he was willing to do the same for me. I think—I hope—we sold some engines for him along the way. That's how you end up getting help, because whether it's sponsorship or advertising, the company expects that by making it known a driver is using or advertising that product, it will yield additional sales. At least, that's what Uncle Sam's IRS expects.

At the time, Kim was working at Pope's Cafeteria, and she took some of her paycheck to buy a neat little Dillon trailer for about $1,700. My dad put up a certificate of deposit as collateral so I could buy a used Globe-Democrat delivery truck for about $6,000.

The pieces of the puzzle just started coming together.

Along with my sidekick Wendy (the dog), I've just picked up my first race car frame and trailer at Dillon's. Most of the money for the trailer came from Kim, and all the money for the frame came from John Childs. I will always be grateful. *(Kenny Wallace Collection)*

Here we are a little while later with the car complete and the trailer looking good. *(Kenny Wallace Collection)*

Although Rusty hadn't wanted me to become a driver earlier because of my value to him as a crew member, once he realized that I was dead serious about driving he spent a lot of time talking with me and being a sounding board as I worked out what I wanted and needed to do. I'd spent time in my pick-up running around the St. Louis area—which was my "thinking time" in an otherwise hectic life—deciding whether I should go dirt or asphalt racing. Rusty and I agreed that because I was just beginning my driving career at the somewhat advanced age of 22 (whereas most of the guys I was going up against had begun at 16, if not earlier) I needed to accelerate the process if I wanted to get back to NASCAR as a driver.

I can't say that it was critical to me to get back to NASCAR. The big deal was I wanted to drive a race car and in retrospect simply looking beyond that fact, I think I've made two critical mistakes in my driving career. I'll get into the other one when I talk about Winston Cup racing, but the first one was in not getting experience driving a Hobby car or Late Model at the quarter-mile dirt tracks around St. Louis. From the bottom of my heart, I wish I'd done that.

We had several really great tracks there—I-55 Raceway in Pevely, Missouri; Tri-City Speedway in Granite City, Illinois; Godfrey Speedway in Godfrey, Illinois; and St. Charles Speedway in St. Charles, Missouri. I could have learned how to improve my driving skill by following and racing with some grizzled veterans who probably still know more than I'll ever learn.

The other advantage of racing on dirt is learning car control. I've never been totally comfortable with car drift—meaning the car's rear end wanting to come loose on you. That's just a given in dirt racing and it's part of the reason drivers like Jeff Gordon, Tony Stewart or a young guy

It took me almost 20 years to get my dirt-car racing career on track, but I so love it—and all that I'm learning as a driver on dirt—that I'll continue for as long as I can. *(© Kirby Laws Photo; Kenny Wallace Collection)*

like Carl Edwards isn't at all bothered by that. They've got all those laps wrestling with a dirt car.

I don't know if dirt experience would have made me a better driver, but I'm convinced it would have made me a more comfortable driver. And now that I race on dirt, I'll also add that it's damned fun, too.

But in the winter of 1985-86, Rusty and I felt like the better route was asphalt, and the only asphalt track in the area, Lake Hill Speedway, had closed, so getting asphalt experience meant going on the road with ASA. In our defense I'll also note that at that time, the ASA was the feeder series for Busch and Winston Cup racing, and although new drivers in NASCAR didn't tend to be as young as they are today, it was still very difficult to break in if you weren't in your 20s. Just ask Dick Trickle who didn't go NASCAR until he was 40. How brilliant could his NASCAR career have been if he'd started at a younger age?

Not everybody agreed that going ASA was the thing to do. My other brother Mike said, "You know, Herman, I'm going over to Tri-City Speedway and run a 25-lap feature and probably win $1,000. You're going to go to Canada and you're probably not going to win. You're gonna run fifth and make $1,000, but look what it's going to cost you to go do that."

It pissed me off. I replied by saying, "Mike, you go to Tri-City and run your 25-lap race, but in a couple of years I'll be at Daytona and you'll still be in St. Louis."

We were both right.

I could have learned a lot about hustle and controlling a cranky race car if I'd followed Mike to the dirt tracks, but I did make it to Daytona a whole lot sooner than he did because I took the short cut. That wasn't really the precise plan—I think we've established that I wasn't good at

When Mike told me how smart he thought it was to stay home and race, it was hard to argue with him. He had excellent equipment and towed it with this beautiful enclosed trailer. He was The Man at Tri-City Speedway at the time. *(Kenny Wallace Collection)*

the planning thing—but Mike's comment spurred me on. And if it hadn't worked out and I spent the rest of my driving days running ASA—or the short tracks around home—it wouldn't have felt like humble pie, because, dammit, it's still driving a race car!

All Points Bulletin: I'm Going Racing and I Could Use Some Help

Like Rusty, once Mike accepted that Herman was gonna do this, he helped me out by giving me about 20 by 30-feet of his garage to keep my car. Bear in mind that Kim, Brooke and I were living in a one-bed-

When Mike realized how serious I was about getting my driving career going, and knowing that I didn't have a garage, he gave me part of his, which he designated—as you can see— as Herm's Place.
(Kenny Wallace Collection)

My two favorite cheer-
leaders during my first
year on the ASA circuit—
Kim and baby Brooke.
(Kenny Wallace Collection)

room apartment and the landlord wasn't likely to be happy with me taking up parking spaces in the lot for my stuff. But I wore out my welcome at Mike's after a time, and I moved on to a good guy named Dan Althoff, who gave me some room at one of his dump-truck shops for a while.

That was pretty much the standard for the three years I ran ASA. I was always operating on the edge, always depending on the kindness of friends who, I guess, felt sorry for ol' Herm. We never did get to move into a nicer home, much less a place with a well-equipped garage. But basically, I needed a welder, a band saw and a drill press—and somewhere to park them. I didn't need a "break," a manual machine that allows you to bend up sheet metal to make body panels, because I went down to Valley Park, where a guy had a beautiful, eight-foot long break that he left outside all year long. I would just go down there and bend what I needed.

Come to think of it, I'm not sure whether he knew I used it or not.

I guess he does now.

Anyway, after working all day at O.K. Vacuum, carving out time for baby-bottle prep and tickles with Brooke, I spent just about every other waking moment building that damned race car.

(Side note: Another argument for giving Kim a medal. She not only took on most of the responsibility for our little family, she did it with good humor. I do recall one night that she came down to whichever garage I was in at the time and she kinda strutted around the race car. "So," she teased, "is this the mistress you've been messing around with?"

But that was far as she went with complaints, and that's a whole lot less than I deserved because I was obsessed. Flat-out, blinders-on, freakin', obsessed with that thing.)

And the guys who ended up helping me through those ASA years were working stiffs, too. No paid mechanics until right at the end, no unemployed kids living at home or skipping school. Dave "Dog" Wirz had helped Rusty and now he was helping me, as were Dave Munari, Mike Mittler, A.C. Tucker, Big Steve Shear, and, of course, John Childs. There were other people who helped out as they could, but this was my core, and there were nights when they just flat didn't have time to come down and help out.

I got pretty creative. I mean, as all racers will tell you, there are tasks that require more than one person. Like bleeding brakes. Or loading a full tool chest on the trailer. Or holding washers on the back side while you pop-rivet body panels in place.

So, I would go to my 12-year-old cousin Timmy Wallace's house and I'd tell him, "I need you to hold washers on the back of pop rivets tonight," and he would help. I don't think I threatened or promised anything, but I sort of think the desperate look on my face probably conned him as well as anything else. I mean even a 12-year-old knew that I was doing this on a wing and a prayer—and a lot of favors.

It wasn't the Evil Gang riding again, but there were similarities as some of the same guys went racing with me. That's Dog Wirz on the far left, Dave Munari, John Childs, A. C. Tucker, Harold Pitts and Steve Shear. *(Don Thies Photos; Kenny Wallace Collection)*

A Test Harder Than the S.A.T.s

Rusty wanted me to test the race car before I ever drove in an actual race. Bear in mind that my total driving experience to that point consisted of a single instance of driving a street stock on a dirt track a couple of years earlier and now I was going on a big, mean ol' half-mile paved track at Cincinnati. Didn't take a freakin' genius to figure out I probably wasn't ready.

So, Rusty rented the track at Cincy and the first day I worked by myself. I had come in with the advantage of the knowledge I'd gained working on Rusty's ASA crew. It had been only a couple of years earlier so the technology hadn't changed all that much. I knew from working with Rusty and Paul Andrews that if you got a Dillon car, which I had, you needed to cut off the top, right rear shock mount and move it an inch. And then cut the bracket off for the rack-and-pinion steering and move it up two inches. For Rusty's driving style, and for my learning phase, that meant an almost perfect handling race car—if not a guarantee of a well-driven car.

Anyway, on the second day, Rusty came in. And, I'm pleased to note that the test times I was turning in were about as good as the ones he did. But, when I came back to the pits, Rusty told me that I was "arcing"

By the time Rusty won his first Michigan Speedway race, I was out on the road with ASA, so I was no longer an important part of his race team. But since I was racing nearby the night before I stopped by the track and saw the race—and they let me into Victory Lane afterward to be part of the family photo. *(Judy Wallace Collection)*

the corners too much, meaning I was letting the back end of the car drive me through instead of leading in with the nose, and that I was going to bust my ass if I didn't stop it.

I was not intending to prove Rusty right, but showing my brother is every bit as smart as people think he is, I drove down into turn one, arced it, and spun the son-of-a-bitch so I backed it super hard into the wall and then smacked the driver's side. Bad enough that I was dizzy for longer than I admitted.

Rusty and the guys set a record running out to me that would do the NCAA track finals proud. Other than being goofy between the ears I was fine, but the same could not be said for the car.

A friend, Cecil Frost, had chromed a bunch of parts on the car for free, and the car was . . . or had been . . . just beautiful, but there was hardly a chrome piece on the car that wasn't bent or busted up. There wasn't *anything* on the car that wasn't bent, it seemed.

About 30 minutes later, after we'd figured out how to load the car for the long trip back to St. Louis and certain I was okay, Rusty draped his arm around my shoulders and said, "Well, pal, welcome to the Big Time."

That's my brother. A considerate asshole.

Unintended Success

It was a major thrash, but I got the car fixed. And I made that first race at Cincinnati, where, I'm happy to say, I kept it out of the wall and got

Credit Card Magic

The ASA appearance and prize money didn't always pay the bills. At the time what they paid, compared to other organizations, was darn good, but let's face it—wreck, blow a motor, misjudge in any way and the repair bills are likely to exceed what you take home. So, I would find myself sometimes standing at a motel check-in desk, opening my wallet to pull out the credit card, and wondering how the hell I'm going to pay the bill when it comes.

But, of course, you don't pay the bill. You mail them the $20 that keeps them from sending the sheriff to arrest you in front of the neighbors.

You know what? When I was reaching for that credit card, I would always see the photos of Kim and Brooke that I carried in my wallet. And that always, always gave me pause. I'd look at those beautiful faces and I'd remember why it wasn't enough to be just a race car driver. That was enough for me, for sure. I just needed that "fix" I got behind the wheel and I was satisfied.

But I needed success for my girls. I needed them to feel like the sacrifices in time and money had been worth it to pursue my dream. I could have been the troll under the bridge as long as I got in a race car every week, but my family deserved better. There had been people who told Kim she was crazy to let me drive race cars. They thought I should have been satisfied to be a good crew man or a good vacuum repairman, and there's nothing wrong with those professions—there's never anything wrong with making an honest living of any kind, in fact. Pay your bills and you should always be proud.

Kim ignored the naysayers. She probably even ignored her own common sense at times, but she never made any threats or demands on me.

So, when I looked at those photos in my wallet, I knew exactly why I was out on the road, busting my ass trying to climb the ladder in racing and be more than just a contented also-ran around home.

I'd fold that wallet, put it back in my pocket and try to make it just one more step on the road to the life my girls deserved.

In the early days of my racing career I carried a photo of Kim and Brooke, but as time went on, the wallet photos included all the girls. From left, Brittany, Brandy and Brooke. (Kenny Wallace Collection)

a respectable mid-pack finish, too. I managed to finish ahead of several guys with tons more experience, so I didn't feel half bad.

And there were people who made me feel really good about the decision to run ASA, starting with the series owners Rex and Becky Robbins. In fact, they seemed downright happy to see me. A couple of years before this, they'd known me as Rusty's tire changer, but Rusty had been good for the series, drumming up a lot of excitement with his style,

My very first ASA race at Queen City Speedway near Cincinnati, Ohio. This is after I'd destroyed the car practicing, but as you can see, we got it back together and looking good. *(Roger Grevenkamp Photo; Kenny Wallace Collection)*

on-track and off. They already knew me well enough to trust me to carry on the family tradition.

And they knew I was broke.

Several years later, I ran into Becky again and I told her, "You know that all those checks I wrote for pit passes were bad, don't you?"

"Oh, yeah," she laughed. "That's why I held them for a few days after the race."

Here's the deal. John Childs paid a lot of the expenses getting to the track and the motel bill, which was a very generous thing of him to do above and beyond buying my car. And the crew always paid for their own meals and incidentals, but Herman picked up the pit-pass tab, which was only fair. I got the prize money (which went to pay repair bills), the credit and praise (when it was forthcoming), and the slings and arrows (something rookies learn about real fast).

ASA at the time also had a three-tier program to help their regulars with some guaranteed support since it was expensive to be running all over the place. Back then the top tier got something like $1,200 per show; the second group got $800 and the bottom group got $600.

That $600-a-show kept me going, and I can't thank the Robbinses and all the other folks at ASA enough for putting that program together. My career would have come to a screeching halt almost immediately if I hadn't had those checks to deposit each Tuesday after the races.

But promised money aside, we hadn't really planned to run the entire ASA circuit. I mean, we'd put our car and team together in a hurry, the driver was really inexperienced, money was tight, and we all had time clocks to punch on Monday morning.

Fate had another idea.

We planned to skip the second race of the season at Kalamazoo, Michigan, but it was rained out anyway. And for some reason I can't recall, we decided to go to the third-scheduled race at Cayuga, Ontario, Canada, even though it was even farther away from St. Louis than Kalamazoo.

Behind me in 1986, one of the great minds of racing, ASA President Rex Robbins. *(Kenny Wallace Collection)*

Larry Phillips

If you want to sort the diehard, long-time racing fan from the Johnny-come-lately, throw out the name Larry Phillips.

He never became a NASCAR Grand National or Winston Cup star because he didn't need to. Larry was making a living driving on the short tracks back in the day when he, Dick Trickle in the upper Midwest, and Richie Evans on the East Coast, were among the very few who could. And they made such a good living doing what they loved that they had no need to prove that point on other circuits.

Larry did a whole lot more for our family than just helping Dad burn down the garage when I was a kid. And he was probably the biggest influence on Rusty besides Dad. The trickle-down effect means that he also had a big influence on me because of what Rusty taught me.

Here's something really important that I learned from Larry: *Not everybody is going to love you.*

So what.

Larry outran so many good drivers that he was considered a bad guy by a lot of other competitors and their fans. And he hadn't been to charm school so if he didn't like you, he didn't care that you didn't like him. You couldn't psyche him into feeling bad about it either.

Today, a lot of drivers take crap because they don't stop to sign every autograph request, never mind you couldn't make it to the car in time for the start of the race unless you left the garage area at 3:00 P.M. on Thursday. If Larry was counseling the drivers, he'd say, "so what."

I know, because I once saw him carrying on a pretty intense conversation with another driver when a fan came up and very rudely demanded his attention. Larry ignored the guy for about as long as he could, but then he finally reached into his pocket and pulled out a coin that he handed to the "fan."

"Here's a dime," he barked. "Call somebody who cares."

I could never bring myself to agree that rudeness deserved rudeness, but I did learn that if you're going to make a living from racing, the racing better be your number one focus instead of the marketing and P.R. And even more important, I think, was that you COULD make a living from racing even if you weren't the most beloved character at the track. You may have no idea of what a revolutionary idea that was back in Larry's day.

Larry died a few years ago from cancer. You know what? I'd give about anything to hear him snarl at me one more time to get my shit together.

You have no idea how rare this photo is—Larry Phillips was usually photographed scowling or deadpan because this was his business and his livelihood. And he took it all damned serious. *(Rocky Rhodes Photo; Kenny Wallace Collection)*

And there we finished fourth. Our second race—only my third race ever in my life—and against some of the very best short-track racers in the entire country, we pulled off a fourth place finish!

What the hell! We decided, let's go for it, the whole *enchilada*, and try to make the entire season, a decision made easier by the knowledge that I had an on-site, traveling guardian angel in Dick Trickle.

Rusty, proving yet again that I couldn't have a better brother, had called Dick and asked him to watch out for me, tutor me a little and generally be sure I had my shit together since Rusty wasn't there to do that for me.

Almost everybody who's ever paid the slightest attention to racing has heard of Dick, if not for the 1,000 or so short-track races he's won, then for being the punchline of ESPN Sports Center for years.

Now, here's how I feel about that.

I'm a punchline for my laugh. I've also been told that I'm not serious enough for NASCAR racing.

Well, I am as dead serious as anybody who's ever sat in a race car when it's time to fire up the engines. I just don't think you have to be a stick in the mud when the engines shut down, and I refuse to live my life the way some public relations flack tells me I'm supposed to. If Kim or Mom or Dad or Rusty or Mike or somebody else I love thought it was a problem, I'd address it, but they're fine with Herman just as he is. So, I'm tired of easy punchlines.

Dick Trickle is his name. That alone is not an easy joke. It's his name and it's attached to one of the most talented race drivers who ever got in a race car. Period. End of sermon about that crap. Beyond that, though, it's really important to note that Dick also possesses a sense of humor to meet—or exceed—mine since he's almost as famous for that as he is for winning races.

At Cayuga Speedway in Canada, Kim and I pose for a shot prior to the race. *(Don Thies Photos; Kenny Wallace Collection)*

For example, one night after the races I was teasing him because his shirt was unbuttoned and, well, the man doesn't have any hair on his chest.

"Hair don't grow on steel," he barked at me, and how can you argue with that?

Everybody who raced in the upper Midwest in the '60s and '70s, ASA in the '80s or NASCAR in the '90s has a Dick Trickle story to tell. He's a living legend because he was the whole package—a fascinating person as well as one of the most accomplished drivers I've ever known.

And while he's notorious for his sense of fun, on the track he was all business. My mom has said that Dick is an "old soul," meaning that there is depth to him that is missed by all the people who just enjoy his humor. It also meant that when Dick took on the task of looking after Herman, he took it seriously.

I had some really great moments that year, in large part because of the coaching I got from Dick. I had a habit of knocking off my front fenders out of impatience, and it pains me to admit that I was too quick to blame other people when I wrecked, but Dick kept bringing my attention back to where it needed to be. "You must first finish to finish first," he told me more than once. He also told me to "race the racetrack," which meant to stop worrying about what was going on around me and do what I knew was right and what my equipment could handle for each given track.

And I ran well in several races. That kept my morale up, too. Finishing fourth in my very first race at Milwaukee and then having the great Joe Shear tell me, "Man, I was so sick of looking at that damned Childs Tire on the back of your car," was one of the high points.

Being able to run well at such a variety of tracks, from the flat one-

My earliest experience with press conferences came in ASA. Waiting our turn while seated at the table are Mark Martin, me, and Dick Trickle. At the time, Mark was gaining credibility, Dick was a real star, and I was just happy to be at the table even if I didn't look like it. *(Kenny Wallace Collection)*

On this day I was following #36 Joe Shear at the Minnesota State Fair, but there had been a day when Joe followed and couldn't pass me all day. That was one of the important points in my career, because if you can outrun Joe, you are a race driver. *(Kenny Wallace Collection)*

mile at Milwaukee to the super-fast, half-mile high banks at Salem, Indiana, was just the greatest. And when I managed a fourth place finish at the fabled Winchester 400 to end the season, I had a smile plastered on my face all the way to the banquet in Nashville where I was crowned the 1986 ASA Rookie of the Year.

And that smile lasted until the second race of the following year.

At the 1986 ASA banquet I was named the Rookie of the Year and posed for photos with Mom and Dad *(Don Thies Photos; Kenny Wallace Collection)*

7

Balance a Checkbook? Get Real, I'm a Race Car Driver

I WAS MINDING my own business.

After a rookie year that included probably too many wrecks, but none very bad, I'd gotten pretty good at taking care of my equipment. There are several obvious reasons, beginning with fatigue at having to fix all the stuff I broke and probably ending with good advice from my mentor, Mr. Trickle.

So, even though I was on an unfamiliar track for the first time, I was just taking care of business when I came through the tri-oval. It was Sanair International Speedway, the second race of ASA's 1987 season, and I was running in the money. And then the guy in front of me torpedoed an engine. Not just a little dropped valve or even a rod through the oil pan. It was a total, catastrophic failure that sent parts flying off his engine block, including pieces of the block itself, I think. And before the yellow flag could come out, I ran over a piece and cut down my left rear tire.

Stuff like this happens all the time. I'd been in races already when I couldn't avoid debris on the track, but the car had been controllable. I had never before so totally had the control of a race car taken out of my hands, not even that practice session at Cincinnati.

The car spun sharply and before I could put together a simple, clear thought about what had happened, I slammed into the retaining wall. I hit so hard that it almost knocked me out. In fact, I was so dizzy that I started hearing people talking in French.

And then I remembered that we were near Montreal, and in Quebec people do speak French. It just took a few seconds for that fact to come back to me. I think it dawned on me as I walked back to the pits while the track personnel figured out how many tow trucks it was going to take to load what was left of my car and how the remains were going to fit on my trailer.

Kim was with me that day. I always want her to go to the races with

These are never happy memories, but after this wreck at Sanair in Canada, I was seeing double from having my bell rung. And I was looking at a junked frame on the only car I had. This wreck ended up being a test of character, but I think we passed because two weeks later we were back on the track. *(Don Thies Photos; Kenny Wallace Collection)*

me, and although there are weeks when she says, "Time out!" and gets a little space for herself or for the girls, this was an instance when she had gone to the track with me.

Considering how little she enjoys foreign travel, it's amazing she was there. I mean, I talked her into going to Japan when we raced there in the late 1990s, but she passed on Mexico. I think she went to Canada because it's North America with an *"eh?"* on the end of it.

I was knocked so stupid that I can't even remember the look of relief on her face when she saw me. I mean, I'm goofy at the best of times, so anything that is approximately the same is okay. Besides, I didn't tell her how bad my bell had been rung.

Dick Trickle also came to check on me. I can't tell you how good it was to hear something in English, even if it wasn't real comforting. He looked over the mangled mess that had been my race car and in that Trickle bark of his, said, "Well, what are you going to do now?"

I knew Dick well enough by this time to recognize what he hadn't said. He hadn't said, *"Do you have the balls to keep going with this deal?"*

So, I looked Dick right in the face and said, "I'm going to fix it, and I'll see you at the next track."

He almost grinned. He didn't tell me that was the right answer, but then he was probably going to wait to see if I was a man of my word. He might have heard the bell ringing in my head, too.

My number one cheerleader.
(Kenny Wallace Collection)

But, what he couldn't have realized was that his question was exactly what I needed. Dick probably saved my career because instead of coddling me, he challenged me.

Still, it was a long, damned drive home from Montreal. Over 1,100 miles, in fact, and in those days I was still the truck driver, too. That's a long, long time to be chased down the highway by a trailer full of wrecked car. Long enough to be devastated—and hopefully, get over it.

If you've seen my television face, you may find it hard to believe, but sometimes I can really get down in the dumps. I'll talk a bit about that in another chapter down the line, but I have to say that at this point I had never really felt sorry for myself—I was never truly depressed, I think, because at a very young age I'd been through some pretty demoralizing wrecks with Rusty and I'd learned that it wasn't the end of the world. Even when you're broke. It's tough. It's a major obstacle, but if you want to race bad enough, you can figure out how to do it.

Driving down the road at three or four o'clock in the morning was when I did most of my thinking in those years anyway. Between punching a time clock, working on the car and trying to find a little family time, these late (or were they early?) hours behind the wheel were my time to figure things out.

On that long drive home, here's what I remembered: Rusty was trained by Larry Phillips, who taught him to be fast and to have the attitude that absolutely nothing is ever going to get you down and keep you there. And who did I learn from?

And if Larry and Rusty hadn't been enough, the cavalry, as far as I

Even in my third year on the ASA circuit, I realized that I still had a lot to learn and I was still listening to Dick Trickle any time he had advice.
(Kenny Wallace Collection)

was concerned, came in the form of Dick Trickle, who damned sure believed in himself, too.

I'm not a religious person, but I am spiritual. That means I don't feel a need to follow the dictates of any particular religion, but still in my life I have felt at times that I've been touched by God. When my children were born, when I walked away from bad wrecks, sometimes just when I realize how lucky I am to be alive and walking in these boots, are some of those times. I do believe in God, and I do believe that I am an overachiever. I'm the poster child for never giving up. There are several really accomplished race drivers I could name who would have walked away from some of the stuff that's happened to me in my life, and they would have called it quits. But either God has thrown a few obstacles in my way because He knew I could handle it and make the best of things as I could, or He was there to guide me when the obstacles appeared. You all can argue among yourselves how it is, but by the time I pulled into Arnold, I was too exhausted to figure that out by myself.

I knew my attitude had changed because of this challenge, and it was a whole new way of doing things for me. All the meticulous care I'd lavished on my race cars to that point went right out the window. If I was anal about getting everything just so during this repair, I couldn't be back on the track literally for months. So, my plan of attack was to squeeze an entire winter's worth of building a race car into two weeks' time so I could make the next race as I'd sworn to Dick that I would.

Two Weeks . . . zzzzzzz . . . Without Sleep

A lot of race car drivers have done a major thrash to get a car fixed and ready to race in less time than it had originally taken, so I'm hardly alone in one of these deals. I know there's more than a few guys out there reading these words and shaking their heads in memory of their own little nightmare. You learn a lot about yourself and what you are capable of doing when you are presented with a seemingly impossible task.

I had a good team on my side, including Jimmy Huisken, who was now supplying my race car chassis, and he basically stepped aside to allow Herman full access to all that was needed. With Jimmy's blessing I started bending tube, firing up the welder and using his jig ahead of other customers. I paid for the materials, but by doing the work myself I was able to save a lot of money, and even though I was a disaster at balancing the checkbook, I was well aware that there wasn't enough in the bank to pay for a complete new rolling chassis built by someone else. Race car drivers are notorious for pretending stupidity when it comes to budgets because, well, frankly, we're going to spend every dime we've got and all that the credit card company will allow us. Plus whatever we can beg and borrow from friends and fans. The problem, when you've demolished a car like I did, is that you don't have enough friends and fans, even if they outnumber the Mormon Tabernacle Choir. This was major.

Building the frame is just the start. It takes so much time to bolt on all the suspension, put the engine in, plumb it, run the electrical, and hang a body, that you need to allow even more time for that than building the base.

I knew that, so when the frame and cage were done, I didn't even prime-paint it. Just took off for home in the middle of a rain storm, no less. When we got home, the damned thing was all rusted up, but who cared?

We set a world speed record getting a coat of flat, black paint on it just so it wouldn't rust through before the end of the season, but it wasn't pretty. And up to this time, I had made "pretty" something of a priority. I'd learned that at Rusty's knee, because he'd always, but always, taken pride in his cars. It's not a bad idea, either, because you want potential sponsors to feel like they're going to be proud to have their name on your beautiful car. I had always wanted my cars to look really, really good, but at this point I realized that, look, I don't have enough hours in the day to make my shit look good. I got to go racing. And I realized from all the cars I've seen in my life that ugly shit still looks good in Victory Lane. Larry Phillips had managed to keep racing night after night because he only paid attention to the stuff that mattered—the things that made it go, stop and turn. Many a night, he drove the butt-ugliest car at the track—right into the winner's circle.

Two weeks after obliterating my one and only race car at Montreal, I showed up at the next ASA show. I pulled into the pits, backed that brand-new car onto pit road . . . and just about collapsed.

In 1987, after fixing my car a few times, I gave up on the two-tone red-and-yellow color scheme and went to an all-yellow car as it saved a lot of time in the paint booth. I'd learned from Larry Phillips that an ugly car always looks beautiful in Victory Lane. *(Kenny Wallace Collection)*

It's entirely possible to go two weeks without sleeping, but I wouldn't recommend it. Especially if you are going to then put on a firesuit and demand total concentration of your exhausted mind for 200 laps.

But I got through it, in large part because even at the most unbearable moments, I never, ever once wanted to give up driving a race car. I wanted it so badly, in fact, that I had Easy Ed, my sign-painter, craft a poster for me. It said, ***"Tough times only last a while. Tough people last forever."***

Back in a corner of my renovated Globe-Democrat truck, I hung Easy Ed's sign. Not where other people could see it, because it wasn't for show. I hung it in a corner where only a few people like Kim, my crew and I knew where it was.

It used to be that every race team had a sign painter instead of buying graphics. Clear back to the days when Rusty raced locally, ours was Easy Ed. He always made sure that the Wallace race cars looked good. *(Kenny Wallace Collection)*

When you've got motivating words like that and a guardian angel like Dick Trickle, who applauded my return to the track, there's no chance you'll give up.

Guys You Want in Your Mirror, But Sometimes Hate to See There

The first time Dick gave me that advice about having to finish a race was at a 400-lap show in Anderson, Indiana, my first year. Boy, that's a tough, tight little track that beats on you mentally as well as physically—but I found out about the physical part first hand—and what a role other drivers can play in such things.

I looked in my mirror during the race and Mike Eddy, The Polar Bear, was about a half a straightaway behind me on the back stretch. I'd already heard about his reputation, and it was something like this: *Don't dick with him.*

There are several drivers where you can say that's the case. I found Jack Ingram was that way when I went to the Busch Series. Robby Gordon is another one. The late Dale Earnhardt Sr. was the ultimate example, but back in the ASA days, everybody knew that if Mike Eddy was coming up to *race* you, that was one thing, but if he was going to *lap* your car, you just needed to get out of the way.

This night, Mike was coming up to lap me. And me, thinking I'm going to be the good guy and get out of the groove, waited until coming off the fourth turn to do that. I hadn't looked in my mirror again, so I didn't realize how fast Mike was coming up on me or that he'd gotten out of the groove to lap me.

So, I ran him into the outside retaining wall.

And even though his car was junked, he was talented enough to peel that car off the wall, stay wide open, run right down into turn one and return the favor.

A week later, I called him up and apologized. He told me, "You ran me into the wall. My night was over. I wanted to make sure your night was over, too."

I couldn't argue with that.

I hadn't approached Mike after the race because I figured he needed time to cool down (and I was right), but Trickle beelined down to my car afterwards. He looked up at the scoreboard, and asked me, "Where did Gary St. Amant finish?"

St. Amant was my adversary in the battle for Rookie of the Year. I looked at the scoreboard, too. "Gary was fifth."

"That's right. And how many laps down to the leader was he?"

"Two."

That was the first time Dick laid on me the need to finish a race. Gary had piled up a bunch of points on me just by staying out of trouble. And then Dick taught me another lesson: "I was running with Mike for that position," he said, "and he was feeling the pressure from me."

Racing is like the Army in that you can spend a lot of time hurrying up so you can spend almost as much time standing around. But at least we have some very interesting characters, in this instance Gary Balough and Butch Miller. *(Kenny Wallace Collection)*

I wasn't competitive that night and yet I was trying to hold them off. I took out Mike—unintentionally, of course—and I might have taken out Dick, too. How smart was that?

So, from that night on I made it a point to use my head, no matter how racey I was feeling. Race when you got the horse under you, but take her out of the groove when you don't.

Besides Dick Trickle, probably my closest friend during my ASA years was Gary St. Amant, and if you don't know who he is, you should, so I'll tell you about him. Gary was the very first real rival I ever had in racing, and he was proof that you can race your brains out against a guy on the track and then hang with him afterwards.

There were a lot of guys I would have liked to consider rivals, like Trickle, Eddy, and Bob Senneker, but I was nowhere near to being in their league at the time. So, when this real nice, young guy came out of Ohio with some pretty stout racing genes, and his approach was kind of similar to mine, it was natural that we clicked. Kim still talks to his mom Ruth a couple of times a year, and we love it when we can get together.

Gary's dad Bud had been crew chief for one of the true short-track greats to come out of Ohio, Don Gregory, so I felt like Gary had a real advantage with his dad turning the wrenches. But since both of us were learning how to drive 200-lappers instead of 25-lappers, and we were a couple of puppies following the Big Dog (Trickle) around, we developed driving styles and instincts that are almost identical.

Gary went on to win ASA championships because when he had the choice between bumping a guy out of the way for the win or settling in, he'd finish second. (Echoes of "you must first finish to finish first," you know.)

He was the demonstration of the dilemma drivers who race for a living face: You can go win this race and maybe make a couple thousand dollars more, or you might destroy your race car and spend way more than a couple thousand dollars fixing it.

Dick Trickle

I'm wearing you out, talking about Dick Trickle, I know, but, honestly, without his influence I would have been lost along the way.

I would marvel at how he could be such an outrageous character and yet have his act together where racing was concerned. Part of the secret was because he was so frugal, something he learned, I'm sure, from the folks back home in Wisconsin. I never did ever meet anybody from there who wasted money or opportunity.

Dick would go racing six nights a week, and you can do that only if you take good care of your equipment on the track as well as off, and you really love what you do. People say you can't win the 1,200 races Dick is supposed to have won, but if you race as much as he did and you are just flat that good—well, yes, you can. And he did.

I would also marvel at how he could win so much but yet have so much fun. He explained to me that *to win, you don't have to be miserable.* You just have to work hard.

After he went to NASCAR, things didn't go as well as he had hoped. But he was older, the competition was so tough, and he didn't have the rides it took to win. You have to realize that in NASCAR Winston Cup, which is now the Nextel Cup, the difference between Victory Lane and

43rd place was often some tiny flaw in a tire or a set-up, or five horsepower, or some such minor deal. It was—and still is—that close.

So, after Dick joined the senior circuit, he found it a different world from the one he left behind. There was nothing fair about it, and I can recall these young—25-or-so years old—crew people on other teams who would make fun of him because he was an older guy, struggling to get the job done. Lack of respect existed 15 years ago, but it's only gotten worse.

For example, my brother retired just last year. Already, he can walk through the pits of a NASCAR Nextel Cup race and few stop him anymore. A year earlier, he could barely take a step without being asked for an autograph or a photo, but without that uniform to identify him, Rusty can go clear through the pits, anywhere he wants, without recognition or the respect he's earned.

Man, that's sad. And it happens to other past champions who've retired, too. It's as sad as NASCAR fans missing out on Dick Trickle in his heyday when nobody could touch him. The difference? NASCAR was not a big deal in those years to a guy from the upper Midwest. And in the grand scheme of things with regard to Dick's career, it still isn't.

In this sequence, you'll notice that Dick Trickle is doing the talking and Kenny is doing the listening—until the end. And then I couldn't be quiet any longer, but I'm sure I was asking a question rather than telling him anything, because, really, what could I tell him? (Kenny Wallace Collection)

Probably my greatest rival when I started on the ASA circuit, Gary St. Amant (right) became one of my closest friends. Our families remain in touch to this day.
(Don Thies Photos; Kenny Wallace Collection)

Gary is still one of the top short-track asphalt drivers in the country. And I truly believe he could have been a NASCAR star if he really wanted it, but he has always liked what he does. And he does it so well, you can't argue the point. I called him out on it once, but he's just happy where he is and what he's doing. And happy is what it's all about in the end, isn't it?

Another of the incredibly smooth drivers I recall from those days is Bob Senneker, the Blue Bird. He got the nickname because his race cars were the most beautiful shade of shocking blue, and they were pearlized so they always shimmered in the light.

Not incidentally, Bob won something like 500 feature events, and he did it without beating and banging on people. If he could pass you, he

I can't believe I got to hang out with Bob Senneker, one of the greatest drivers in the history of asphalt short track racing.
(Kenny Wallace Collection)

passed you. If not, he passed you next time. And frequently, he did it by being just a whole lot smarter than everybody else. I mean, he was an engineer before there were engineers in racing. Everybody else would have an Ed Howe car or a Dillon chassis, and they would go straight up with the recommended set-ups for suspension. Bob wouldn't even have the normal rear suspension. At one point I recall he had what's called a wishbone suspension, which was totally radical.

Bob would let me talk chassis with him, and that was just huge to me. Here I am, still wet behind the ears, and a guy who was going to be a champion with like almost a hundred ASA wins would let me ask him all kinds of questions. And out on the track I tried to drive just like him because it was so neat to see how well he could read the track and the competition.

What I didn't try to do was sit in a race car the way he did. If you never saw Bob race, think Dale Earnhardt Sr. Remember how low down into the cockpit he always sat? Well, so did Bob. You could barely see his helmet, and I'm not sure how he saw over the hood of the car, in fact. I never did ask him why he mounted his seat that way and sat like it was an airplane, but I speculate that it's an advantage to keep everything low in a short-track, asphalt car. A lower center of gravity makes the car faster. We were trying to get as much weight low down in those cars as we could until the rule makers made us build them more like passenger cars again.

Probably the biggest rivalry that existed at that time was between Senneker and Eddy. Talk about opposite personalities and styles. But it worked for them, it worked great for ASA, which could promote the heck out of the competition, and it was a blast for all of us who got to see it happen.

I'm really proud that I got to be friends with both of them. Yeah,

Through Rusty's short-track years and mine, the one constant was the support and encouragement of John Childs. It's no stretch to say that neither of us would have gone on to better things if not for John's help. *(Kenny Wallace Collection)*

The competition during my ASA years was as intense as any I ever encountered at any level of racing, so I worked long and hard on my car. But I hadn't lost my sense of humor, so just for fun one day we dragged out the director's chair and I pretended to be a bad-ass boss. *(Kenny Wallace Collection)*

even after that deal at Anderson with Mike, we managed over time (and a few beers) to become pretty good pals. I still like him a lot. I think I figured out that what happened on the track was a mix of his strong personality and how he came up in racing.

Mike learned on the short tracks. Running 25-lap features where they inverted the field and he had to start in the third or fourth row meant he had to get up and go right at the green flag. You had to get it done, and you had to get it done *now*!

Mike didn't go out there with the purpose of spinning you out, but if he got up to you and you were slower, where most guys would give you a lap or two to get out of the way, Mike might—I stress the word, *"might"*—give you a half lap. And then he was going to put a bumper on you and move you out of the way. And if you could drive at all, you'd recover and go on. And if not . . . well, don't look for Mike to come down with a beer in hand afterwards and apologize. You were between him and the prize money, and that's what put the groceries on the table at his house.

What I learned from Mike was very helpful in dealing with the next car owner I drove for. It was just a brief one-race deal in the Busch Series, but if Mike wrote the chapter on tough-as-nails driving, Dale Earnhardt Sr. wrote the book.

8

The Yo-Yo I Rode In On

WHEN I THINK ABOUT Dale Earnhardt Sr. as the ultimate superstar of racing—and he was—it just amazes me that we became good friends. Little Kenny who stole soda bottles for French-fry change from back porches all over Arnold still lives inside me and sometimes can't quite believe some of what's happened over the years. Maybe there are people who are surprised to be friends with me, but I really doubt it. When it comes to making pals, I'm easy. Senior wasn't, which brings me back to my original observation.

Getting information from Dale. A priceless moment, especially since I can't do that anymore. *(Kenny Wallace Collection)*

It was another friendship that put me in his Busch car, the closeness he had with my brother Rusty. So, anybody who thought I got to NASCAR with help would be right, but it's fair to note that there's no shortage of people who get to audition. I agree with those who believe there are very talented drivers who don't ever get a shot even though they could drive the pants off a lot of us. But in life—in all sorts of careers, most sports, almost anything you think of—getting ahead is a matter of networking and taking opportunities when they are presented. You don't honestly think that when Rusty called and said, "Hey, Herm, do you want to run the Busch Series?" I was going to say, "Gee, bro', I'm not sure it's my turn for a try-out."

Hell, no. And every other driver worth his helmet would do exactly as I did. The fact that I've run (and won in) Busch for 17 years and Winston/Nextel Cup for 13 years probably means that I can do this, and I can do it on more than coattails.

By late in the 1988 ASA season, my third year on that circuit, I had accumulated some pretty stout statistics and demonstrated that I could do reasonably well with limited equipment. Don't get me wrong—everybody who was helping me with the car was giving me as good stuff as they could, but we didn't have spares and that probably impacted how I raced to a degree. I had to be more conservative than a guy who's got enough parts back at the truck to build another car, and a paid crew back at the shop to fix the mistakes.

A lot of people were noticing. I was getting feelers (and encouragement), but there was nobody I could expect to be more comfortable with on this journey than Rusty. Maybe to prove a point I should have tried to move up to Busch with somebody else, but let's face it, with

1988 was my final year in ASA, but at the start I didn't know it was going to turn out that way, so at tracks like Grand Rapids, I was running wide open and hoping people would notice. *(Don Thies Photos; Kenny Wallace Collection)*

It wasn't unusual to encounter Dale Earnhardt Sr. in public, but the most meaningful times were those instances when we got to talk alone. *(Kenny Wallace Collection)*

Rusty as my guidance counselor I had a comfort level that went back to the cradle.

He told me at the time that, "If you want to be at Daytona next February, you have to be approved by NASCAR."

To get the ball rolling, I had to race with NASCAR, and the logical starting point was Martinsville. A racey, half-mile flat track, Martinsville isn't all that different from a lot of the tracks I'd run with ASA. And since Rusty's arrangements for my ride in the coming year with a team he'd chosen weren't yet complete, I needed a car to complete this "test" in.

Enter Mr. Earnhardt.

I got on a plane and flew to Charlotte, and, to be honest, I was kind of running in a fog *(can this be real?)* because unlike my first time down that way I now knew what was what in racing and just how high the stakes were. A lot of thoughts were rambling-jambling around inside my head when I went with Rusty out to the Earnhardt home.

The original home.

Today, the Dale Earnhardt Incorporated (DEI) shop is called the Taj Mahal, out of respect for what Dale accomplished as a racer and for his wife Teresa's exceptional good taste. It's the benchmark by which every other garage is measured and usually doesn't compare.

But in 1988, there was no DEI. Dale was already a multi-time Winston Cup champion and ran a Busch team, but he did it from the small, two-car garage behind his mother's house. And when I walked in that day, I realized that it was a monument as much as a garage.

This was where Ralph Earnhardt ran his shop. Dale had never touched a lot of what was in there. There were all kinds of things Ralph had put there, hanging from nails in the rafters—spare parts and stuff— and they were covered in cobwebs. Obviously, these were things that weren't useful anymore but Dale hadn't been able to bring himself to take them down and get rid of them. So, it was pretty cool, in a strange sort of way that I totally understood, to walk in and find the latest, great-

Dale Earnhardt Sr.

It didn't seem right after Dale died to talk about him. For a long time, the hurt in my chest just wouldn't go away. But it's been long enough now that I can tell you a little about the guy I called the original Marlboro Man, because everything that commercial tried to pretend, was Dale Earnhardt for real.

If he liked you, he invested time in you. For example, I can remember him calling me and then picking me up in his motorhome for the drive down to Darlington very early in my NASCAR career. It was an opportunity for him to talk without prying eyes or ears.

"Kenny," he said, "the most important thing you're going need in NASCAR is a good crew chief. It will make all the difference for you. And the second thing you need to remember is that there are thousands of great race car drivers all over these United States. They're hid away at every race track—it's just that we're the ones who were lucky enough to make it here."

Beyond that great lesson in remembering to be humble, he also quickly stopped me from using a certain term. In my typical hyperactive manner, I said to Dale after a race, "I *beat* that guy!"

And he told me, "Don't ever use the word 'beat.' You 'out-ran' him. That's important because next week, you'll feel a whole lot better if he 'out-runs' you instead of 'beating' you."

There's a zillion stories I could tell, but I choose to save them for Dale Junior, actually. He's been quietly collecting stories about his father these past few years, holding on to his own memories and borrowing some others.

But here's one I just gotta share with you. It's the perfect example of Senior's sense of humor.

We built a go-kart track behind our house in

The infamous water truck that Dale Earnhardt gifted for our go-kart track. We started out with just a little track behind the doublewide, but then it progressed to a huge event. And when James Brady showed up one day (shown with Mike and me) we knew it had gotten too big. (All photos: Kenny Wallace Collection)

North Carolina, and I found out that it wasn't the dirt that cost money—it was the dump truck to move and haul dirt. Well, Dale let me use his dump truck to get the job done and then he asked me if I wanted a water truck, which, of course, I was going to need.

A few days later, I'm running a Busch race but he's off, so he shows up at the house and can't keep from laughing as he and a buddy left behind a "truck" that had to come off the rollback because it wouldn't run. I didn't know this, so when I got home and Kim told me Dale had left a water truck, I was so excited. Even though the truck wouldn't run, I could use the tank to store water.

Well, that damned thing was so rusted out that when I tried to fill it, the water just spurted out all these thousands of tiny pinholes!

And Earnhardt wasn't done with me. The following week at the race track, he had Teresa bring the truck title to me. "I'm going to take it to the scrapyard," I told her. Understanding his sense of humor, she just laughed and handed the title to me anyway.

I couldn't leave it at that. So, I rolled the tank out into the field and painted a white #3 on it.

But, even though he enjoyed a laugh at my expense now and then, I would have come to love him so much anyway for one simple reason: He was absolutely wonderful to my wife. He called her The Brown-Eyed Girl, and he spoke so sweetly to her—always made her feel special. Even when she wasn't around, he would always want to know what was going on with Kim.

So, when we heard over the airplane's squawk box, sitting on the runway at Daytona that horrible February day in 2001 that he was gone, tears came out of the Brown-Eyed Girl's eyes like they have very few times in her life.

And I had no clue of how to comfort her because there was a huge, aching hole in my heart, too.

est equipment mixed with stuff that hadn't been touched in nearly 20 years. Dale Earnhardt's garage bridged the gap between the past and the present like I hadn't seen—or have since, either. It's sort of what they tried to do with the barn scene in the movie *Days of Thunder,* but with typical Hollywood excess, got wrong.

It's Dale Earnhardt Sr.'s final race, Daytona 2001, when the day was still sunny and happy for us all. That's me in the #27, brother Mike in the #7 and Rusty in #2. Ricky Rudd is in #28, Jerry Nadeau in #25 and Matt Kenseth in #17. *(Jim Edwards Jr. Photo)*

Tony Eury Sr. and Tony Jr. were there that day, and at some point it dawned on me that we were taking out the custom seat that belonged to Dale Earnhardt, and putting in one for me. *And if I couldn't fill his shoes, how the hell was I going to fill his roll cage?*

A few days later, we went to Martinsville, and I ran the race with Dale Earnhardt Sr. and Rusty Wallace as my spotters *(how cool and how scary is that?)*—competing with each other, trying to tell me what to do. The saving grace is that everything happens so quick at Martinsville you don't have time to figure out which one you're going to listen to, because a lot of what happens there—happens. You'd like to think you were in control, but, really, it just happens.

That day, Dale is telling me to go for it, stand on the gas, don't take no shit from anybody else on the track, and Rusty is telling me, no, *no,* don't do that, *don't tear up the car!*

See the deal is, Rusty had rented the car for the day. Whatever I tore up, even if it wasn't my fault, was going to be covered by Rusty. So, Dale doesn't care. But I really think—no, *I know*—that even if Rusty wasn't running the tab, Dale would want you to go for it. Don't let anybody fool you about Dale running conservatively for points later in his career—he was always going for the win, and he couldn't help himself, even after so many years behind the wheel.

Well, I started 26th and finished 11th, Rusty didn't have to mortgage the house to pay Dale, and NASCAR seemed to approve of the job I'd done.

Maybe best of all, a great friendship was born.

And We're Off to the Races— Or, Are We?

I went home walking on clouds. And even though it meant breaking up that little gang of mine that had been running ASA, all the guys, all the sponsors, all the help I'd gotten were just about as happy as I was. I mean, they all felt they had an emotional investment in what I was doing, so if I was going to Charlotte, in a roundabout way, so were they.

But you didn't really think it was going to be that smooth, did you?

I went down a short time later to meet the team that Rusty had found for me. Ironically, the car owner's name was Don Miller, but he was from North Carolina, unlike the Don Miller from St. Louis who eventually put together a race team he co-owned for quite a while with Roger Penske and Rusty.

The team I was going to, however, was even more down-to-earth than what I'd seen at the Earnhardt garage. Dale's garage was the way it was because he wanted it that way. The Miller garage was the way it was because that's what they could afford to do.

It was nothing personal against them—on the contrary, I liked the group—but I had some real concerns. I'd been to Charlotte before and it

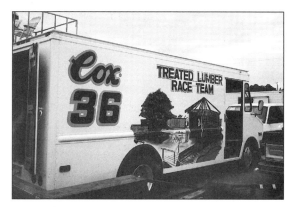

When I came to North Carolina, Rusty told me to bring everything from my ASA operation that I hadn't sold. So, Kim and I stuffed everything into our converted newspaper-delivery truck (shown as the Childs & Wallace Racing truck) and headed down, where the truck got a fresh paint job. *(Both photos: Kenny Wallace Collection)*

didn't stick. This time, coming as a driver, I'd better show some stuff or I was going back home to St. Louis without it being my choice.

A couple of days later, Rusty called me. He'd been a little upset because he'd gone to all this trouble to find his little brother a ride, and little brother wasn't as thrilled as Rusty maybe thought he ought to be. But after reflecting on it a bit, Rusty understood. So, the new deal was that we'd build our own team.

Cox Treated Lumber had agreed to sponsor me on the Miller car, and they weren't at all opposed to coming over to this new team, especially with Rusty's name involved.

Jim Ruggles would rent us motors, and David Ifft would not only lease his shop to us, but would be crew chief, too. Only catch was that I had to bring my spare ASA equipment, and what I didn't already own, was gladly given to me by John Childs, so no problem there.

We were on our way!

I didn't bring just things to North Carolina for the Busch team Rusty had put together for me—I also brought Tony Fraise to work on the crew. *(Kenny Wallace Collection)*

The Tax Man

I had never in my life had a cash sum of $14,000, but after selling the race car, trailer, her car and some other things, I had fourteen grand burning a hole in my pocket as Kim and I loaded up for Charlotte. Man, we were finally going to have some breathing room for the first time in our marriage.

Well, when we hit town I bought a little used car for Kim to drive around town, a little piece of shit that cost about $2,000. No way was I going to have her and Brooke stuck totally on foot, especially since I knew from past habit that I would end up working long, long hours.

Then Rusty's bookkeeper called me into the office one day and told me that I owed the I.R.S. $12,000. I still don't know exactly how that happened—I must have made more money with the ASA than I'd realized, and, no, I hadn't been making quarterly payments to the government.

They have no sense of humor, no patience and no willingness to give you any significant time to get the money. Especially when you have it in the bank.

So, I wrote the check to Uncle Sam, and Kim and I were back to scratch. At least we were already familiar with the concept.

Between you and me, it's no good to try to keep the money and get some interest on it. You might get 25 cents, but the government will charge you 75 cents in penalties.

Brooke in front of the Phoenix I bought for Kim when we first moved to the trailer park in North Carolina. We thought we had some money, but it turned out that the Tax Man got the rest. (Kenny Wallace Collection)

We thought.

Kim and I loaded everything we had into the converted Globe-Democrat panel truck, right down to the ironing board. By this time I had an enclosed trailer, which I'd bought with mixed emotions because the original open trailer represented a lot of hard work and love from Kim. But she understood as she always has, so we got all the race car parts in the new trailer. Who knows how much that sucker weighed, but I'm sure glad I didn't have to go across any truck scales on the way!

Along with baby Brooke, we brought Tony Fraise (son of Midwestern driving ace Steve Fraise) and his girl friend, because Rusty said to bring EVERYTHING from my ASA operation, and Tony was my paid (a term used loosely and laughingly) mechanic by this time. Honestly, I couldn't help thinking of my Green Acres days once more, except it was in reverse. All we were lacking on the road from Hooterville was Arnold the Pig.

You know the great thing about coming from pretty humble roots? When you're young and don't know any better, you have no idea of how funny you look. About all my little group had going for us was ambition. We were a sight otherwise, but there was such anticipation (both good and uncertain) propelling us down the highway. We were just old enough by now, and beat up enough by life experiences, to not be totally stupid. But let me suggest that the next time you are in a truck stop and you see a young family with a loaded U-Haul or pick-up truck, smile at them. Many of us have had one or two of those times in life when all we own in the world would fit in a 15-foot truck, and we're off searching for a better life. Even if you get a big smile back, you can bet there's some quaking in the boots going on.

I know this first-hand.

While Kim got us semi-settled in, I went to work at the garage like I was the lowest-paid, lowest-on-the-rung shop rat to ever set foot in Charlotte. Some people might call it running scared.

And, Lordy, they would have been right.

We got equipment together and went down to Daytona to practice, and, *wow,* what a rush! During the test sessions I traded fast time with Rob Moroso, who was one of the fastest-rising young stars in Busch racing then. (Sadly, Rob died in a highway accident the following year, but at that point he had as promising a future as anybody, so he was the perfect benchmark to measure yourself against.) We came back to Charlotte figuring that the Florida sun wasn't the only hot thing around!

And then NASCAR did its annual good-will tour of the garages. It's a pretty good idea, when you think about it. They bring in the templates and check to make sure you're legal. Spend a little time talking with you so everybody knows where they stand and you avoid ugly arguments at

During that first season on the Busch Series, my most constant rival for Rookie of the Year was Rob Moroso. But that didn't keep us from being friends, and here he is watching the antics of my daughter Brooke with an empty bottle. *(Kenny Wallace Collection)*

The boss and me in our Cox Treated Lumber shirts. *(Kenny Wallace Collection)*

the track, where maybe a media person with a long lens picks up that all is not well in heaven.

At the time, Robert Black was the Busch competition director, and, my rookie status showing once more, I didn't even know who he was or why he was there. But after he said that I couldn't race at Daytona because I hadn't been approved, I made it a point to find out just who he was and what the hell was going on!

Rusty and I called Les Richter, who was the main cat at NASCAR in those days, behind Bill France. More importantly, if you wanted a fair answer about what was going on at any level of NASCAR in those days, Les was the straight-shooter you talked to.

Les said for us to come on down to Daytona and have a talk. You can imagine how long that plane ride was for me. Under the best of circumstances I'm hyper, but when things get crazy, I get crazier. I don't know if Rusty threatened to tie me to the plane's wing so he wouldn't have to watch me fidget, because I was so wrapped up in this Catch-22 running around in my head. *You can't get experience without racing, and you can't race without experience.*

Ya think?

Well, as it turns out, even though we made the argument that I had turned some fairly impressive times during practice, along with a solid race at Martinsville, not to mention having Rusty in my corner, what got me the okay to race was—the resume.

I'll bet some of you didn't know that you have to submit a resume to NASCAR in order to race at the higher levels.

Our original instructions at the time I was going to drive Dale's car at Martinsville included sending a resume of my racing career, which Kim, my mom and I put together and forwarded. And then we promptly forgot about it because we figured it was what happened on the track that mattered.

Well, Les felt it was significant that I'd raced ASA and done well. ASA might have been just a feeder series in Daytona's eyes, but it was a critical proving ground and they were all smart enough to recognize that racing at places like Winchester, Salem and Michigan were excellent experience.

So, after sweating bullets and wondering what I had ever done to deserve so much frustration, I was finally cleared to race. But in all honesty, when we got back down to Daytona in February, I couldn't quit looking over my shoulder. Every time it looked like somebody from NASCAR was headed in my direction, I looked for a bolt-hole. They were NOT getting me out of that garage, no matter what else there was *that I didn't know about!*

You Have Got to Be Kidding Me, I'm Starting the Race Where?

I qualified for the pole of the Goody's 300 at Daytona.

I don't know who's writing this script but even *Ricky Bobby: Talladega Nights* fiction couldn't surpass the surprise that I was on the pole. I'm sure a lot of people in the pits thought it was because of the car, and I don't think I can argue with that. I just simply didn't have enough experience to "carry" a car that was ill-handling or had missed the set-up in some way. Between Rusty, David Ifft, Tony and the rest of our small crew, we'd managed to nail the preparation exactly right.

I was walking on air.

Herman the German, from little old Arnold, Missouri, was going to pace the field at the mighty Daytona International Speedway. What had the world come to? And, yes, it was the Busch race, but do you know some of the other drivers in that race? Dale Earnhardt Sr., Geoff Bodine, Dale Jarrett, Harry Gant, Donnie Allison, Ken Schrader, Darrell Waltrip, and my brother Rusty, along with all the regulars, who may not have been as well known but were every bit as good.

Come race day, and I had never been that nervous in my entire life. Not when the Boogie Man jumped out of the weeds and scared Mom and me. Not when the gorgeous Miss Kim Poole walked into the classroom. Not even when I turned the wrenches on Joe Ruttman's Winston Cup car at Daytona.

I am pacing the field in my very first Busch Series race as a full-time regular. It's Daytona and my heart was pumping about 1,000 beats a minute. *(Kenny Wallace Collection)*

As an aside, I'll tell you that these days I'm far more nervous at any of my daughters' softball games, wanting them to do well, but in 1989, at age 25, I had little enough of significance to compare to, and the focus of my life at that point was getting established as a race car driver. I just hadn't really stopped to think about a launch that was square in the middle of the spotlight.

Wisely, the rest of the field in that first Daytona 300 let the wild child go. I was determined to lead a few laps, and I did. *(Kenny Wallace Collection)*

The Truth Shall Set You Free

There are plenty of funny people in the NASCAR pits. Guys and gals who can trade one-liners with real comedians, in fact. But there's really only one guy, Ken Schrader, who has "wit."

According to the dictionary, wit is, "the keen perception and clever expression of connections between ideas that awaken amusement and pleasure." There's also something about intelligence and wisdom, but that might be taking it a step too far in this case.

I've known Kenny well all my life, but this is the instance when I understood that he goes beyond just funny, all the way to witty.

I had just managed to corral the Goody's 300 pole at Daytona my first time there, and shortly afterward Kenny came up to me.

"Congratulations, Herman, on the pole."

I was so excited that my feet were barely touching the ground, so I was a little effervescent, shall we say?

"Schrader, you've been there for me the whole time! You are like my brother!" I exclaimed.

Kenny is never comfortable with anything that focuses attention on him, and to add to the squirm factor, here's a bunch of media types standing around taking this in. And, even though I can sense that he's a little uncomfortable, I'm so high I can't stop myself, so I said, "You always took care of me, Kenny, *you always took care of me!*"

He put a hand on my shoulder, looked me in the eye and said, "No, Herm. Your family always left you behind at the track, and I got stuck bringing you home."

I get harassed about my laugh all the time, but you know what? It's that damned Schrader who's responsible for unleashing it because he's always saying something hilarious. Here he's also entertaining Bobby Labonte, Mark Martin and Jeff Gordon. (Kenny Wallace Collection)

I think I jumped the start of the race a little. Not intentionally, but I'd reached the point that there was just no reining in the adrenalin. I've never needed drugs or alcohol to get high. Drop a green flag, as far as I'm concerned, and there's nothing to exceed the feeling, and with all that incredible accumulated talent behind me, believe me, the green couldn't come out soon enough.

I was determined that if I never did anything else in my life, I was

The Card Game

I'm told that during qualifying for the 1989 Busch race at Daytona, there was a serious poker game going on among some Winston Cup heavy hitters. The television was on, but the volume was turned down. Still, when the announcer said that rookie Kenny Wallace had fast time, they all put down their hands and looked at the television screen. This included Bud Moore, Jake Elder and Tony Glover among others. Bud is a legendary car owner, Tony has crew-chiefed some great drivers including Ernie Irvan during his heyday, and I have already introduced you to Jake back in my original NASCAR stint.

I guess Jake just shook his head, watching me go around on my cool-down lap, and said, "I'll be goddamned."

I had told Eddie Thrapp four years earlier that the next time I saw him I would have a helmet in hand.

Well, I didn't. I had it on my head.

Of course, a little success and suddenly people come out of the woodwork, from relatives you never knew you had to people wanting to collect on old debts.

"Hey, Herm," Tony Glover said the next day, "remember when I loaned you $50 in Las Vegas back when?"

Yup.

"Well, pay me back, you son-of-a-bitch."

And I did.

They are trying to figure out why I didn't go faster during practice at Daytona, but, man, the first time you go out on that track, it better intimidate you like it did me, or you're just plain stupid. Of course, I couldn't explain that to the crew. (Kenny Wallace Collection)

going to lead that first lap. Thank God the rest of the field recognized a wild-eyed child when they saw one!

I led several laps, in fact, but then the car began to push. I never have over-estimated my ability, so I didn't assume for even a minute that I could overcome problems with the car. When it stopped being perfect, I accepted it and just continued to run as best I could.

Then, there was a red flag almost at the very end of the race, and we were sitting on the front stretch waiting for the okay to re-fire when I realized I was hearing a noise that wasn't related to my hot, tired car. I looked over at the fence, and it took a minute to register, but there was a guy I knew from St. Louis, waving "hello."

My concentration level had been so absolute on the race car that it had taken a while for me to register that there were probably 50,000 people sharing the same real estate—and I even knew a few of them.

From that surreal moment, I remember little because I was limping along by then, making it to the last lap in spite of a broken valve spring. Even so, I still managed to eke out a very respectable 10th place finish. Not bad, huh? But while I was in my little world trying to gain some respectability, there was a race going on. And, boy, what a race!

Dale Jarrett tried to pass Rusty high for second place on the last lap, but then he was in the wall. And there were people who thought Rusty put him there.

About ten minutes after the race, I crossed paths with Earnhardt. I smiled, he smiled, and then he said, "You better get ready. NASCAR is mad because they think Rusty put Jarrett in the wall on purpose, and they may not let him drive in the (Daytona) 500 tomorrow."

What????

I wasn't even a tiny bit happy at the thought of driving in the Daytona 500.

I was terrified.

My heart was somewhere down around my ankles, which were shaking like leaves.

Man, nobody in that whole place knew better than I did that I was

My very first pit stop at Daytona, and my brother is pitting in front of me. So, I had no room—and no clue. Now you can't do this, but the crew just ran out on pit road and did the job! *(Kenny Wallace Collection)*

NOT ready to drive in the biggest race in the world. Some guys come to NASCAR, full of themselves and convinced they can conquer the world right from the get-go. But the smart ones know they need experience, and I may not be the smartest one ever, but I at least knew that much.

Fortunately, it was only a matter of minutes before I got the reassurance that Rusty was going to get his hand slapped, but he would be allowed to drive in the 500.

And I could quit cowering in the corner, figuratively sucking my thumb.

It was an incredible roller-coaster ride for the launch of my Busch driving career, but I was headed for a year in which I would race with Bobby Hamilton and Jeff Burton for Rookie of the Year honors, and then snag it at the end. I would win three poles and come close to winning a couple of races, too. It was very, very heady stuff, and I was headed for even better days.

Or was I?

9

Demons and Darlings

FOR MANY YEARS, the Busch Series has been my saving grace. It has been the source of my greatest triumphs behind the wheel—and it has been where my heart has been broken. I suspect 17 years doing anything will yield highs and lows for the person living the life, and if I'm remembered only as a solid Busch Series driver who was the Super Sub in Winston and Nextel Cup, I'll live with that. Larry Phillips once reassured me that even one win in Busch was the equivalent of a hundred short-track wins, simply because there were at least a hundred very talented race drivers at the short tracks who would gladly trade places with me and walk a mile in my shoes.

If I looked happy, I should. I was posing outside my brother's beautiful shop in North Carolina where his team fielded Busch Series cars for me several seasons beginning in 1989. The Busch Series has always been very, very good to me. *(Kenny Wallace Collection)*

You can believe that I was appreciative of the opportunities coming my way when I was still pretty inexperienced as a driver. But I never, ever, even for a brief moment looking in the mirror as I shaved, thought that I was God's gift to the racing world. I knew that I got a real shot at racing in the Big Leagues thanks to some lucky breaks and good connections, but I also realized that a lot of guys have done that and then disappeared after a season or two. If I was going to continue racing with NASCAR's elite drivers I had to prove I belonged there.

So, one of the earliest things I did was seek out Jack Ingram. Just as you didn't mess with Mike Eddy in ASA, you never jacked with Jack on the Busch Series level. I was told that he was the epitome of the short-track racer who worked his way up, and having come up the hard way he expected respect and courtesy on the track. Hell, he'd earned it. But, even as he wanted you to use your head racing him, he wasn't going to cut you a lot of slack if you simply made a mistake. Every position meant another dollar in the bank to keep him going, so no matter the cause—stupidity or a simple error—you didn't want to screw up Jack.

Here's a story I heard that demonstrates what I mean. Back in Jack's earlier days he got in a beating-and-banging match with Bob Pressley.

For those who think I'm just a big goof—well, I have my moments. And then I have my moments. (©*Steven Rose, MMP Inc.; Kenny Wallace Collection*)

Oh, Brother

Brother acts are nothing new in NASCAR. It's great to share experiences with the guys you grew up with, and it means that you have somebody else to root for if your race goes sour. But, you can also expect that your career is always going to be compared, first and foremost, with them. If you have the most wins and success, you feel compelled to apologize; if you're the one who's chasing the rainbow, you will always wonder just exactly what you have to do to shut up the naysayers.

Michael Waltrip and I really understand each other. People think that we are trying to out-do our brothers, when really all we wanted to do was what our brothers were doing.

The Nemecheks were a lot like us, too. The younger brother John was like me in that he put a lot of stock in being happy off the track. He used to come over to the go-kart track and have a lot of laughs with us. Joe, on the other hand, was Big Brother like Rusty was for us. Joe has always been real serious, and that makes it hard to know him really well. Since John died, Joe has a big hole in his life, and he's even harder to know.

The other three-brother family racing in NASCAR is the Bodines, Geoff, Brett and Todd. They're a lot like us, too, but while youngest brother Todd is very much like me off the track, we're quite different on. Todd is another of those guys you don't want to see in your mirror, but he's a winner and you can't argue that point.

Like us, they've sometimes been under the microscope, but these days we've pretty much passed the torch to the Busch brothers. One big difference, though—none of us early guys ever had P.R. coaches.

However, we all had mamas who would box our ears when we acted out!

A wonderful homecoming night at Tri-City Speedway was a reminder of what we're all about. (Kenny Wallace Collection)

Bob's son Robert became one of the real stars in Busch racing later, but Bob was a terrific driver in his own right.

Anyway, this fender-banging episode cost Jack a championship. So, he turned his car around on the race track and ran wide-open, head-on into Bob.

Point taken.

Well, I didn't have a chance to talk with Jack during the craziness that surrounded us at Daytona, but when the Busch Series moved on to Hickory Speedway, I went early so I could carve out a few minutes with him.

He was Old School, and I say that with utmost affection and admiration. He had invested his money in his race car, so he was towing with a Chevy Dually and an open trailer. Everything he had was invested in the car—not the stuff to get it there. And because there had been years when he didn't have a lot to put in the car, he'd worked hard to make himself a really good chassis man. That means, he had figured out how to wring out everything he could from the equipment he had. I can remember leaning over his fender and seeing "RFH" on a spring. He told me that he'd run that spring for the last ten years at Hickory, and he knew that if the car wasn't handling, it wasn't that spring.

From Jack Ingram, I learned that sometimes it's as important to know what's NOT wrong with your car as trying to figure out what is.

Because I was willing to listen to him, and probably because I treated him with respect off the track as well as on, he became a really good source of information. And that brings me to another point—racing has no shortage of accomplished, experienced drivers willing to share at least some of their knowledge, but it isn't always because they are un-

I made it a point to get to know Jack Ingram when I started Busch Series racing. There was nobody who was tougher to deal with on the track—or off, if you crossed him—but his guidance in Busch was as important to me as Dick Trickle's had been in ASA. *(Robert Harris Photo)*

The body language should tell you something. I had never been so nervous in my life because we had done something to the car that was in the gray area of the rules and I just knew we were going to get questioned on it. We'd found out something that another competitor was doing that helped him have an advantage and he'd not been caught. Well, nothing came of it, but it was a sweaty palms moment. *(Kenny Wallace Collection)*

selfish. If the rookie kid shortens the learning process, he's also a lot less likely to tear up your equipment as well as his own in a stupid, avoidable wreck. You maybe don't tell him all your secrets, but helping him helps you, too.

One of the big things Jack taught me was that you could improve your car's handling by how you ran the throttle. At different spots on the track, you can actually be faster by running quarter-throttle or half-throttle instead of stomping on the gas all the way and then have to stomp on the brake to stay out of the way. I've heard it called "slowing down to go faster," others call it *finesse,* and it's a valuable lesson.

Jack also taught me how to move slower cars out of your way without wrecking them. Believe me, he knew how to do the latter, but if he liked you, he was a master at the sweet spot. You would just be running your groove and all of a sudden you were up a lane, and you didn't know how you got there. But then you'd see Jack motoring on by and you knew that he had you. The bump-and-run that's so popular now, even in Nextel Cup where the drivers are supposed to be better than that, isn't necessary. Just spend a little time watching tapes of Jack Ingram or Harry Gant. They didn't hit you. They moved you out of the way and there was no way in the world you got mad at them and wanted to fight. They were just the best at making progress smoothly.

Harry Gant taught me a few things beyond how to move a competitor out of the way without destroying his car. Our first encounter was at Talladega back when I was crewing for Rusty in the NASCAR Grand American Division pony-car days.

It was my introduction to 200 mph, so it would be memorable any way you look at it, but Rusty won the race. And in the process he had

Harry Gant is a gentleman, humble and considerate. I can't think of anybody better to try to follow as an example. And, whether it was his intention or not, he taught me some good lessons. *(Robert Alexander Photo)*

outrun Richie Evans and Harry, among others. Harry was the first driver to come down to our pit afterwards. He shook my hand even though he didn't know me.

Harry also gave me a valuable lesson in humility. We were signing autographs at the Lebanon, Missouri, race track, pretty early in my career. It wasn't arrogance—it wasn't even a conscious thought—but I signed my name pretty large on a shirt. There wasn't a lot of room left, so Harry looked at the shirt and then he looked at me in a way that brought my attention back to the shirt, and then he said, "*Boy*, let me teach you how to sign."

And he wrote his name in a way that left plenty of room for other autographs—from bigger stars. It was a reminder that even if somebody wants your autograph, you may not be the ultimate driver for them. For sure, even bigger stars are out there and they are probably going to be willing to sign the object, too. Leave room for them.

Respect. And humility, too, because you could congratulate Harry on a win and he'd turn the conversation to the house he was going to build tomorrow instead of dwelling on what a wonderful job he'd done.

You can deal with the less wonderful Sundays better if you don't take the "good" out of context. It's sort of like—if you puff yourself up when you win, then you ought to crawl in a hole when you lose. And in our sport, even the greatest drivers lose more—sometimes a lot more—than they win. So, if you don't want to spend a lot of time in a hole licking your wounds, you need to keep it all in perspective.

It was a great education from a great man.

Brandy

It didn't matter what was happening with my racing career, Kim and I were having children. Brooke had made us a family in 1986, but just over two years later we found that we were growing again.

At the time, we were living in a singlewide mobile home, settled now in North Carolina, and according to the sonograms we were going to have a boy.

Brooke had been a tough delivery for Kim, but our *little boy* suddenly required an emergency C-section after a long labor. Apparently the boy we had been promised left some apparatus behind because I leaned over to Kim and told her, "Um, it's a girl."

First thing through our minds was, "Oh, gosh, we painted the room wrong," because it was blue. But after that moment of silliness, we counted fingers and toes, and realized that we had another absolutely gorgeous little girl. Far too pretty to have been a boy.

If you have children, you know that each one is unique, and if you don't have kids let me confirm that fact for you. Here's the difference between the girls, and it's just as true today as it was when they were four years old and two years old: If we were outside on the porch and there was a big bug, Brooke would literally scream and run away. Brandy would smash it. I've always claimed that Brandy gets mad at us sometimes because we left her in the labor room too long. Truth is, she's just the female version of me, heaven help the world.

Brandy has been blessed with that sense of adventure that usually works in her favor—and occasionally doesn't. She's the one we got called to school for. She drives too fast because she thinks she's bullet-proof. She's a wild child who loves to sing and dance, and is justifiably full of self-confidence. But, if you have any need at all for a smile or a laugh, Brandy is the person you want to hang with.

A classic middle child, Brandy came into this world saying, "I don't wanna!" I'd say, "Come here, Brandy, come to Daddy," and she'd jut out her chin and lower lip and say, *"I don't wanna!"*

Of course, she would eventually come over, but it had to look like it was her idea.

On her christening day, Miss Brandy poses with her godparents, Uncle Rusty and Aunt Patti Wallace. (Kenny Wallace Collection)

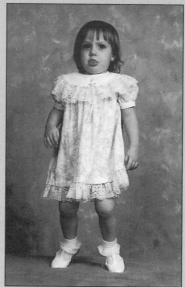

This photo sums up my darling Brandy's personality from a very young age—it's gonna be my way or the highway! (Kenny Wallace Collection)

And Then I Crawled in the Hole

That first season on the NASCAR Busch circuit was a rolling high. I really feel in my heart that Rusty believed I could be a Cup star if the cards fell just right, and so, even though 1989 was the year he won the Winston Cup championship, he was like a proud papa. He kept his hand on the team's pulse so that David and the crew, which by now included my cousin Timmy, and I all felt very connected. There's no question that the second and third place finishes, the laps led, the Rookie of the Year award, and the sixth place in points came in great part because we had feedback coming from Rusty, unquestionably one of the best drivers to ever sit in a race car.

And then 1989 slid into 1990. Once again, we were *right there,* right on the cusp of winning but just missing because of this or that dumb little thing that would occur.

The season went on.

And on.

And on. And pretty soon the whispers started: *When is Kenny going to win?*

And the more ominous one: *Can't Kenny win? Can't he get the job done?*

I admit that I had to think long and hard about whether to discuss this time period or just gloss over it. Yeah, it was tough, but look at the good things that have happened in my life, so how can I be hung up by a brief, tough time?

Well, when I made the commitment to do this book, I agreed to tell the whole story. Not just the public-relations, pretty part. And if you

Fraise wasn't my only secret weapon from back home—I also brought out my cousin, Timmy Wallace, who worked for us a while and is still a good crew man in NASCAR. *(Kenny Wallace Collection)*

The public relations machine at NASCAR really knows what it's doing—most of the time. And sometimes they come a cropper—Bobby Labonte, Jeff Gordon and I were the original Young Guns of NASCAR. And we hated every second of this stupid promotion. *(Kenny Wallace Collection)*

think that even the great stars of racing never have bad times, you've bought into a lie.

That Mark Martin and Tony Stewart sometimes wrestle with demons is no secret. That the demons sometimes win is known. I'm here to tell you that they—and I—are hardly alone in this.

I remember being at Loudon, New Hampshire, before a race several years ago and sitting in the back of a pick-up truck with Jeff Gordon waiting for driver introductions. During these brief periods, you spend time with another driver and nobody else is around to overhear or interrupt. You hope you're waiting with somebody you like, and in this

I've even driven open-cockpit cars a couple of times, although I'm not sure how much indoor racing counts on the tally. In 1992, I ran at the RCA Dome in Indianapolis in a USAC versus Outlaw Midget race, but the flywheel bolts broke on the car so it was a short night. I did get a good laugh with then-fellow Busch driver Jeff Gordon. *(Kenny Wallace Collection)*

Tony Stewart

Tony Stewart is one of the greatest race drivers of all time. With Tony, it's as much about his passion for racing as it is his success, and he's won in everything he's gotten into from a midget on a quarter-mile dirt track to IROC to road courses, and, of course, NASCAR. If nothing else, you would have to respect his record.

But I happen to like the guy even more than I respect his winning ways. And I'm intrigued by him because he's such an enigma. There probably isn't a more complex person in our sport. The stuff going on inside him must be wilder than Cirque de Soleil.

An article I read about Tony in *ESPN* magazine speculates that Tony is a product of wanting his dad's approval but feeling he was never good enough. If that's true, boy, can I ever identify with that. It doesn't mean you don't love them— just that you spend a lot of your life trying to live up to somebody's expectations besides your own.

More media conjecture is that when the Indiana native won at the Indianapolis Motor Speedway, his dad wasn't satisfied because it wasn't the Indy 500.

I don't know about any of this because I've never had this conversation with Tony, but it's

public record that he's struggled with explosive anger and knee-jerk reactions to stuff that's happened on the track. So, it's created some public relations problems as fans want to love him, but some just can't quite get there because of his strong personality.

He was forced to confront it, and I really respect how he's been able to deal with all those issues. It's worked, because when he finished 11th in the regular season in 2006, he smiled and granted all sorts of interviews; the Old Tony would have stomped off to the hauler and let people think what they want. He has always been able to see through the phonies, but sometimes he didn't even do the reasonable stuff because he couldn't handle what was going on inside himself.

I do know this. At one point when he was especially miserable, my brother Mike pulled him aside and asked him why such relatively petty stuff was eating him up. And then Mike told Tony about the day he backed up his race-car trailer at home in St. Louis—just another average day, without a care in the world—until he realized that the trailer had backed over his toddler son, Mikey.

Tony has said that Joe and J.D. Gibbs, three

I don't know anybody in racing with more natural talent than Tony Stewart. But it's good to see the intensity that makes him so competitive on the track is being tempered off the track these days. He still barely tolerates foolishness, but he's learned not to sweat the details so much anymore. (Bruce Bennett Photo)

psychiatrists and several therapists couldn't get through to him the way Mike Wallace did that day. No matter what's happening at the race track, no matter how many stupid questions are hurled your way by the media, no matter how badly your fellow competitions treat you, it can't compare to what Mike had to deal with.

And that put it all into perspective.

This beautiful toddler playing with Uncle Kenny is Mikey, my brother Mike's son. And anytime you look at Tony Stewart and marvel at how calm and controlled he is these days, you'll know that Mikey's fate is at least part of the reason Tony has learned to control his emotions and stop sweating the small stuff that used to bug him so much. (Kenny Wallace Collection)

case it was no problem. I know the tee-shirt-and-jeans Jeff Gordon at least as well as the wine merchant who can co-host the heck out of *Regis and Kelly*.

And suddenly, out of the clear blue sky, Jeff said, "God, Kenny, I wish I could laugh like you."

Unlike the people who think my laughter means I'm not a serious racer, Jeff was telling me that he wishes he could just let loose and let a laugh roll up from his toes completely without inhibition.

But, of course, he can't. He's been the center of controversy of some kind or other since he was a little kid, and while his life is a good one, he's always got to be on guard. Half the grandstand loves him, and the other half hates him for no better reason other than that they don't understand him. I'm glad that he's come to terms with that, but he made my knees go weak with his comment. Here I'd practically cut off my arm for just one of his Winston Cup or Nextel Cup wins, and he's telling *me* that he envies at least part of *my life!* Millions of dollars and incredible professional success are no guarantee of a completed life, but it seems like he's happier these days—and it's got nothing to do with winning.

Nobody's life—not even the Earnhardts'—is perfect. We all wrestle with our own personal difficulties, and it's usually a private deal. But I've been nothing if not honest, so welcome to my personal demons: My life

And then I ran a mini-sprint at the Charlotte Arena. A split second after the photo was taken, #98 (me) spun out #99 (Kenny Schrader). But he forgave me. *(Kenny Wallace Collection)*

has always been driven by the intense need to drive race cars and the need to live up to the extremely high standards of being a race driver named Wallace.

In late 1990, I was pretty sure that I hadn't done what I needed to do to have that respect. You see, in the Wallace family, even though there's no overt pressure to be a winner, nonetheless you are *expected* to win. Remember, we're the family who would drive home in total silence

Family is everything. These are the people you get the maddest at because they know better than anyone how to push your buttons. But these are also the people who know exactly how to make you feel like king of the world. My mother, knowing what a tough time I'd had trying to come out of my brother's considerable shadow, once met me at the door with this sign when I came home from a win. It gave us all——including Rusty——an inside joke and a great laugh. And being greeted in Victory Lane with my daughter's squeal of delight is absolutely the best that life can give me. *(L: Kenny Wallace Collection; R: Robert Fairman Photo)*

Maybe because his racing career has had its share of ups and downs, too, my brother Mike understood what a Busch win at Rockingham meant to me. So on my victory lap, he made the sign I'm holding, and then he stayed in Victory Lane because he understood how important it was to me to share such a happy moment. *(Both photos: Robert Fairman Photos)*

from the race track on the nights that Dad didn't win, *because, we hadn't gotten the job done!*

Sometimes, I want to sit my dad down and say, "Who taught you to be so damned hard on yourself? Who was it? Why do you need the wins so bad? *Because you passed that hard-ass, need-to-win attitude on to me.*"

I was standing in the garage area in 1990 with some good statistics and the respect of most, if not all, my fellow competitors, building the base for a solid, long-lasting career.

And I was absolutely miserable because I had not won.

Overreacting, you think? But how would you feel if the following had happened to you?

The guys on Rusty's Blue Max Winston Cup team took pains to tease him about our effort. One of the crew guys asked one day, "Hey, how come that Busch team ain't won yet?"

"That Busch deal is a pain in my ass."

Rusty didn't know I heard that. Or how devastated I was. Or how much more pressure I was putting on myself because of it.

I don't question Rusty's love. I have often wished he could express it vocally. Mike is better at understanding my need to hear the words once in a while. When I won at Rockingham in 2001, Mike hurried up in the pits and wrote a sign that said, *"Herman, you are the man!"* He wasn't bothered at all to hold it up in front of the world.

But even Mike and I have a different approach to racing. He's always viewed it as a way to make money, shades of Uncle Gary, and he's very sensible when it comes to the business side of racing. I admire him for that, and I don't doubt his love of racing, either, but if you put me in a

In a rare moment of relaxation during the hectic summer of 1989, when Rusty was on his way to the NASCAR Winston Cup championship and I was in my rookie year on the Busch circuit. *(Kenny Wallace Collection)*

race car I honestly forget there's a purse paid out at the end. I haven't been stupid about the money I've made racing, but it doesn't drive me.

Rusty certainly understands how I feel about racing. But he feels that the need to openly express affection is corny. You have to pretty much assume Rusty cares for you because he'll never put his arm around you. He'll never tell you he loves you. He learned at the knee of Larry Phillips, and he learned well, that if you win—or even if you don't—it's just expected that you take it in stride. And considering all that Rusty has done for me in my life—the opportunities, the advice, so very many things—I would be a total idiot if I didn't realize that it's his way of expressing love.

Still, I'd trade a Nextel Cup victory for Rusty just telling me—out loud—that he loves me. But at this point in my life I'm resigned to both being pretty much out of my reach. And I won't curl up and die. It's just part of being a grown-up that Mick Jagger and the boys were right about when they sang, *you can't always get what you want.*

Okay, Herm, you big wuss. In 1990, you're struggling because people are starting to question your ability, and your Busch career is maybe a drain on your brother instead of a joy.

But it wasn't just Rusty. I kept waiting for my dad to tell me that I'd done a good job in a race. That the wins were going to come. That I was just this close to reaching the summit.

And he never said it.

I can remember Rusty and him talking about other drivers. It was Dad and Larry Phillips both speaking when Rusty opened his mouth and said, "Well, he's *(insert a name here)* a good driver, but he just can't finish the deal. You know, he just can't win."

I would think, if my brother and my dad are thinking that about another guy who can't seem to get the wins, then does that mean they

Rusty put his 1989 championship trophy in my office at Wallace Racing as inspiration, but you know what? I think it really ended up being pressure more than anything else. *(Kenny Wallace Collection)*

don't respect him? Does it mean he's not talented or worthy? And if I don't win, then does it mean that I'm in the same category with the guys they don't respect? Are they not going to want me around? *Am I not good enough to be a Wallace?*

Well, of course, I know better now. And if I hadn't been so insecure at that time, I would have known it back then. Just as I love them, flawed humans as they are, I also know that they love me, flawed as I am. Nobody's perfect, so when you aren't getting what you need from one place, look in another.

For me it came sometime later and was in the form of Don "The Snake" Prudhomme, who probably has no idea at all that he saved my

I was so happy to see Ron Capps win a Wally (trophy) at Gateway International Raceway near my hometown of St. Louis, for his car owner, and my very good friend, Don Prudhomme. *(Les Welch Photo; Kenny Wallace Collection)*

Brittany

Kim's mother is one of ten children in a close-knit family. So, I guess I shouldn't have been surprised when Kim said she wanted to have seven kids. And it follows that it wasn't a huge shock when Brittany was born two years after Brandy.

This time we knew that it was going be a planned C-section, and I figured that I'm Mister Tough Guy by now. I got queasy when each of the other girls was born, but, hey, I'm almost qualified to be an obstetrician by now, right?

Well, hell, I fainted.

Kim's hollering, "Is he okay, *is he okay?*"

At least, I think that's what she was saying. Could have been, "Let him lay, *let him lay,*" for all I know. I was still trying to get my sea-legs back under me.

After our wonderful little Brittany was born—and I don't know how this is possible, but here was a third girl with yet another distinct personality of her own—for reasons too complex and personal to relate here, Kim had her tubes tied. But after the Oklahoma City bombing in 1995, and the loss of all those precious children in the federal building there, Kim was moved to feel she wanted to try again to have more babies.

She went through a pretty harrowing deal with the surgery, and we tried, even going so far as in-vitro, but it didn't work. When we realized that it just wasn't going to happen, I took her in my arms and said, "God is telling us that we've got three beautiful girls, and it's time for us to move on."

Kim got all teary-eyed and said, "But, Kenny, I wanted you to have a boy."

I would have enjoyed it, I'm sure, but we were meant to have girls. That's just the way it is, and I can assure you that I've enjoyed the softball games every bit as much as I would have baseball games. Everything we do together, whether it's just going out to eat, sitting around the house teasing each other, intense conversations about boy friends, or taking nice trips together, this is truly what I was meant to do in life. It's 100 percent more important than anything I'll ever do in a race car, and I hope it doesn't sound like bragging but I think Kim and I (okay, mostly Kim) have done a damned good job. The girls aren't perfect but if they were, what would they want to do with their old dad?

When I think about having three girls instead of a mix of boys and girls I can't help remembering the line from that Rolling Stones song, "You can't always get what you want, but if you try real hard, you just might get what you need."

I only have to walk in the door at home to realize that I've got what I need.

It's time for Brittany to make her entrance into the world, so Brooke and Brandy come along with Dr. Kenny. But it looks like they would just as soon be at home watching Sesame Street. (Kenny Wallace Collection)

And then Brittany arrived. I had recovered nicely from my fainting spell. (Kenny Wallace Collection)

Brittany's favorite photo. She accompanied us to a shoot, and frankly, the best photo taken that day is this one. (Kenny Wallace Collection)

career and my sanity, and reassured me that I have a right to feel pretty good about my life. Don, who is one of the all-time great drag racers and now is one of the best car owners in the National Hot Rod Association, has long been a close friend of Rusty's. They've got relationships with Miller Beer that go way back, and that's how they were introduced. But they also hit it off, so by association I also got to know Don.

Snake and I crossed paths in Las Vegas some time ago, and he told me, "Herm, you're really starting to show what you've got. The wins are going to come."

And then he looked me in the eye and just floored me when he said, "You know the difference between you and your brother? The fans yell, 'Hey, Rusty, come give me your autograph,' and Rusty might, but he might also say, 'I ain't got time.' They yell, 'Hey, Herman!' and you go over and sign for them.

"*Don't change!* Rusty's damn good, but you're a damned good guy. And what's wrong with that? You're too hard on yourself."

In a family of over-achievers, I just needed a little validation that I mattered.

Going all the way back to those early days in NASCAR, I realize that it's also always a case of *damned-if-you-do, damned-if-you-don't.* My happy-go-lucky persona that everybody sees is expressed in public, directly as a result of Rusty's advice. Now, don't get me wrong—I really am a happy guy because I have so much to be happy about and I'm smart enough to realize that.

But that laugh—the laugh that makes me stand out in any crowd—is also the noose around my neck.

Rusty's advice stems from something that happened to him way back when. There was an on-track confrontation between Rusty and Darrell Waltrip. Up to that point, Rusty had been a Golden Boy and Darrell was nicknamed Jaws. But this time in the post-race interviews, Darrell—who'd gotten pretty darn media savvy by this time—sounded like the injured party, and Rusty sounded like the bad guy.

The fans turned the tables on them. The people who love Darrell today, knowing him as a wonderful FOX television announcer, may have no idea of what a villain he was considered to be by a fair portion of the fan base back in the 1980s. And you know what? He was exactly the same person then that he is today, which, I want to add, is a terrific guy. But he came in with a whole different image than the good ol' boys running at the time, and being probably the only guy in the pit area who can outtalk me, he ruffled some feathers.

But he learned from it. And so did Rusty. So, Rusty sat me down in the shop and told me, "Herm, when you get interviewed, don't bitch, don't complain. Just do like Bill Elliott and Harry Gant. 'Aww, shucks, 'em,' and don't let on that you'd like to kick that other guy square in the ass.' "

It was—for the most part—excellent advice, as is almost everything Rusty's taught me. I can remember getting taken out of a race when another guy just flat drove into my right rear quarter panel and took us both out.

What did I want to say when they stuck the microphone under my nose? "I wanted to get out of the car and kick that mother******* idiot in the ass!"

And what did I say?

When I was just a scrawny kid trying to make it in ASA racing, Darrell Waltrip did an appearance—and shared some racing wisdom with me. *(Don Thies Photo; Kenny Wallace Collection)*

HERMAN'S TAKE ON . . .

Settling Debts

Rusty wasn't the only family member to invest in my racing career. Although Dad had felt that he was getting older, and being more careful with money I guess because of getting closer to retirement age, he spent some money even though he didn't build a car with me.

I had told him, "Dad, I can't quit wanting to be a race-car driver," and after he saw the dedication and commitment I had, he helped out with some of the bills.

A few years ago, I heard from some folks back in the St. Louis area that dad thought I hadn't repaid the loan. The problem was that I hadn't realized it was a loan, but when I asked him, it was pretty clear that we had misunderstood each other.

So, I wrote Dad a check for $10,000, and I wrote another one for Mom for $10,000, because I figured that she probably did without some nicer things in life so us boys could go racing.

And I learned that a) even with family, you should always get financial terms clear up front; and b) you should thank God and your spouse if you make enough money to repay old debts.

My mom and dad on a very happy occasion— the day that Kim and I got married in 1984. (Kenny Wallace Collection)

"Watch the replay," I smiled.

And really, what can you do? Because you know that at home there's several hundred, if not thousand, racers who would gladly trade places with you. They'd gladly wreck every Sunday. They'd drive the worst-handling piece of crap on earth and smile from ear-to-ear when they got out at the end of the day.

You drive your ass off, you work harder than the guy who won because at least his car was handling or he wouldn't have won, and there's the frustration of not being able to kick *anybody's* ass because you know that the car owner, sponsors and crew are doing everything they possibly can do, so you can't really blame them either.

So, you laugh.

And people, including car owners, think you're not serious.

And inside you're aching, but you can't let anybody see it because the worst thing that can happen to a race car driver, at any level of the sport, is to be labeled a "whiner."

I know that some of the best jobs of driving I've ever done came on days when I finished in the back of the pack, but I wrestled a car that was so bad I should have driven straight to the garage at the green flag. And maybe a handful of people recognize the job done. It happens to all of us, even the really successful guys. So, you deal with it. I mean, at least at the end of the day, I get to go home to Kim and the girls, so—based on what Jeff Gordon, and a surprising number of other drivers have said to me—I'm a winner on an even bigger stage.

If I just wasn't driven to compete, maybe I wouldn't be so miserable sometimes when I realize that time is passing, and while I'm blessed to be making a living doing this, I'm still struggling for respect as much as I was in 1990.

But a few things that have happened along the way have made it possible for me to live with my own unfulfilled expectations. It's just that the good is always balanced by something bad.

Like in 1991.

10

The Intimidator Serves Spaghetti

HOW CAN A SINGLE YEAR be the best—and worst—racing season in a guy's career? Let me tell you how it happened for me.

During the off-season, still wrestling with personal demons, I recognized that Tony Fraise and I were trying to do too much, and we didn't have the experience we needed. I had seen some other drivers, including my brother Rusty, who had been smart enough to let go of total control so they could concentrate more on driving and on being less mentally exhausted when the green flag dropped.

Finally! Standing on the door in Victory Lane at Volusia County Speedway. *(Kenny Wallace Collection)*

I've seen thousands of Victory Lane pictures with a pretty trophy girl, but I think I may be the only driver to also have a clown. *(Kenny Wallace Collection)*

This is the car in which I finally broke through to the winner's circle. Part of the reason was because we'd hired Steve Byrd. *(Both photos: Kenny Wallace Collection)*

So, when veteran mechanic Steve Byrd quit Steve Grissom's Busch team, we snatched him up as quickly as we could. The difference was just amazing. We went from competitive to COMPETITIVE almost overnight.

And then, on March 24, 1991, it finally happened. I broke into the Busch Series winner's circle at Volusia County Speedway. I know that there have been scores of race drivers who've been as happy as I was that early spring afternoon, but I doubt there's been more than a handful who have ever been as relieved.

I wrapped my arms around Kim in Victory Lane, and I whispered pretty fiercely in her ear, "Oh, baby—*it's finally over!*"

What I meant was that awful, unending worry about whether I could ever get the job done. I could look in the mirror and not imagine my dad or my brother tsk-tsking over my shoulder that I was wasting resources. It had taken what seemed like a long time, but finally I could call myself a Wallace.

Then, on July 14th, I took New Hampshire International Raceway into my heart as I led the most laps and won my second Busch race. And then on Monday morning, my telephone rang.

It was Dale Earnhardt Sr.

"Hey, congratulations on that win!" he told me. "I was getting on my plane during the race, but before we took off, I made the pilot wait so I could be sure you got the win. You did a great job. Why don't you come on over to the shop for lunch to celebrate."

Well, I got the greatest kick from that phone call. As much as I want (and still want) my dad's and my brother's approval, I also wanted Dale to be proud of me. He gave my career the kick start it needed, and he had

A few weeks after the Volusia victory our team won again at New Hampshire International Speedway. Does a win matter to the crew? You be the judge. *(Both photos: Kenny Wallace Collection)*

consistently been friend and mentor. It was important to me that Dale feel good about the win, too.

I got in my truck and ran down to the shop. He had a little picnic bench there, and even though everybody else had finished lunch, I'll be damned but Dale sat there while I ate cold spaghetti and a salad. He told me how important it was to "close the deal." That when I won, I'd closed the deal, and that was important.

I spent most of that year walking on air. Man, it felt *so great* to go to the track and know that I had a legitimate shot to win every single time. And beyond that, to actually close the deal. But if life to this point had taught me nothing else, it was that the piper is always waiting to be paid.

We returned to New Hampshire late that year for the second Busch race. And, in the blink of an eye, I experienced one of those life-altering moments a person has maybe only a couple of times in their lives.

Loudon had been good to me, and even though the car wasn't great that day, we were still stout and protecting a 90-point lead in the standings over Bobby Labonte, with whom I'd been trading the lead all season. Going down the backstretch the left rear trailing arm welds broke. I went screaming into turn three and hit about as hard as it was possible to do. I cracked three ribs and knocked myself out and it all happened so quick there was nothing I could have done to prevent it.

After helping me get out of the car, the corner worker suggested we sit down on the pavement while we waited for the ambulance to arrive, and, boy, am I ever glad he did. It wasn't enough to smack my helmeted-

Bobby Labonte

Bobby Labonte is a major part of my life. Bobby is that damned nerve I got twitching in my eye, as well as a swift kick to my backside.

See, the deal is that we came up at the same time. And I so wish I could dislike him because he seemed to get the better of me too many times, but it's impossible because he's one of the really great guys of all time in NASCAR and a wonderful friend.

We raced as hard as anybody could race for the 1991 Busch championship and traded the lead back and forth most of the season. But with about five races to go, I had a lead of almost 200 points. Then I blew the motor at Darlington. Next, Ward Burton's throttle stuck at Indy, and he bounced off the wall right into me. And, of course, there was my Loudon crash.

Here's the kind of guy Bobby is. He didn't

crow about my misfortune, not even in private. Instead, he came to see me at the hospital. And he called me when I got out, telling me, "Hey, Buddy, don't give up on me now. We gotta settle this thing on the track, not off."

He really meant it. He didn't want to win that championship by default any more than I wanted to hand it to him. And I would be so much better in my mind if I had been outrun, out-strategized by Bobby and his team instead of losing from the sidelines.

But, all that aside, I've been very happy to have seen his career do so well. Bobby and Terry Labonte are the class acts of NASCAR. And Bobby driving for the King, Richard Petty, is really cool. You'd feel funny about a lot of guys getting into the legendary #43, but Bobby is exactly the right one.

If I had to finish second in the 1991 Busch Series, I'm glad it was to a real class act (and good friend) like Bobby Labonte. (Kenny Wallace Collection)

head on the concrete wall—at least by sitting down I didn't have so far to fall when I passed out again.

Kenny, Kenny . . . . I could hear a long way off, like the voice was coming through a tunnel. In addition to a concussion, I had positional vertigo, and even though I tried, by the end of practice the following week it was clear that I couldn't drive. Rusty had to get in the car for me, and that was just enough to kiss the championship good-bye.

Alan Kulwicki

Alan Kulwicki was like a mad scientist. All kinds of people in positions of power and accomplishment in ASA and NASCAR tried to tell Alan how he needed to do things, and like Dr. Jekyll, he just ignored them and did his own thing. I'm really glad it worked out so well for him in his too-short life that his name is on that Winston Cup championship trophy.

Most people don't know this, but Alan asked me to come to work for him back in our ASA days when he was one of the toughest young competitors Rusty faced. I didn't want to leave Rusty, but I always appreciated that Alan thought that much of me.

In 1989, he asked Rusty for help in locating a crew chief, and Rusty suggested our old pal from St. Louis, Paul Andrews. It was a real meeting of minds—they were just about perfect for each other. Paul calculated so well that final 1992 race day at Atlanta exactly how many laps Alan needed to lead—and when to stay out on the track—so he could get the bonus for most laps led. It was brilliant strategy on their part. I can't help wondering what more they would have done if that plane hadn't gone down the next spring with Alan on board. Man, we lost an icon that day.

Frank Sinatra could have been singing about Alan in that song, "My Way." And I'll tell you an example of how:

A lot of us who drive race cars believe in God, but even if we have faith we don't have a lot of organized religion among us. Sunday mornings, you won't find a lot of NASCAR drivers in the pews of churches around Charlotte for the obvious reason we're on the road nearly every weekend of the year. But on the day we had our daughter Brandy baptized, when we turned around from the font I spotted Alan sitting quietly in the back.

Alan came from Wisconsin and he brought his Midwestern values with him. It wasn't at all unusual for him to go to church, not just in Charlotte but wherever he might be.

And I'll bet St. Peter remembered that when Alan arrived at the Pearly Gates.

The late champion—and friend—Alan Kulwicki. He brought a 1957 car from his collection over to Wallace Racing for us to see. That's also his shop in the background. (Judy Wallace Collection)

Putting the Championship Loss in Perspective

A decade later, both Adam Petty and Kenny Irwin lost their lives in the exact same place where I had crashed at New Hampshire in 1991. I spent a little sheet time in a hospital, struggling with positional vertigo to go with a concussion and cracked ribs.

After I got back to North Carolina, I realized I still had a problem. I could look straight ahead or at a certain angle, and everything was fine, but if I looked in the other direction, everything whirled around so horrendously that I was physically sick. I can remember waiting in the doctor's office and Kim trying to catch my vomit in her hands. She didn't freak out, she didn't find an excuse to leave me sitting there on my own even when I told her it was okay.

"I love you too much to leave you here like this," she told me, but, really, she didn't have to tell me—ever again—how much she loves me. Talk about proof of caring.

Years later, when I drove for the wonderful folks at Square D, they asked if I would like to see the sports therapist that they were sending all their salespeople to, and I said yes, not because I necessarily thought I needed to talk to this guy, but because it seemed like a real teamwork kind of thing to do.

Turned out to be a very interesting look into my own psyche.

I had been carrying around inside a lot of latent anger and frustration because the crash had destroyed any chance of winning the '91 Busch title. And if I'd won that, maybe it would have opened a lot of doors. Maybe things would have been different on the Cup level. *Maybe, maybe, maybe.*

I'm well over the whole "maybe" thing. Because I also realized that God's hand had surely been on me that day. A few centimeters this way or that, and I would have had the same fate as Adam and Kenny, since my helmet made contact with the concrete wall. It's hard to think I was a lucky man that day, but I have only to look at those families walking around with huge holes in their hearts and I know just how blessed I was.

People have asked Mark Martin how he will feel if he finishes up his career without winning a Winston/Nextel Cup championship, and he replies, "Well, I'll still get up in the morning."

It's a mark of me as a competitor that I so desperately want to win races and championships—that I'm torn up I haven't done more—but when you think about all the what-ifs, the close calls, the wrecks that maybe I shouldn't have walked away from through the years, well, thanks to Mark Martin, I can sum up just how all the misses in life stack up against the might-have-beens.

Most people don't know this, but the late Kenny Irwin (shown here center) worked for Wallace Racing in the early 1990s. He used to disappear all the time to go drive race cars, but I guess if anybody could understand the need to do that it was the Wallace boys. I lost a championship in a wreck at New Hampshire, but Kenny lost his life in a later wreck at the same spot. (Kenny Wallace Collection)

After this deal happened to me, it meant that nobody at the Atlanta track the following year for the Cup championship knew better than I did how Davey Allison felt when all he had to do was finish the damned race to take the season title. And Ernie Irvan spun out in front of Davey, and Alan Kulwicki's name will be on the champion's trophy forevermore. I knew *exactly* how Davey felt.

You know, we race drivers have cracked crystal balls. If we could really see what is going to happen in the future, we'd probably all retire and suck our thumbs in the corner somewhere. But we ignore what happens to us and what might happen, and we never stop trying to force good things to occur. Kim will say something like, *there was a huge pile-up on the 100th lap, and if you hadn't fallen out earlier, you might have been right in the middle of it and gotten hurt.* And I'll reply, *Kim, I would have loved to be in that wreck.*

We racers haven't got an overload of common sense, because ultimately, we just want to race. And we'll park intelligence to do it. Even knowing what happened—how the best year of my career for 99 percent of time turned into a huge pile of crap at the end—I'd still do it all over again, right up to and including the wreck.

Dick Trickle taught me that we drivers justify everything, and he's so right. I can look at my life and realize that I lost a championship the last day of the season, I have wrecked bad a few times, and I probably am never going to get a championship-caliber ride in my 40s, but if there's a race next week, I'll be there, helmet in hand. I'll get out of the car afterwards, laugh out loud, kiss my wife, have a beer, and repeat the whole process the next week. Because you know what—and here's the justifying, Dick—running last beats the hell out of being the world's best vacuum-cleaner repairman. That's not true for the world's best vacuum-cleaner repairman—who never would have been me anyway—but that's the way it is for me.

Introduction to Cup Racing

I got one race behind the wheel of a Winston Cup car in 1990, but Davey Allison ran out of brakes and punted me into the wall, so it was hardly a deal for trumpets and flowers in my path. The following year, however, Kyle Petty broke his leg in The Big One at Talladega, and he couldn't race for a little while.

Felix Sabates hired me to run those few times and we did okay. It was a learning curve, but I got good finishes. When Rusty decided to fold the Busch team at the end of 1991 after a solid season, another guy stepped forward and bought the team. He was going to field both Busch and Cup cars for me.

In December 1991, however, the new car owner was arrested for defrauding his investors. It seems he was taking the money and spending

My very first Winston Cup ride and I'm not hanging my head—it's time for the invocation prior to the race. I got punted into the wall during the race, so there's nothing very memorable about this day. *(Kenny Wallace Collection)*

it on Cup cars instead of re-investing in the business. He wanted to be a big shot in NASCAR, and his investors wanted growth return on their money, which wasn't going to happen.

So, here I was, literally a handful of weeks out from the Daytona 500—and unemployed. Rusty had done so much for me in the past, but this time it was beyond a quick and easy brotherly fix, even though, thanks to Uncle Gary's great connections within his business world, we had good sponsorship lined up with Dirt Devil.

Enter Felix Sabates once more, and he purchased the remains of our team. I will always be grateful that he helped us out at such a critical

Dirt Devil sponsorship really helped us, and among other accomplishments we picked up the pole at New Hampshire Motor Speedway. *(Kenny Wallace Collection)*

time. If I had gone through the 1992 season without racing at all—much less winning, as we did—it's possible my career would have been done. Maybe somebody else would have ridden to the rescue, but it was so close to the season beginning that I was totally screwed, I suspect.

Feeling that it would be spreading out the money too far, Felix decided to fold the Busch operation and concentrate on the Cup deal. Having been on the stage in New York City as champion with Darrell Waltrip, crew chief Jeff Hammond got the Dirt Devil people really excited about the whole deal.

So much promise.

So little delivery.

We came into the 1993 season with such high expectations, internally and from the press and the rest of the competition, that when we didn't live up to the hype it turned into a brutal year. Jeff and I started openly arguing because we had such different ideas of how to set up the car, and then how to turn things around when the original set-ups were way off. I messed up because I never asked for a different crew chief. And when push came to shove, who was Felix going to listen to, anyway?

Well, I know who he did listen to. And it wasn't the driver.

I was on my way to a personal appearance in New York late in the year when I got a call to come by and talk with Felix. Sometimes, I'm still the naïve kid from Arnold, so I went to the meeting prepared to tell him exactly what I thought the team needed to do to turn things around.

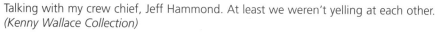

Talking with my crew chief, Jeff Hammond. At least we weren't yelling at each other. *(Kenny Wallace Collection)*

Don't Get on Kim's Bad Side

If you are female and reading this, don't get mad at me, but I think men and women have different approaches to the bad stuff that happens in racing. It's probably because if you are a wife or girl friend, you see things happening to the guy you love and there's absolutely nothing you can do about it. It's the most helpless feeling in the world, I'm told, and it probably shapes what happens in our minds.

When Felix Sabates let me go after our first year, I was hurt, frustrated, and I still feel it crippled my career to an extent. But Felix and I talked things out and we're fine with each other. I don't have a problem with Jeff Hammond either, even though he was the force behind my release. Jeff and Felix had been friends for a long time before I came on the scene and I understand why Felix listened to Jeff over me. Stuff like this happens all the time in racing.

Bearing in mind that just about everybody in NASCAR really likes Kim, and she likes them right back, note that she still hasn't forgiven Felix. She's not the only driver's wife to carry a grudge about what is—bottom line—business.

A friend who's also married to a race driver tells me that she has the 20-year rule, which is that she is allowed to stay mad for 20 years at anybody she thinks has slighted her race-driver husband, but then she has to let it go.

It hasn't been 20 years for Kim yet. I guess I'll have to go on keeping her and Felix on opposite sides of the pit area for a while longer.

The only time you have to worry about getting on Kim's bad side is if she feels you haven't treated me (or our girls) right. And then it takes a long time for her to forgive. That kind of loyalty is something special, I think. (Kenny Wallace Collection)

And Felix was prepared to tell me what he thought the team needed, based on Jeff's thoughts. That was—they wanted a new driver.

I've come to the conclusion after watching a lot of drivers—not just myself—that if a driver who's won a lot of races has a bad year, the car gets blamed. If a driver hasn't won a lot, and it really doesn't matter what the cause, the driver will be blamed for a poor year, even if the next driver—and the next driver, and the next one—have disappointing years, too.

That's what happened with that car. Bobby Hamilton followed me into the driver's seat and had no more good fortune than I did. And if memory serves me right, it was considered to be Bobby's fault, too.

Eventually, Felix sold most of his interests to Chip Ganassi and noted that he'd learned a lot in his years as a car owner, most notably that it's a humbling business, and success in other fields—which Felix could legitimately claim—didn't always translate to success in racing.

A few years later, our mutual friend, Mr. Earnhardt, sat us down to bury the hatchet. We did, but I realized then that Felix didn't have a clue about who I was then or now. He had written a check for $125,000 when he terminated my contract, and he thought all along that it made everything okay.

I know if you're reading this and $125,000 seems like a lot of money, we're in agreement. It certainly kept the wolf from the door and protected my family, so I'm not stupid about it. But I've never been about the money. It's always been about the racing and the challenge to win. I never felt like he gave me a real shot at proving what I could do.

I also felt forever branded. It happens a lot these days. I could name several young guys who will never get another chance in a Cup ride because they didn't produce fast enough. So, I guess I can be grateful that I got my rookie ride in the '90s when it was still possible to get a second chance.

The problem was that a second chance probably wasn't going to be in quite such promising circumstances. I mean, Felix had thrown a lot of money at the operation, we had a champion crew chief, so when it didn't go well, it had to be the rookie driver, right?

Except that the rookie driver got almost zero input on what to do with the car. And I feel no vindication because the car continued to be mediocre long after I was gone. Because, from that year forward, even when I did well, there was always the specter of that rookie year peering over my shoulder and making other car owners wonder whether they should gamble on Herman.

In 1993 at Watkins Glen. I'd been to Bob Bondurant's road racing school a couple of years earlier so I have enjoyed the Glen. (© *Sam Sharpe/ www.THESHARPEIMAGE.com; Kenny Wallace Collection*)

You might see some familiar faces among my classmates at Bondurant's school. A lot of racers have recognized the value of "studying" with Bob. *(Kenny Wallace Collection)*

Super Subbing

My roller coaster career has twice gone uphill—quite a bit, actually—when other drivers experienced injury. It's not the way you want it to happen. Being a Super Sub may prove that you can drive, but in both instances I knew that it was strictly filling in.

During the time I drove for Robert Yates Racing we had a lot of success, but there were some not-so-great moments, too. I got into and spun out Mr. Earnhardt at Martinsville. It wasn't intentional, but try telling that to his (booing) fans. *(Cliff and Christy Metcalf Photo; Kenny Wallace Collection)*

Add to that the strong emotions from the team and the fans, and, man, you want to talk about walking on a tightrope. When I drove the Robert Yates car after Ernie Irvan's serious injury at Michigan, and then several years later for Dale Earnhardt Inc. (DEI) when Steve Park was recuperating, I always knew that the deals were temporary. I would have loved to stay with those teams, but realistically I was just trying to prove that I was worthy of a good ride. Both times, the rides saved and prolonged my career, even if I didn't get in cars quite so well-financed and prepared later. But I did prove a point. A lot of people, and I particularly remember a conversation with Ricky Rudd back then, told me that I did a whole lot better in those rides than they thought I would. I guess the Sabates deal had put the bar so low that expectations could hardly help but be surpassed.

I'm told that Jack Roush was a fan of what I did in the Yates car and asked some questions of other people about keeping me in the car. Even though it was a different team, Jack's influence at all the Ford teams really counts. But Jack tells me that someone very close to me said, "Kenny doesn't need to be in that car."

Still, Robert was gracious about that period and never hesitated to tell the press that, "It was a tough year, but Kenny Wallace did a good job with what we gave him."

It's Not All Bad

Before Ernie's injury in 1994, I was truly at loose ends for a while. I was honored to drive for Bill and Ernie Elliott for a few races in Cup. But I'd seen a really neat Busch Series car that Jeff Burton had been driving. The

The Cat in the Hat, Jack Roush. Not only is he incredibly successful as a car owner, but he has a lot of influence about what happens on all the Ford teams. (Kenny Wallace Collection)

During the '90s I occasionally tested for IROC. Since they were looking for consistent laps rather than variety, it wasn't a lot of fun. But it paid $600 a day, and at that time I was tickled to pick up the extra pay. *(Kenny Wallace Collection)*

#8 FIC car was owned by a successful businessman out of Nashville named Filbert Martocci.

About that time, Rusty had to fly to Nashville to do a television show, so, figuring I could hitch a ride with him, I called Filbert and asked if I could talk to him about his car. He agreed.

Here's where it gets a little funny, and maybe proves that being outside the insulated little world in Charlotte, you don't always know what the gossip is. Filbert thought I was coming to talk to him about putting my brother Mike in the car. At Filmar Racing they thought I was hot stuff and could write my own ticket in Charlotte, when the truth was—with the Sabates fiasco hanging over my head—the only ticket I had was for the Saturday matinee showing of *Days of Thunder.*

In 1994, I hooked up with Filbert Martocci and his Filmar Racing in the Busch Series. We were very, very competitive during the years I was with Filbert, which was a lot of fun, too. *(Kenny Wallace Collection)*

One time it was still fun when we *didn't* win was the night that my brother Mike (#9) won at Indianapolis Raceway Park. *(Kenny Wallace Collection)*

Jeff, and Bobby Hamilton before him, had been frustrated because the car seemed to break a lot. But I got in the car, and I just hauled ass. I mean, it was a beautiful thing. I won three races that year, at Bristol, Richmond and Martinsville, and ran well just about everywhere else, too. I'll never forget the time that Motor Racing Network anchor Barney Hall told me, "Well, Kenny, you won that deal, didn't you?"

I asked, "What deal, Barney?"

"You're running really well, and the team you left behind is struggling every bit as much, if not more, as it was when you were with them."

At the end of 1994, Filbert heard the rumors about Yates considering me for his Cup car fulltime, so he asked—jokingly, I think—*what's this I hear about Yates wanting to hire you?*

Brandy had been practicing sitting on my race car and holding up her finger as #1, but when I actually went to Victory Lane at Martinsville, she wanted no part of the mad scene there! *(Kenny Wallace Collection)*

Isn't that trophy pretty? That's what you get for winning at Bristol—and then when you're showing off the crew nails you with ice water! *(L: © Dorsey Patrick Photo; Kenny Wallace Collection; R: Kenny Wallace Collection)*

I told him that Yates was bouncing the idea around, and Filbert kind of chuckled. "Well, if you think you're going to get out of your contract, I'll sue you for everything you have."

He kept it light and funny, but you know what? I knew he was dead serious. Self-made men rarely joke about being taking advantage of, if that's what they perceive is happening. Filbert didn't want to be my launching pad for a Cup return with somebody else. He wanted to be the one who took me.

So, when we got the Red Dog Beer sponsorship, we thought we could make the move, straddling between Busch and Cup. And when we won the spring Busch race at Richmond, we really looked poised for good things.

But we got to the third or fourth Cup race in 1995 and they said that we weren't going to run the next race.

Excuse me?

I was never told that the sponsorship wasn't cast in stone. Nobody had mentioned that we might have to cut back to a part-time schedule. But we continued to limp along, running occasionally, and it's funny but that period of time is really fuzzy to me. I suspect it's just my way of trying to comfort my ego, which was taking a battering ram at the time. I didn't get drunk and stay that way, but it feels like I did. Like a buzz that allows you to function but you know you won't remember much in the morning.

That was 1995 for me.

From Herman to the Hermanator

Important to what happened next was the Filmar Racing team moving from Nashville to Charlotte for the '96 season. It was tough for crew chief Gil Martin and the whole gang, who uprooted their families, but it had become clear that we needed that interaction with the other teams. To see what was going on and get the feedback we hadn't been getting.

Added to that, we picked up Square D as primary sponsor. We ended up with an eye-catching blue-and-yellow car that people remember to this day, maybe as much because we went from occasional back-marker to a really happening team. We made them pay attention to us by producing on the track.

In fact, we rolled into Darlington that spring ninth in points—and ahead of Rusty.

I have always let Rusty stand an inch taller than me because we got along a lot better that way. Okay, so he really is an inch taller, but you know what I mean. And we have teasingly called him "God," for years because we did whatever he commanded us to do. On the track, his record speaks for itself.

But for this brief, shining moment, Herman the German was outpacing God. So, Earl Barbin, who was from St. Louis and had known us all clear back to the days when I got the original nickname, and who was now working on Rusty's crew, came over to our pit. It wasn't a long walk because we were next to them.

Earl took a silver Sharpie marker and wrote on the brand-new, black jack handle in our pits, "The Hermanator."

I liked that.

I liked that a lot. Herman the German is a funny, hyper little guy from Arnold, but The Hermanator *can race with you!*

For a while, Gil Martin was my crew chief and we did run well. *(Kenny Wallace Collection)*

In 1996, we were ahead of Rusty in points for a while and that's how the Hermanator was born. One of his crew wrote that on our new jack— and we liked it. *(Joyce Standridge Photo)*

Over the years, The Hermanator stuck about as well as Herman the German, and during a slow winter a couple of years ago, I drew up a cartoon Hermanator. A friend in Charlotte had a bunch of stickers made up for me, and now you'll see them around, especially on my own modified and hauler.

But back at The Hermanator's birth, we were just a happy bunch, running down the highway and looking forward to Sunday throughout 1996 and 1997. However, genuine, deeply held happiness behind the wheel never has lasted for me.

The piper was waiting in the wings to be paid once more.

11

Friends, Foes and Filbert

WE MADE CNN Headline News.

I think the screen crawl said "Brotherly Love," or "Brothers 1-2." Something neat like that. But as our whole family sat at the restaurant that Saturday evening, it was probably as happy a gathering as we've ever had. You see, Rusty and I had run 1-2 in the Busch Bash (now called the Budweiser Shootout) at Daytona.

The previous season, I had gotten two pole positions in Cup racing—at Martinsville and at Bristol—and that meant that I was qualified for the race. A special event during Speed Weeks, the Bash at that time was a race you could get into only if you'd won a pole the previous season.

The 1998 Busch Bash was one of the highlights of my professional life. My car didn't have a lot of speed on its own, but in a crowd—and there's always a crowd at Daytona because of the restrictor plate—the #81 Square D Ford handled like a dream.

You have to also bear in mind that in spite of a stellar career, Rusty had known a lot of headaches—mostly, by way of wicked crashes—at Daytona. He practically owned the short tracks and road courses at times during his career, but Daytona was hardly kind to him.

So, as we got to the final lap, Rusty was running the outside line, and Jimmy Spencer (now my *NASCAR RaceDay* television broadcast partner) was on the inside.

I can't begin to tell you how close I came to making it three wide.

I mean I coulda had a cow, I wanted to go through the middle and be the hero so bad. But you know what would have happened? And I know this in my heart—I would have wrecked all three of us and fourth place would have waved happily as he passed on by to take the checkered flag. I know this because the little hole coming off the turn between Jimmy and Rusty closed up real fast and proved my instincts had been right.

No matter how things have gone with my career, I have been blessed to go home to my beautiful girls. That's Brittany, Brooke and Brandy in the mid-1990s. *(Kenny Wallace Collection)*

I tucked in behind Rusty and, since two hooked up together is always faster at Daytona than anybody running by himself, I pretty much pushed Rusty across the line for his first ever win at Daytona. I had such a run coming off turn two that last lap I actually had to ride the brakes to keep from spinning him out, but you don't always win at Daytona even when you're the fastest. Sometimes you're second and it feels really great when the guy finishing first is one of your idols.

And then the good stuff stopped.

Let's go backwards for a moment: We had changed crew chiefs late in 1997. Filbert had let Gil go because of a conflict. At the time, Filbert asked if he could come over to my house, and frankly, after my experience a few years before with Felix, I wasn't looking forward to it. Especially considering that Filbert still lived in Nashville at the time, so he was making a special trip over the mountains to see me. But instead of firing me, Filbert was making a crew change.

"Do you feel like you can't go on?" he asked.

"No. No, we can do it," I said through a sense of relief. I mean, I was happy in the car and I thought we still had some achievements left in us.

So, Filbert hired David Ifft for a while, and it was good being back

In our happiest times, my exuberance got a little carried away and I planted a kiss on Filbert Martocci's cheek. But even in quieter moments, like when I was signing autographs, Filbert was—and remains to this day—one of the finest gentlemen I've known, and maybe our favorite car owner next to my brother. *(L: © Steven Rose, MMP Inc.; Kenny Wallace Collection; R: Kenny Wallace Collection)*

with him, but over time David left and Filbert elevated Newt Moore to crew chief.

I believed in Newt.

Even when the ignition went out during the 125 qualifying race at Daytona and we had no provisionals or championships to fall back on to make the 500. Electrical problems happen all the time in our racing, and you just live with it.

But, here's the deal: When you know that you are going to make the 500 no matter what happens in the 125 you can look forward to Speed Weeks as a vacation for you and your family. When you have to make the 500 through the qualifying race, however, you sweat bullets. It's not a lot of fun, and when you fail, it's just plain miserable.

I didn't get out of bed for two days.

Kim came to the rescue yet again. She forced me to get up and go over to Universal Studios with her, although I'm sure my foul mood ruined it for her. I did feel marginally better when I got back, but I was wishing I could just have gone home with the car.

See, when you don't make a race, NASCAR expects you to load up and scoot. They'll be big about it and give you, oh, four or five minutes—no, really, an hour or two—but if you're not gone somebody is going to come around and kind of hint that the gate is open.

So, the car and crew went home to North Carolina, but I had to hang around for the Square D hospitality gathering on Sunday morning. I just want to tell you that if you've ever thought you wanted to be a big shot race car driver and you'd love the attention, the morning you have to go shake hands with a bunch of really nice people who are really bummed that you didn't make the race, and you feel like you have totally let them down when they deserved so much more for helping you even be here—well, that's about as lousy as you can feel. They will still pat you on the back, and enjoy the machine-gun laugh that you'll trot out because you can't let them see how devastated you really are.

And you know what? Whether it's on the way up or on the way down, every single one of those guys who make it to the summit of NASCAR racing has at least a few of those days, whether it's missing the show or wrecking or getting into a public feud or just something that you have to explain at the hospitality tent that you don't want to.

It sucks.

It really, really sucks, but you paste on a smile, shake hands and smile for the camera even though you'd like to put your frustrated fist through a fencepost. *At least I'm getting a shot at this,* you remind yourself.

And then Earnhardt won the damned race and I didn't even get to put a friggin' wheel donut on the side of his door!

Filbert, You'll Always Be a Favorite

My "brother" Ken Schrader has never been fired from a ride. I've rarely had the luxury to quit one, but it was because of Schrader's influence that I left Filbert.

When Square D and I went to Petree Racing, Andy Petree (left), and Jimmy Elledge, my crew chief, joined me for some publicity photos. *(Kenny Wallace Collection)*

Hanging with a couple of guys who've impacted my career in different ways— Steve Park and Ken Schrader. *(Kenny Wallace Collection)*

Kenny was running for Andy Petree, doing well but recognizing that having a multiple-car team was a definite advantage if for no other reason than the feedback. They put together sponsorship from Oakwood Mobile Homes and there was the fact that Andy had been a champion crew chief at Richard Childress Racing, helping Dale Earnhardt on the way to a lot of records.

Filbert had been as kind and good a man as I had ever known in the racing world. Even through ups and downs, we'd remained close. He had occasionally spoiled Kim and me with nice surprises—like the time he paid for a romantic cruise on the Finger Lakes near Watkins Glen so we could celebrate our wedding anniversary in style. It wasn't easy to ask Filbert for a release as a result, and he didn't make it easy on me. I think it cost $50,000 to get out of the contract, but Square D had me on a personal contract and they advanced the sum. Since the Oakwood Homes thing fell through, they were also going with me to Petree.

But as much as I loved racing with Filbert, by the end of 1998 I knew that we had gone as far as we could together. That last little leap over into winning just wasn't going to happen. Plus, between Andy's incredible storehouse of knowledge and the chance to team up with Kenny, I knew it was worth the financial cost. And I knew that teaming up with Kenny meant there wouldn't be any backstabbing going on.

If you buy into the public relations stuff in racing, you might believe that all teammates love each other and work hard to make sure they all share information. Or maybe you think, well, they don't necessarily like each other a lot, but they still are going to work together because the boss isn't going to allow anything less.

During the time I was with Filbert we scored several pole positions including Martinsville and Bristol. *(Both photos: Kenny Wallace Collection)*

Don't be naïve. There have been in the past, and currently still are, instances of drivers doing everything they possibly can to undermine a teammate and get him fired. I've seen it, I've been a victim of it. It happens more than you would suspect, even on teams that appear to be getting along reasonably well. It's just that if you get to the Cup level, you're probably fairly smart in addition to being talented as a driver. And if you're smart you can figure out how to subtly stick it to the other guy.

And sometimes it's not so subtle. Look at what happened between Rusty and his teammate Ryan Newman. I mean, I give them credit for not even pretending. They could have been a couple of phonies, but, hey, everybody knew it wasn't Playtime on the Playground at Penske Racing. And think about the supposed "friendships" at Hendrick Motorsports in 2006 when Brian Vickers was finishing out his contract.

So, stuff happens all the time, but I knew—absolutely without any doubt whatsoever—that I could race with Kenny Schrader and it would be a good thing.

It *was* a good thing.

For a while anyway. Then at the end of that season, even though we'd all had some pretty decent results, Kenny took me aside and apologized because he was leaving Petree for a good ride in the MB2 Motorsports car.

Now, this is the mark of the kind of man Schrader is. He was genuinely worried that I would be hurt and disappointed that he was moving on. And to an extent, I was, but you know, you can't help but be happy when someone you respect—who's been helping you for many years—gets an opportunity that seems very promising. If the roles had

The Square D car—no matter who I was driving for—was always a memorable car. That blue and yellow design stayed in people's memories. *(Kenny Wallace Collection)*

been reversed, I would have probably thought about it long and hard, too—and maybe gone.

Maybe should have gone.

Maybe should have stayed with Filbert.

See, Andy did a lot to help us out. He went out and got good people for our team, but here's a sample of how the season went: We were in Phoenix and Barry Dotson was my crew chief. A thunderstorm broke out, but we're in the desert, right? I'm running near the front and I keyed Barry for directions.

"Well, I've never seen it rain very long in the desert," he said.

I agreed, so we pitted for fuel and tires. And I'll be damned but what it didn't rain out. We still got a good finish of eighth, but we had a shot at a win and finished under the caution instead.

And it seems like everywhere I go, patience runs thin. I tend to drive for start-up teams, and no one wants to accept that it takes a while to establish a start-up. A driver can come into Hendrick or Roush and make an impact pretty quickly—or not, as some have come and gone—but when you start from scratch it takes a while.

Not everybody wants to wait.

I understand, but it's been hell on my progress. And when it rolled around to 2000 and we still hadn't broken through into the win column, Square D—to their credit—went to Andy and asked, "What do we have to do to run better?"

I believe they were thinking about hiring away talent from other teams, but what Andy must have heard is Talent, as in capital T—a driver.

And, according to Square D, he told them that maybe they could get Mike Skinner.

Skinner has a quite a record in NASCAR Craftsman Trucks, and he was Dale Earnhardt's teammate at Childress in Cup racing for several

When Kenny Schrader and I were teammates at Petree Racing, it was one of the best teammate situations I've ever been in, and it went a long way toward solidifying our lifelong friendship. *(Kenny Wallace Collection)*

I really enjoyed this team, but typical for my career I was working with several guys early in their careers, and they went on to become talented crew chiefs—for other guys. *(Kenny Wallace Collection)*

years—where they didn't get along and it probably hurt Skinner. He was in the hunt a lot of races, but couldn't quite punch through to Victory Lane, and Earnhardt didn't care.

Well, when the word got back to me, I was pissed. God, it makes me sick even now to talk about it because it all turned out so bad, but I called Andy and asked if he wanted to split. And he said he had to talk to Square D.

A few days later, Andy called back and told me, *let's go another year.*

But because I had another opportunity, I let my hurt feelings get the better of me. What happened next, I'll take 98 percent of the blame, because I should have stopped to think about the fact that we'd improved and that I just plain liked Andy. I hadn't enjoyed having Joe Nemechek

No matter how goofy I may act when I'm out of a race car, once I get in I'm as serious about the business as anybody who's ever strapped on a helmet. And you can take that to the bank. *(Kenny Wallace Collection)*

Know what I really like about this photo? I'm racing at Watkins Glen—in the rain—and I felt totally comfortable. It was really fun to do something different like this. *(Kenny Wallace Collection)*

as a teammate the way I had with Kenny, but I suspect there wouldn't have been many people I would have gotten along with the way I did Schrader. We still had real possibilities but I was feeling ready to cast the net once more.

Rusty called me over to his trailer one day and told me that I needed to go with Eel River Racing, another new team funded by a New England businessman—but this was the attraction: Barry Dotson, with whom Rusty had won his Winston Cup championship in 1989, and with whom I'd had some fun racing a few times at Filmar Racing—was going to run the show. Pretty hard to pass that up, especially knowing that Petree Racing was lusting after Skinner.

The Winner Who Was Never Officially Champion

I've had a lot of bad luck and misfortune in Cup racing, but I've always been happy-go-lucky in spite of it. Mark Martin, on the other hand, has won a lot of races and been a hero to so many people over the years, and yet it's hardly a secret that he has been seen as melancholy.

So, it's probably pretty weird that we became good friends. Part of it is just length of time. We go way back to Rusty's ASA years, which were also Mark's. And while Mark has known success, he also was the guy who went to NASCAR and then had to fall back to ASA for a while and get more experience before going back to Charlotte and sticking. *(Sound a little familiar?)*

I have always admired and respected Mark, for many reasons. When you listen to him, it sounds like he puts every ounce of soul, bone and muscle in his body into racing. That his body is molded into the car and becomes a part of it.

And it's true. When Mark says, "I'm wearing myself to my knees," you believe him.

There's a misconception about Mark that when he was young his dad just bought him everything and made the path easy. But while Julian Martin was a big part of the whole deal, I watched Mark work every bit as hard as the rankest, most-afraid rookie of all time. I mean, there were times you couldn't find him because he put his little 130-pound body inside the frame and was tearing up the suspension or re-jetting the carburetor. He learned about all there is to know, and while he always gives a lot of credit to his car owners and teams, the truth is that he knows so much he can literally look over their shoulders and tell them what to do—but he's so good about it that nobody seems to mind at all. And that's made him a tremendous success.

Another thing about Mark is that while most racing fans know he is a fitness fanatic, few are aware that in his youth he was a wild man to challenge the rest of us. But Mark never does things by halves. If he's going to race, he's going to race harder than anybody, and if he was going to party— well, you get the picture. But Mark is so disciplined and determined that he simply stopped all that stuff at a young age. He is still very funny and a great guy to socialize with, but he keeps himself in an iron grip.

Mark is also partially responsible for who I am. When I was a crew man on Rusty's ASA car, things were pretty intense, as I've noted. And being hyper, I would get caught up in the craziness and fly off the handle. I'm not proud of that in retrospect, but part of the reason I got it under control was that one day—when I was blowing off steam—Mark told me, "Boy, you sure do complain a lot."

Talk about stopping me in my tracks. And, I don't know that Mark was trying to hold up a mirror so I'd realize how I sounded, or that he even thought I was worth the effort. Or if he was just tired of listening to me, but just as Rusty had an impact on how I present myself to the public, there's also always been in the back of my mind this little picture

A very special, long-time friend Mark Martin and his lovely Arlene. *(Kenny Wallace Collection)*

Julian and the Gun

There have always been parents who lived their lives through their kids. Still goes on. You can just go on down to your local quarter-midget track and you'll see a few people who've decided the kid is their retirement plan.

Not everybody lives through their kids because they don't have a life of their own or because they couldn't do things themselves. Some just follow the kids' dreams and help make them happen—and then enjoy it along the way, too.

That would be Julian Martin. With a successful trucking business in Arkansas, Julian had the resources to put Mark in good equipment, and he did from the time Mark was about 8 years old,

but he made sure that Mark kept a good head on his shoulders, too. Then, for many years, where you saw Mark, you saw Julian.

And he lived it all with incredible intensity. I can remember a particular instance back in the ASA days when Mark was blowing everybody away in a 100-lapper at Springfield, Missouri, but the engine coil quit working before the end. Then, afterwards, we all went to a Denny's and ate.

But when we came out of the restaurant, Julian went over to the trailer and took the coil out of the race car, put it on a fence post—and shot it several times with a .22 pistol.

Now, *that's* intense.

We've run a lot of laps together through the years, and it means that I'm one of the lucky souls who remembers Mark Martin in his young and carefree days. At least, what passed for carefree for the ever-intense and talented driver. (Kenny Wallace Collection)

of Mark Martin telling me I complain too much. And because I thought he was absolutely wonderful—as a person, as well as a driver—it just cut me off at the knees. No way was I going to be a disappointment to Mark.

Of course, I had to do something positive for him. Two decades passed, but a couple of years ago I was on the set of the post-race television show and I heard Mark being interviewed by someone else. I guess I shouldn't have been surprised at how defeated he sounded, in spite of running very well, because one time he had called me over to his race car and said, "Herman, I really can't stand people."

What he meant was he couldn't stand that everybody in the world seemed to want something from him, to the point that there was nothing left OF Mark FOR Mark. A lot of the NASCAR stars end up feeling that way at times—not just Mark.

I'll bet nobody will argue with this—one of the great things that's happened since the drivers hang in the motorhome compound these days is that we get a chance to know each other better, like I have Ricky Craven, and the King Richard Petty, and it tends to carry over to the pits and the track, too, like with Jeff Burton. And then I get to wrestle Jimmie Johnson for his Nextel Cup trophy! Not really, but we do horse around now and again. *(All photos: Kenny Wallace Collection)*

But after that post-race interview, I went on-air and said—among other things—that, *"Mark is such a pessimist and he is so miserable. And I don't know how a man can run in the top five so consistently and be that miserable."*

Well, Mark heard me. He came up to me the following week and said, "Herman, you really helped me. I'm a better man this week. I'm going to win this race."

And I told him, "You're damned right you're a winner. Now, go get 'em!"

He didn't leave it at that. During his acceptance speech for being in the Nextel Cup top ten in 2005, he stunned me by saying—on national television—that Kenny Wallace had helped put his life into perspective and made him appreciate that he has so much to be grateful for.

That was humbling. I guess I'm still amazed that I impact anybody's life, but to know that my ramblings had helped a great guy like Mark, really got to me. I mean, he had it inside of himself—he's such a great person anyway—that it just needed a nudge. And who would have thought it would be Herman who would bring it out?

I bring up Mark at this point because as we have gone through our lives together at so many points, those times when I hit the skids and things sometimes seem rough I just think about Mark. It's not that he doesn't appreciate the great things that have happened to him—he does recognize that very clearly—*it's that he's so terribly hard on himself.* He thinks he should have won more, won easily, done this, done that. *He never cuts himself any slack.*

And God gifted me with the ability to love life. It's not that I don't have moments maybe even darker than Mark does, but just that I can deal with it and move on, and the world isn't usually any wiser that Herman had a bad day.

Considering what happened to me in 2001, I would think at times about Mark Martin's approach, from getting control of my life to whether I had a future as a race-car driver or not.

12

DEI and I

I WAS ABOUT 10 FEET from the manager's door when I heard a voice say, "We missed the race because Kenny's just not into it. He give up."

The mixture of pure anger and intolerable hurt I felt on hearing these foreign words from a familiar voice stunned me. I didn't move for a moment. And then I finished coming around the corner of the team manager's office at Eel River Racing and looked Barry Dotson right in the face. His eyeballs got big as silver dollars when he saw me step into the room. And frankly, I don't remember what was said from that moment forward because my brain shut down. Rage will do that to you.

I laugh a lot. But I go inside myself a lot, too. My brain is always tussling with what the car needs, what the crew needs, what I need to do. I'm not racing just because I can. I'm racing because I can't imagine drawing a breath without racing in my life. *(Kenny Wallace Collection)*

You see, Barry was like family to me. There's no way that Rusty could have won the 1989 Winston Cup championship without Barry, and there were so many instances ever since when we'd shared great moments, on and off the track. You believe that these are the people who are going to back you 100 percent, 100 percent of the time.

But Barry's back was against the wall. He had this massive reputation—well-deserved—but come 2001, the brand-new Eel River Racing team was not living up to expectations. There had to be a reason, the owner believed, and logically you turn to the team whip, which is the crew chief.

Again, as I have so many times throughout my career, I recalled the words of Dale Earnhardt Sr. on that comfortable cruise down to Darlington in his motor home, telling me, "You have to have a great crew chief. It's the most important thing to making your career succeed."

I assumed that he meant a great crew chief would concentrate on car preparation and bringing together a group of people who were going to communicate with each other, and treat each other with the kind of respect and support you see in the great baseball and football teams. Auto racing teams may not be as visible through the ranks, but just as you don't want a weak relief pitcher or a pass receiver whose attention span wanders, it's absolutely critical that everybody on a racing team pulls together and gives his all. The successful ones work out tensions, problems, miscommunications, whatever happens, and the last thing that a team needs is to have the coach (i.e., a crew chief) tell the owner—or the media, or anybody else—that the weak link has been identified and it's this person.

Here's the truth of the matter. I have yet to meet the race driver at any level of the sport who has "given up." What happens is that sometimes you get in a car that handles so freaking bad that you have to slow down because you're not willing to kill yourself. You're not willing to wreck yourself and your fellow racers finding out just where that crossover line into disaster is located, because you know you're way too close to it anyway.

As God is my witness, I had not given up on that car, that team, that crew chief or that owner. But I don't think I've ever felt sicker in my life, because of what Barry meant to me personally.

We had made the Daytona 500, but only on luck. We didn't have a provisional because we were a new team, and I had been a nervous wreck during all of Speed Weeks because I knew the car wasn't fast. I really doubted our ability to get in through the Twin 125 race, but somehow we did. Then in the 500 we ran well back in the field, but we were a well-back-in-the-field car at that time.

From there, it went only downhill. And after finding out that the guy who was supposed to be my biggest cheerleader was actually putting my neck on the chopping block ended any hope of it all working out. It took a little while longer, but eventually Rick Mast got in the car—and did no better. Nor did Mike Bliss when he followed Rick into the seat.

It meant that eventually Barry was gone, too, and Rusty, feeling all kinds of mixed-up guilt over what had happened, hired Barry. But whatever chemistry and magic they'd had in 1989 was gone. Before long, Rusty let Barry go, even though it hurt like the dickens for everybody, and Rusty apologized to me for having encouraged me to try the Eel River ride in the first place.

And let me finish this by saying that I still care very deeply for Barry. In part, it's because he lost two children in an accident, and having lived through the accidental death of my nephew, it creates a bond that no race car can break. And what we all experienced back in 1989 was a period of euphoria that no later deal can destroy. So, even though my heart still aches that Barry didn't have faith in me, I know that he's had too many heartbreaks of his own, too.

The Rainbow's End—Sort of

As all that was going down, the good ol' Busch Series was riding to the rescue—yet again.

Literally a few days before the Daytona 500 I got a call from Gere Kennon, crew chief on the Busch car owned by George deBidart, a really talented communications and television principal. George had invested money in a team and Gere called to say, "Hey, Herman, our driver just announced he's quitting. Would you be willing to drive the car at Daytona?"

I told him to go over to Eel River and get one of my seats. They put it in the car, and the very first time I ever sat in it was at the big track. But it was golden—we finished in the top ten and everything was clicking as superbly on the Busch circuit as things were going badly at Eel River.

I ended up in the car for the season, and we finished in the top ten of points. But importantly for all of us associated with the team was the introduction of a new sponsor—Stacker 2. It's no exaggeration to say that Stacker 2 took a racing career that was fading into the background and turned me into a household name for a lot of auto racing fans. I'll tell you more about the whole Stacker 2 experience in the next chapter.

Meanwhile, there were more changes and challenges on the horizon. During the Darlington Busch race, Steve Park had his steering wheel come off as he exited the pits, and after slamming the outer retaining wall he was t-boned by another driver. It was a wicked, bad wreck resulting in severe head injuries that nearly claimed his life.

This had more ramifications than just that race. Steve—one of the good guys of the sport—had been hand-picked by Dale Earnhardt Senior to be his first protégé at DEI. And Steve—in true storybook fashion, had won the next race after Dale's tragic demise. A season scripted in tandem by Walt Disney and Stephen King, I think.

Two guys very, very important to keeping my career afloat, car owner George deBidart (left) and crew chief Gere Kennon. It meant a lot to me to be able to take them to Victory Lane because when the Eel River deal went sour, these were the guys who picked me up and helped prove that I could drive a race car. *(© Steven Rose, MMP Inc.; Kenny Wallace Collection)*

With about 30 laps to go in the Darlington Busch race, my crew chief Gere came on the radio and told me that Paul Andrews from the #1 Pennzoil car was there. "He says Steve is hurting pretty bad, and they want to know if you can drive the car tomorrow?"

What happened the next day lifted the lingering sense of gloom that had been hanging over my Cup career for some time. I got in Steve's car, started dead last and was up to 9th by lap 30. Of course, we couldn't just cruise along—the heat exchanger, which was an oil cooler inside the

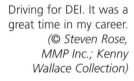

Driving for DEI. It was a great time in my career. *(© Steven Rose, MMP Inc.; Kenny Wallace Collection)*

Dale Earnhardt Jr.

I don't know how many people really know or understand Junior. There are folks who adore him to such distraction that they don't really see the guy behind the steering wheel. He's just such an icon that they can't see or accept any flaws, and really, it's the flaws that make us all a whole lot more interesting as people.

And there are people who are so turned off by Earnhardt-mania, they assume he's skating along on his name. And that's no more fair to Dale than not allowing him to be human.

I do know a couple of things about him that I'll share here. One is that he is so smart and far more sophisticated than you'd think a young guy from rural North Carolina should be. But he grew up in that household and he saw all sorts of people trying to use his daddy. So, even when you think you're getting to be buds with Junior, if he thinks you're getting too close or stepping too far into his territory, he will tell you so. He's got a lot of friends, but really only a small circle of close, trusted friends—and when you're that famous, that's what you have to do.

He's also as diehard a racer as I know. I can remember back when he was still a kid, there was a bunch of us who liked to spend our winter months racing slot cars. Short-track asphalt driver Dave Mader set up the tracks and we'd get a huge crowd of drivers, crew chiefs and mechanics, and you'd think it was Daytona instead of Dave's garage. We had purses, too—it paid like $25-$30 to win!

Dale had to sneak out to join us. He told me, "My daddy doesn't want me doing this. He thinks it's for kids."

But, hell, we were all just a bunch of overgrown kids anyway, and he wanted to race and win every bit as much as the rest of us, no matter what level it was. Then, that carried over to the real thing. He's never—not even once—coasted on the track because he has a guaranteed ride forever. He races like they're gonna take the pink slip BEFORE the checkered flag.

I've raced with Junior in Cup, but I really *raced* with him more when he was in the Busch Series because I have always been in more competitive rides there. I can remember thinking right from the get-go that he had talent and desire—and it's pretty hard to stop that combination.

He's also always handled himself so well. He's a kid who's been able to put things into perspective in spite of all the pressure on him. Example: we were at Sears Point in 1999, I think it was, and he had to take a provisional. He was upset. I could see he was really down in the dumps, and I asked him what was wrong.

"Well, I'm supposed to be this 'superstar,'" he said with sarcasm, "and I have to take a provisional."

That drew the picture for me right then. He felt he was letting everybody down.

I'm telling you, Dale has always been about 25 years older in his mind than in actual years.

I don't have very many autographed pictures of other race drivers, but in my St. Louis home hangs this shot of Dale Junior and me. The inscription says "A true friend at the end of the day. Hats off, dude." The feeling is mutual, dude. (Kenny Wallace Collection)

radiator—cracked and allowed the water to come out. But here's the thought that was in my head that day: *"What the hell have I been driving the last five years?"*

Thoughtful observers of Cup racing probably are already aware that there are some pretty significant differences between teams, and that the top tier groups like Hendrick, Roush, Childress, Yates and DEI, have got their acts together. I knew that every team I had driven for had given me the best they could, the best they had to offer, but I also knew that we were missing some elusive elements that kept us from being routinely competitive. And when I sat in the Pennzoil car, I had all my thoughts confirmed.

This also served to restore my self-confidence, which had been taking a pretty awful beating. I realized that, yes, I can drive. It's more than a great, burning desire in me to drive race cars—it's something I really can do.

Possibly the best weekend of my racing life occurred that year, at least as far as results are concerned. It was even better than pushing Dale Earnhardt across the line for his last-ever win at Talladega in 2000—yet another race I had nearly won, but became more memorable to the racing public in general because of the circumstances.

At Rockingham, I passed Jeff Green and Jason Keller on the last lap after a restart and won the Busch race. And in the Cup cars the next day, I led much of the day and ended up a really close second to Joe Nemechek at the checkered flag. My spirits were lifted so high—much higher than I had ever thought would happen again. I may never have another weekend like that, but all the self-doubts and wondering that had been eating away at me were lifted off my shoulders because I found out that if you have a first-rate Busch car and a first-rate Cup car, it becomes much more than just the thrill of participating—it's an achievement.

A day I will never forget—I'm in the Square D car and I pushed Dale Earnhardt (outside) across the finish line for the final Cup victory of his storied career. *(Kenny Wallace Collection)*

I got to lead the field, but honestly, we ran very well wherever we were at during the time I drove the Pennzoil car. *(Kenny Wallace Collection)*

The following year, I got to run the DEI car at Daytona and we ended up in The Big One wreck that took out a bunch of us. We didn't cause it, but we couldn't avoid it either. But even though we were doing well, there was an extra person always "riding" in the car with me—Steve Park. I'm told that Tony Eury Sr. wanted to keep me in the car through the rest of the season and give Steve more time to recuperate, but Ty Norris wanted to bring Steve back. In retrospect, Tony was probably right. Steve got some good finishes, but without sufficient time to recuperate, and after another bad wreck, Steve has never had the chance to prove over the long haul what an extraordinary talent he is. There are some eerie similarities between Steve Park and me, beginning with having the same birthday—August 23rd. Steve is also a well-grounded and considerate person who can drive the hell out of a race car—always could, and I believe, still can.

Who knows what he would have accomplished in Nextel Cup if not

I substituted for Steve Park when he was injured and instead of being a wedge it turned out to be the beginning of a great friendship, as you can see. *(Kenny Wallace Collection)*

for the Busch Series accident he had at Darlington? I came around the track in my car and saw that they had the tarp up around his car, and that's never a good sign. In fact, it's the kind of thing that just makes your heart fall to your feet.

But Steve fought back. Took a long time for him to heal and during the time that I was driving his Cup car, he would sometimes come around the hauler. I could always tell that he was trying to put a brave face on things, but he was bummed. I've been bummed enough times in my life to recognize it in another person.

I always made it a point to reassure him that I was just the caretaker of his ride. I would have loved to remain in the car, and he was no fool—he knew that—but I wanted him to understand that I would never engage in back-stabbing or do anything to try to take the ride away from him in any kind of underhanded way.

The argument will go on forever about whether they brought him back too soon, or whether he should ever have come back, but what nobody will ever argue about is what a great guy Steve Park is.

Let me say this about the DEI experience: Dale Senior had always treated me very well, from that first day in his daddy's garage. I also consider Dale Junior a good friend. I was blown away by the support and encouragement I received from everybody on the team at DEI, but most of all, I am grateful to Teresa Earnhardt. At any time, she could have sent me packing, because, believe me, there's never a shortage of talented drivers who would like to climb in a DEI car. But she is a classy lady and—at the most painful time of her life—she treated me as a valued friend and employee.

Stacker 2 Moves Up

Sponsors move the sport. They have for a long time and I'll tell you more about that a little later, but at this point in my career when Stacker 2 said they wanted to go to Cup, we were going to Cup.

All of us have nothing but respect for George deBidart and the job he did in building that Busch team, but it was clear that the resources weren't quite there for the Cup level, and Stacker 2 wanted to make an immediate impact. They'd certainly turned the racing world on its ear with a radical approach to weight-loss advertising, so there was no reason to think that they couldn't do the same in Cup.

Especially when it was revealed that we were going to Cup with Bill and Gail Davis. They are two of the nicest, lowest-key people in racing, letting on-track performance speak for them. I have to say I also looked forward to being Ward Burton's teammate.

But when we got on the track it was like a damned dog that couldn't get out of the mud. It's not like we ran really bad. It's just that we couldn't seem to hitch into gear and get where we needed to be. Part of the reason, I believe, is because of the changes made between 2002 and 2003.

During this period I got to do some racing outside NASCAR. In 2001 I finished second in the race, but in 2002 we won the Charter 250 at Bristol. And I told the team we didn't have any place left to climb on the ladder! *(© Jeff Sandt; Kenny Wallace Collection)*

I came to the team at the end of '02 and ran very well, I believe because I had Tommy Baldwin as the head honcho running the show there, Phillipe Lopez as my crew chief, and Chris Rice as my shock man. But going into the new season, they let Tommy go and moved Chris over to be crew chief on Scott Wimmer's Busch car. There was a lot of other reorganization at the time, too, and it proved yet again how critical it is to get the entire team firing on all cylinders.

We were good.

We weren't great.

If you have a bunch of good people, but you spread them out over several teams, you dilute the talent. And the mediocre results backed that up.

And before we could get ourselves sorted out, Bob Occhifinto, president of Stacker 2's parent company, came to us with the news that the company was facing a lot of challenges. Ephedra, an ingredient in some of their products, was being banned. State governments and individuals were lining up to file class-action lawsuits, and instead of spending more money on racing, Bob was looking at spending a lot of it on $500-an-hour lawyers.

The shake-up was that Stacker 2 would cut their support about in half. And that was a huge blow to the Cup effort, so it became clear that we would have to drop back to the Busch Series.

The good ol', life-saving Busch Series, yet again.

Okay, sometimes I understand why I don't get taken seriously. Who else at the Kansas race would take time during driver introductions to pose in Oz? *(Copyright Steven Rose, MMP Inc.; Kenny Wallace Collection)*

But, you know what? Chris Rice was going to remain as crew chief on the Busch car, as they moved Scott Wimmer up to Cup (and Ward out). So, we went from an also-ran in Cup to real competitors in Busch, and it wasn't all about money. It was about chemistry, too. Chris and I remain great friends, at least in part because we ran so strong. It was a good year and that's all there was to it. Even though we held our breath about sponsorship all year long, I'd already spent part of my career on life-support, so I was able to live in the moment. I knew that it was time to enjoy the good finishes, and not worry about tomorrow until tomorrow.

And I threw in a few Cup races driving for Michael Waltrip. He was trying to get some coverage for his sponsor Aaron's, and really, if you can't have fun going to the race track with Mikey, there's something seriously wrong with you.

I drove for Mikey Waltrip a little, too. We were fifth at Talladega—but then I got penalized for passing Sterling Marlin below the yellow line. But if NASCAR had looked a little closer at the tape they would have seen that other cars pushed me down below the line. *(© Steven Rose, MMP Inc.; Kenny Wallace Collection)*

Why Don't I Quit?

With Stacker struggling, we knew that we had to look for more help. At the end of 2004 we found it in Greg Pollex and ppc Racing. Greg had come into the sport in the 1990s with football quarterback Mark Rypien and Busch driver Chad Little, but in 2000 he formed his own team. And while they weren't swimming in Jacksons and Grants, they had outstanding support from Ford. Enough that our reduced Stacker 2 budget could get us competitive.

And that we were, with the additional help of AutoZone Auto Parts when Stacker finally had to call it—temporarily, at least—quits. We had a couple of really good seasons, so much so that after I battled Jeff Burton lap-after-lap at Darlington, Rusty called and said, "Damn, Herm, you looked good!"

You're always looking for your big brother's approval, so that was a real kick.

One of the biggest deals of that time was the Wallace Family Tribute 250 at Gateway International Raceway, just outside St. Louis. There have been very, very few races throughout Busch Series history that included a racer's name, and I believe we're the only family. Shop 'n Save grocery stores underwrote the deal, and it was fantastic. They had started out talking about it being for the brothers, but I told them they had to include our folks and our wives. Being a class operation, they did exactly that.

The local sports commission dedicated the day to Rusty, we had some grandstands dedicated in our family name, but—get this—it was also Kenny Wallace Day in nearby *Hermann,* Missouri!

They played a great DVD prior to the race on big screens in front of the largest crowd in the track's history. One of my teachers from high school came and kindly refrained from discussing my checkered educational career in any detail. But what I really remember is that when I

The whole team had a good time during the press conference to announce AutoZone's sponsorship of our Busch Series car. And it was a really good association. *(Jim Compton Photo)*

Wallace Family Tribute

When the Gateway International Raceway set up the Wallace Family Tribute in 2005, our family was very honored. Happily, Whelen Engineering had stepped in a few weeks before with needed sponsorship on my car. *(Both photos: Jim Compton Photo)*

During the Tribute, I couldn't help thinking about Tri-City Speedway just five miles down the road where, for a while, my dad was the king of the hill, and got this whole thing started. *(Rocky Rhodes Photo; Kenny Wallace Collection)*

looked at my parents I remembered all those nights just five miles down the road at Tri-City Speedway, where the Old Man of the Mountain, as the announcer called my dad, got it all started. Five miles away on Route 203, but how many thousands of miles to get there?

We'd had to take Stacker 2 off the car at the Chicagoland Speedway race two weeks prior, for legal reasons. But the Whelen company stepped in to make sure we could race that night.

And we didn't include the other Wallace "brother," Kenny Schrader. Kenny's career deserves attention and appreciation, but hell, they probably invited him, forcing him to turn it down in case the rest of the family left me at the track and he had to bring me home again.

I'm not sure how many people appreciate how much Missouri has meant to NASCAR racing, but here's a partial list—I'm in the Aaron's #00, that's Columbia, Missouri's Carl Edwards outside me, Valley Park's Ken Schrader in the #49, and my brother Mike in the #4. *(Jim Compton Photo)*

Last Gasp?

I have been asked why I don't quit Cup and Busch racing. Some observers have suggested—in sometimes cruel and crude terms—that I ought to stop because the odds for winning have pretty much passed me by. And that only proves to me that these so-called experts or fans don't have a clue of what drives drivers.

I'm not talking about just me either. I have no clue how people arrive at the idea that it's somehow more honorable to pick an arbitrary date and walk away from the very reason you get out of bed in the morning. Some guys can do it. Some guys can't. We've established which group I'm in, and nothing said by a yuppie who came to auto racing

Is there anything more beautiful than the ballet of a good pit crew performing a pit stop? *(ASP INC./Walter Arce)*

Kenny Schrader

There have been Schrader tales peppered through this book for a good reason: Ken Schrader is one of the most important people in my life. I can sum up his place by saying that if I found out he was upset with me over anything at all, I would be crushed. His opinion matters more than almost anyone's.

As children, we knew each other well because our dads raced at the same places and we hung out together, too, even though he's a little older than I am. But in our young adult years we kind of drifted apart as we tried to establish careers and families.

Somewhere along the line—and it happened gradually, I think—I took the blinders off and realized that not only did he share my love of our hometown, St. Louis, but that we'd often experienced similar joy—and frustrations—in racing. The good stuff was great, but the bad things just remind you that no matter what you do, you can't always control your future.

Personally, I consider Schrader one of the greatest drivers of all time. He's got the versatility to get in any kind of race car and get the absolute most of out it, whether it's a winner or a dog that'll run better than anybody expected. And I totally get the fact that he is obsessed with racing. He does the Nextel Cup thing because it pays a lot of bills—and yes, he does enjoy it, especially since he's teamed up with the legendary Wood Brothers group—but he lives for the dirt racing. Now that I've discovered how much fun it is, dirt racing has become yet another bond between us.

There's very little in life that I enjoy more than lights-out at I-55 Raceway, the 3/8-mile dirt track he co-owns with Ray Marler in Pevely, Missouri. It's just south of Arnold, and a very well-run facility. But, after all the fans have gotten their autographs, wished us well and headed for their cars and home, Kenny, our crews, friends and families wheel out the cooler, the benches and the racin' lies! Life gets no better than this.

Ken Schrader is truly my other brother. In fact, I can talk with him as I can with almost no one else in the world, and I respect his opinion about any matter we ever discuss. So, it follows that when I was offered a ride with a new start-up Nextel Cup team out of Denver, Colorado, I asked Kenny's thoughts.

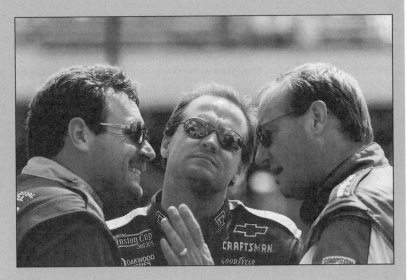

Robert Pressley (left) seems to be really into what Ken Schrader is saying, but I know it's about time to get out the shovel. Seriously, though, Kenny is one of the drivers to whom I've always looked up—and over—and in front of—and occasionally even behind. (Kenny Wallace Collection)

"Take the ride," he said.

"Why do you think I should do it? I'm sure it will be a struggle from the start and we'll probably miss some races."

"If you don't do good, nobody's going to think anything of it. Everybody knows how hard it is to get started in Cup racing," he told me.

"But if you do good, everybody will say, 'Hey, look there—Herm's doing a good job.'"

With a simple phone call Kenny put a good spin on something I wanted to do anyway. And if I've got his stamp of approval, hell, it doesn't matter what almost anybody else thinks.

After a NASCAR Night of Stars at Schrader's I-55 Raceway, the gang gets together for photos. We are (from left): David Reutimann, Schrader, Matt Kenseth, Martin Truex Jr., me, nephew Steve, Brendan Gaughn and Rick Crawford. We had a ball! (Joyce Standridge Photo)

webcasting 15 minutes ago is going to change my mind. Nor even a respected journalist—or the love of my life, who would really like for me to be home more often. I am so hopelessly, totally addicted to racing that I'll go on doing it until I can't do it any more.

In Kenny Schrader's autobiography, he noted that there was a guy who was offered Busch and Craftsman Truck rides when he was released from his Nextel Cup ride, but turned them down. In Kenny's words, that meant this guy wanted to be a Nextel Cup driver. All those of us who want to just

Times change. At one point, I was smiling in Victory Lane because I'd won, but you'll note from the other photo that seeing the torch passed to another generation brings just as big a grin. Since I have three girls who aren't interested in being drivers, I've taken a real interest in my nephew Steve and his first ever ARCA win in 2005 was reason to celebrate. *(Both photos: © Steven Rose, MMP Inc.; Kenny Wallace Collection)*

get in a race car and drive, even when there's no hope, even when you're talking street stocks at the local track—well, we're race car drivers.

I agree with Schrader, and I don't know why that makes us objects of occasional ridicule. A real race driver is going to drive anything and everything he possibly can that he feels is safe. You're going to look over the roll cage and the seat and how stuff is put together. You pass on the true shitboxes, but if you are willing to drive only equipment that you believe is capable of winning a race, that makes you a short-sighted fool. And here's why: A lot of the *can't-win* cars are owned and crewed by some of the best people who ever walked the earth, who love racing with all their hearts, and are thrilled just to be part of the circus. Why would anybody want to miss that?

So, I took a Cup ride with a great guy by the name of Barney Visser, who has no intention of leaving Denver, Colorado, for Mooresville, North Carolina, no matter how many times he's been told he will never win in Nextel Cup unless he does. Furniture Row is a terrific and successful company that wants to be part of the scene and has no illusions of where their place is in the grand scheme of things, especially as so many other teams and sponsors try to break in.

In 2006, I was going to be at the track anyway to do television. If I didn't make the show, well, I had to be there anyway. And if I did get to race—what a great bonus.

So, tell me again what's wrong with that?

13

Play Ball

ONE OF THE MOST valuable lessons I ever learned in auto racing came when I was about 14 or 15 years old. Rusty had just hooked up with Roger Penske, and I learned this: Most car owners in the big time are wealthy, but they don't bankroll their cars. That's why they are wealthy—they don't spend their own money. So, you see, the old joke about the best way to make a small fortune in racing is to start with a big one is true. And there are some car owners spending their own dime—I've driven for a few of them, in fact—but the truth is that people like Jack Roush, Rick Hendrick, Richard Childress, and some of the others have lasted for so long in significant part because they not only didn't spend their own money, they figured out how to deposit at least some of the sponsor money. Smart.

Beyond understanding that I needed sponsorship, I also learned that it's not just a matter of somebody giving me money either. When I was

Same team, different sponsorship, which gives a whole different look to a race car. But imagine a car without major sponsorship, and you might as well think of a disappearing car because that's what happens without the support. *(Both photos: Kenny Wallace Collection)*

a kid back in St. Louis, I thought that was the way it worked, but I found out before I ever started looking for help that in fact the most critical part of the equation is figuring out what I need to do for my sponsor after he writes the check.

Sometimes, it's pretty straightforward, especially in short track racing where barter is as much part of the bargain as outright assistance. For example, a sponsor might "give" me some race car parts, but in turn I buy a few more. He breaks even on the deal because I've bought some things, but I come out good on the deal because I'm buying at his cost. The difference (the stuff he gave me) is worked out by advertising on the side of my race car (which is tax-deductible for him) and maybe some personal appearances, too. It's pretty simple—and very effective. It's been working like that at the short tracks since the horseless carriage.

As you go up the scale, however, it gets progressively more complicated—and maybe a little more interesting, too. At the NASCAR level, it's big business, in fact. Sponsorship begins with the car owner negotiating the package for the team. This is the graphics and stickers you see all over the car and the cost can be as low as supplying parts (in return for fairly inconspicuous stickers) to $20,000,000 a year for a major sponsorship on one of the big teams. A lot of sponsors are paying out $10-12,000,000 a year and that's just to have their name on the car big enough to get referred to during the race by the announcers as, for example, the ABC Chevy or the XYZ Ford.

Beyond that, the sponsors normally produce commercials with direct tie-ins. The commercials cost $50,000-$250,000 to create, and then they will spend $25,000-$250,000 to place each spot during the pre-race, race and post-race broadcasts, depending on a lot of factors. Just after the green flag at Daytona, obviously, is one of those big-ticket times. Immediately after Jimmy Spencer and I spar on the pre-race show is a lot more affordable.

And then they pay the driver.

I'm not aware of any instance where a sponsor didn't work out a contract with the driver, but there have been times when it went sour during a contract period. See, all those millions paid to the team were for the *team*—the car owner, the employees, the paint job on the car, but the driver is a whole separate deal that's negotiated by the sponsor and the driver (or his representative).

Depending on the driver and his record, for a few thousand dollars to a few hundred thousand, you can get your company's name on the driver's uniform and mentioned when he thanks sponsors for helping him get on the track. For a million—or more—you get some serious loyalty. Bear in mind that the sponsor deal is totally separate from winnings. If you are as big as Dale Earnhardt Sr. was, you make many times more on collectibles and sponsorships than you ever do on the track. In fact, Senior is still one of the biggest moneymakers in auto racing because his memory continues to be strong with so many loyal fans.

The Phone Bill

Nowadays you can get a phone plan with unlimited long-distance calls, but back when I was trying to break into racing as a driver, every call counted. And even with the best plan I could get, I wanted to dig a foxhole and climb in every time the bill came. Kim totally understood, but sometimes I think she wanted to kill me. Or at least strangle me with the phone cord.

It wasn't unusual for the phone bill to be $600 a month, at a time when $600 was real money, and you had to talk for days to run up the bill that high. It was so much because I collected a lot of names and numbers when I was working for Rusty, and I had reached a point where I needed help to get my career off the ground. And here's how it would go:

"Hi, Phil *(or Sam or Mike or fill-in-the-name)*, this is Kenny Wallace."

"Hey, Kenny, good to hear from you! Haven't seen you for a while!"

"Good to talk to you, too. I'm doing good, but I wanna be a race car driver and I ain't got no money. Wantin' to know if there is any way you could help me out."

"Well, by gosh, I think we could do something."

Not all $600 worth of calls went that well, but you get the idea. And what it would be—the guy on the other end might agree to give me three tires, but I had to buy the fourth. Or I'd get a couple of shocks and buy the other two at cost. Stuff that like.

I'm not complaining one bit. They all did as much as they could, but when I hear NASCAR Cup guys whine about sponsors opting out, I can't help remembering back to the early days and how happy I was to get a couple of coil-over springs for free.

It's wild these days. You see a few of the evergreen sponsors like DuPont, Goodwrench and the beer companies, who've stayed in the game forever. But most sponsors come in, spend big bucks and get out in less than a half dozen years.

We can break your advertising budget in no time, I promise.

See all those stickers on my first ASA car? Well, there's hundreds of dollars in telephone bills run up getting the equipment those stickers represent. (Don Thies Photos; Kenny Wallace Collection)

This was really cool—I won at Richmond and in Victory Lane they asked about the dog's head on the hood. I got to announce that everybody needed to watch that space because something neat was coming. And that's how we introduced Red Dog as a sponsor. *(Kenny Wallace Collection)*

In putting together the package, you negotiate how many personal appearances you'll make, how often there will be a hospitality deal at a track where you'll visit with the sponsor's guests, whether you'll do commercials, and if you'll visit the company's facilities.

That's why it gets really interesting when a team splits up. For example, UPS felt their identity was so deeply connected to Dale Jarrett that they've gone with him to Toyota, rather than staying with the Robert Yates Racing team where they were for so many years.

And image is everything.

When Kurt Busch had a run-in with deputies during a traffic stop in Phoenix during the 2005 racing season, it made headlines—not least of which was because he was portrayed as being combative and difficult. The worst thing that can happen to any athlete or celebrity is to be quoted in the newspaper as saying, *"Do you know who I am?"*

That assumes that you think you're somebody special and should be treated that way. Worse, alcohol was suspected as part of the deal, and while Kurt tested at 0.017—which is way, way below the 0.08 legal limit—it kicked in that whole image thing again. He was innocent of drunk driving, but the perception hurt him. Next thing you know, Roush terminated the two races left on his contract, and Super Sub Kenny Wallace got to drive the car. (Which was a fabulously prepared ride, I might add.)

You see, there's a "morals" clause in our contracts. They may not be in movie stars' contracts any more (and considering what some of them do, maybe there should be), but the deal is pretty open to interpretation in our instance. We can be let go—even if we're innocent—just because the company feels we are reflecting poorly on them. Innocent until proven guilty works in a court of law, I believe, but in the court of public opinion, you're dead meat, and it's questionable whether you'll *ever* get a reprieve or pardon.

And it's totally changed how we live off the track, causing the birth

Behaving

There was a time when the best place to see a race car driver and get an autograph was at the hang-out bar. Every race track had one, and frankly, because it was time to let down your hair, guys were a lot more likely to pose for pictures and sign things since they weren't at "work."

But what happened was that if you didn't qualify good on Saturday, and the media reported back—and your sponsor saw the report that you'd been in the bar on Friday night—well, that became the reason you didn't run so well so it got to be a handy scapegoat.

There was some serious hell-raising that used to go on by a few guys, but, really, for the vast majority of guys it was just like it is for the factory worker who punches out and then heads to the corner tavern to have a beer and relax. Most of us just saw it as a little social time—not as an excuse to get crazy or misbehave. But as I've said, you have to think about image or they will find somebody else who will. If you embarrass the sponsor's company, you're done.

Everybody has become more circumspect in how they behave off the track. I don't think we've got any closet alcoholics in racing. It's not been a place for guys into drugs either. A couple of suspects have come and gone—but they've gone quickly. Too much on the line for that kind of stupidity. But if you like a nice cold beer after the races, you go to your motorhome.

Or, if you're really lucky like I am, your best friend owns his own dirt track and after they shoo everybody out and lock the gates, you, your friends and crew get to pop open a cold one and be as stupid as you want.

Which in our case, can be pretty stupid, but at least the cameras are put away.

Hanging out in the motorhome compound with my dad. I liked the party life when I was young but these days sharing laughs around a camp fire with Dad is as much fun as I'm looking forward to having. (Martha Nemechek Photo; Kenny Wallace Collection)

of the motorhome compound at the race track. It used to be that we'd all go raise hell at a local watering hole—and, boy, some of those stories are legendary—and the local cops would escort the racing crowd back to the hotel to sleep it off.

But nobody—I mean, nobody with a lick of sense—does that any more. No one is going to cover for you, and if you get caught it can cost you literally thousands, if not millions, of dollars. I don't know a race driver today who wants to raise hell that bad.

We sit around the campfire in the compound, drink responsibly, if at all, and guess what? We found out that the bench racing is just as much fun as it ever was. Alcohol might fuel the lies and they get a little bigger, but we're all still just as full of shit as ever when we get to re-telling race tales.

It's perfectly okay for us, it's great for the companies who have images to maintain, and we get to thwart the bubble-headed, bleached blonde who goes in front of the news camera and dishes the dirty laundry. Foiled. Have to look elsewhere.

Square D and Stacker 2

I have never minded being the spokesperson for my sponsors. Okay, let's be honest—I thoroughly enjoy it. Herman the German-Ham never met a camera he didn't like. And I've never been scared or intimidated by a microphone, but it's all genuine. I truly love to do this stuff, and there's nobody in racing who enjoys meeting fans and doing sponsor deals more than I do. I view it as a true bonus to being in racing.

The two sponsors with whom I've been most identified so far in my racing career also demonstrate the differences in what you may be called upon to do. Square D didn't have a product to sell as such, and Stacker 2 most definitely did.

Square D, going beyond the spokesperson thing, wisely created a great-looking, memorably designed race car. And then they figured out how to use me, which was visiting hospitality tents and going out to meet the companies to whom they supplied materials. Like DuPont, Square D is not selling a single identifiable item or line of things but a

Acknowledging the fans, because, really, where would we be without them? *(Jim Compton Photo)*

Even when you have great sponsors, occasionally you get special race sponsorships, as we did with the rock group Aerosmith. That got attention, I'll tell you. *(Kenny Wallace Collection)*

With Brad Whitford of Aerosmith (and that's Austin Petty, Kyle's son, over my shoulder). *(Kenny Wallace Collection)*

whole umbrella of products that the consumer may have no idea is part of what they're buying. They are a billion-dollar company bringing electricity into your home from the pole. They supply a lot of other materials you see (or don't see) and you never think, *hey—that's Square D.* It was my job to convince small electrical companies, or even larger firms that needed electrical products, to buy Square D. So, our approach was different in satisfying the needs they had, and I think we did it well. They stayed in racing, even after I left the team, and that's usually an indication that they felt they got value for their money.

Stacker 2 was a whole new ball game for me. For racing in general, come to think of it. This was an aggressive company that looked to our team to expand their market and spotlight specific products. If they wanted to promote energy and weight loss, why not use the most hyperactive driver in the sport?

And then we hit the airways.

Rusty used to tell me, "Dammit, Herman, I can't turn on the racing shows without seeing your ugly mug!"

But we changed the face of auto-racing-related television commercials, I think I can say without being immodest. There had been humor before—Budweiser and Miller, among other companies, have always marketed with a sense of fun —but nobody had ever utilized a driver like Stacker did with me. We were so far out there on the limb, there was no reason to go sawing on it. It was a high-wire act with no net.

It was also a break-through, and I think Stacker can take credit for more and more companies figuring out how to use drivers effectively,

One of the things you often do for your sponsor is appear in advertisements. Here crew people set up reflectors to assist with lighting for a photo shoot. *(Kenny Wallace Collection)*

whether it's the wonderfully deadpan series with Dale Jarrett and the Big Brown Truck or Darrell and Mikey Waltrip's truly inspired Aaron's ads. Even Matt Kenseth—who's certainly not as outrageous as some of us—was well-used in the Crown Royal responsible-driver ads. Jeff Burton has a silly grin when the Allstate Insurance lady asks about all those wrecks. And Denny Hamlin never says a word in the FedEx ads but you see his aggressive young guy persona playing out. Those are just a few of the examples of using people's personalities very well. It's so much more effective than just putting a guy in front of a camera to read copy.

Part of the success with our ads—and believe me, they were hugely successful for the company, as well as putting me on the map with NASCAR fans—was in never leaving them on too long. We shot a lot of commercials and we kept running gags through them that gave a sense of continuity. Bringing in other people was a good expansion for the idea, too. The Big Show from WWE Wrestling added a whole new dimension, but I firmly believe that getting Tony Stewart—and he did this as a favor without realizing what an impact it would have on everybody associated with the ads—was the key. Seeing silly ol' Herman trying to chase after Tony's golf cart and the beautiful girls who've ditched me for him—well, it's classic and I still hear about the ads.

We shot the commercials one or two a day, although we got so good at them that eventually we did three or four at a time. They cost the company something like $60,000 each to do, mostly because it takes a lot of effort that doesn't show, from renting lights to catering food for everybody to securing a place to shoot. We had a script, but we were always encouraged to feel comfortable with what we were doing, and it was a blast. A lot of the really outrageous stuff you saw came from just winging it.

Of course, it didn't last. I've been asked if I used the product, and the answer is no, but neither did I smoke Winston cigarettes during the

The commercials I did with Stacker 2 (Big Show from professional wrestling, who's on the hood of the car) were every bit as much fun as they appeared to be in the finished product. *(© Steven Rose, MMP Inc.; Kenny Wallace Collection)*

many years they sponsored our circuit. I still feel a strong sense of loyalty to those who helped us, even if I didn't personally utilize a product. Because of the on-going litigation that Stacker's parent company faces, I can't even comment much here—and you know how Herman loves to talk about everything—but I have no problem saying a big "thank-you" to the company and to its president, Robert Occhifinto. We had a ball for a while there.

My Other Lifetime Love

I've loved Kim since I was 17 years old, but I've loved baseball since I was in diapers. My mom picked me up from Khoury League games and took me to some of Dad's races while I was still wearing my baseball uniform.

A lot of racers don't care about other sports, or if they do it's football, but I am obsessed with baseball's drama. It's a thinking game, much more than simply reacting to what's happening. I get into the games so thoroughly that I can lose track of everything going on around me. Fortunately, Kim is a huge fan of baseball, too, so it's something we can share. And if you are into baseball, and you live or have lived around St. Louis, Missouri, it's impossible to be unaware of how completely the people there live and die for the Cardinals' success.

Me, too.

My relationship with them has changed from devoted fan to devoted participant during the past decade, and I couldn't be more

A real high point in my life—driving a race car and promoting my beloved St. Louis Cardinals at the same time. *(Kenny Wallace Collection)*

thrilled. When Gateway International Raceway was built near St. Louis, there was logic to cross-promotion that neither organization missed. Through Marty Hendin, who was then Promotions and Marketing Director and is now the Vice-President for Community Relations with the Cardinals, and the fine marketing staff at Gateway, the decision to use ol' Herman was a natural because there's nobody who is more devoted to: a) St. Louis, b) auto racing, and c) the Cardinals. It meant a little of my time, but absolutely no effort as far as I'm concerned.

In 2006, the Cardinals introduced a brand new Busch Stadium in downtown St. Louis. I was there opening day, closing day when they won the World Series, and a bunch of times in between. *(Joyce Standridge Photo)*

Doing this work meant that I got to meet some baseball heroes. Now, bear in mind that I don't get sweaty palms very often. Meeting Dale Earnhardt Sr.—yup, that was a Right Guard moment. A few others in racing, too, but generally—and probably because this is what I do for a living—I'm pretty cool meeting racers. But the day I got to go to the Cardinals' KMOX radio booth and meet Jack Buck, the Hall-of-Fame announcer, and his sidekick Mike Shannon, now primary announcer and a legend himself, I was almost beside myself.

Jack said, "Sit down, young man," pointing to his own chair.

His health was starting to fail by then and I felt really funny about sitting down while he was standing.

"Mr. Buck, I can't sit in your chair."

"Yes, you can," he insisted, so you do what you're told.

Mike Shannon interviewed me on the air, and it was so cool because here was a former baseball player, and *he really knew racing!* He was a fan and friend of early NASCAR star Tiny Lund, but, heck, he knew about Lake Hill Speedway, too!

I have found out over the years that a lot of baseball players are at least aware of—and some, like most of the current St. Louis Cardinals' pitching staff—are downright fans of racing. Seems like they really enjoy cars and have admiration for anybody who drives them well, just like I am in awe of anybody who can throw the curve ball for a strike.

Later, I got to meet Stan "The Man" Musial, a Hall-of-Famer who is a god in St. Louis, in part because of his skill but also because he's a wonderful person who has done so much in the community. I was decked out in Cardinal gear, and all I could say to him was, "Would you please sign my shirt, Mr. Musial?"

And he smiled in that warm and wonderful way that has charmed the daylights out of St. Louis for 50 years and did as I asked. He spelled my name "Kenney," adding an "e," and I was so thrilled that I was

One night I got to help call a game on KMOX radio with Cardinals' broadcasters Mike Shannon and Wayne Hagin, which was a huge blast since Shannon is a racing fan. And then I also got to meet actor and broadcaster Bob Uecker, too. *(Both photos: Jim Compton Photo)*

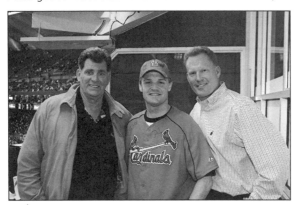

tempted to change my name because there was no way I was telling Mr. Musial that he'd got it wrong.

I have always been surprised when people were nervous around me or hesitated to ask for an autograph. I mean, I'm just Herman from Arnold. I know, because I live with that guy in the mirror every day, and there's no reason to be overly impressed. But when I got to meet some of the Cardinals, I was really nervous. And just as people are sometimes surprised by racers when they meet them, I was shocked when I met some of these ball players I'd been watching on television for years. Like, I had no idea that Scott Rolen is so tall. He's built so proportional that you can't sense his height and size on TV. Same deal as it is with race drivers, I think. And you find out interesting things about their backgrounds, too, like I discovered that centerfield star Jim Edmonds grew up in California two houses down from Robby Gordon—and I'd never had any idea!

Over time, I have become friends with several players. Former Cardinal Steve Kline is a wilder nut than I am so we were a natural. Relief pitcher Josh Hancock is a huge racing fan, so we've done some FOX Sports Midwest shows together and we talk when we can. And I'm really proud to number probably the biggest star in baseball—Albert Pujols—as a friend, too.

That has happened because Albert and his wife DeeDee formed the Pujols Family Foundation, which does wonderful work for other families with Down Syndrome children, and as part of our cross-promotional deal I got started going to their annual golf tournament. Believe it or not, there are people in the St. Louis area who pay big bucks to play golf with maybe the worst golfer to ever come out of the town—me. And then afterwards, there is an auction to raise more money.

(I can't golf worth a damn, but I can spend money.)

I bid $10,000 to spend time one-on-one playing catch and taking batting practice with Albert. DeeDee told me I had done enough just showing up to help with the tournament, but I really wanted that time

One of the great moments of my life. Truth is my first pitch landed in the dirt, but Steve Kline said I deserved a Mulligan so I got to do it again and then it was a strike. *(L, ML, and R: © Jim Herren Photography, Kenny Wallace Collection; MR: Jim Compton Photo)*

That's baseball MVP Albert Pujols third from left, and starstruck Kenny Wallace second from right. *(Kenny Wallace Collection)*

Walking the ramp to the field so I can take batting practice with Albert Pujols. Can you see my knees knocking with nerves? *(Phil Cavali Photo)*

to get to know Albert. He is a hero to me, not because he's such a great athlete but because of what he's done with his celebrity. He's an inspiration with all his work for a wide range of charities in the area and for the way he conducts himself with the fans.

And being a thoughtful guy, he also gave me a pair of outfielder So Taguchi's size 9 game shoes, and a pair of his own gloves. But—and, this is so cool—Jim Edmonds said, "No, his hands are too big for you. Take mine instead."

This is the kind of guy Albert is: The Cardinals won the National League title a couple of years ago, and while his teammates were going wild, popping champagne corks, Albert was helping the janitors tape plastic over the lockers. He's on a first-name basis with almost everybody who works at the ball park, I think because he remembers what it was like to be the poor immigrant kid from the Dominican Republic. Instead of dusting the past off his boots, he embraces it and every struggling kid with a dream.

WE WON!

I know this is an auto racing book, but I have to go on a little more about my Cardinals. First of all, they "sponsor" my short-track car, and I'll tell you about that later on. But I'm glad we didn't do this book any sooner, because I get to brag on my team: In the fall of 2006, the Cardinals won the World Series and it felt almost as good as winning the Nextel Cup would to me!

Bring out the marching band—the Cardinals won the World Series for the first time in over 20 years! *(Joyce Standridge Photo)*

Josh Hancock got us tickets for Game 4 of the World Series, which was scheduled for mid-week. I was in California at the time, but I called Barney Visser with Furniture Row, my racing sponsor, and told him that if he would send a jet to pick up Kim and me and fly us to St. Louis and back, I would do appearances for free in 2007.

He was silent for a few minutes and I thought I'd over-stepped the bounds too much. "You don't have to do it," I finally said a little nervously.

"No, I was just figuring out which plane to send," he said. "You do realize that we'll be *really* busy next year, don't you?"

(So if you saw me in 2007 at a Furniture Row store, I was working off my flight!)

The game got rained out. But, we were so happy to be in St. Louis where the atmosphere was like a Mardi Gras festival, that we didn't mind so much.

Sitting in the stands with another diehard Cardinals fan, Kim. *(Jim Compton Photo)*

Light Fingers and Paybacks

And then I stole two bottles of champagne marked "2006 World Series Champions," which I will keep until I die. There's not enough money in the world to buy them from me, and I knew that as I was slipping them inside my coat. I haven't stolen anything since childhood days when Monty and I took soda pop bottles off people's porches, but I guess my slippery-finger ways came in handy on this night.

As I was surfing the clubhouse, I noticed DeeDee Pujols by herself off to the side. So, I went over, and after we hugged, I reminded her that I'd bid on and won a day of golf with Albert.

"But you know what?" I told her. "I'm a lousy golfer, and I already have some pretty wonderful memories of time I've spent with him. So, instead of me taking up some more of Albert's time, I'm giving the day to you. The two of you spend that day together instead."

The look on her face was worth every cent I spent.

I admit it, I'm a thief. I took that champagne bottle from the locker room after the Cardinals clinched the World Series—and I'm not a bit sorry about it! (Joyce Standridge Photo)

And then the Cardinals won the next game, and Kim and I looked at each other. "Our tickets are actually good tomorrow night because of the rain-out," I said. *"We gotta go!"*

So, we made some calls and rented a plane for $8,000, out of St. Louis through a friend who's an executive at the FBO (fixed-base operation for planes) in nearby Chesterfield. It was worth every single penny.

I'm tight with money—just ask my daughters. They're always ragging me about being tight, but this was important to me. The last time the Cardinals won the Series was 1982, and I was only 19 years old. If I have to wait that long again I may be too old to go.

I told you about turning my body toward the race track when I was a kid in school. Well, I'm a little superstitious as you might have guessed, so during the game, if I had my hand on my cheek and the pitcher got a strike-out, I had to put my hand on my cheek until he didn't. And if I was standing on one foot and they got a run, I had to stand on that foot until they didn't. I was such a nervous wreck that I wasn't even myself—totally immersed in the game and internalizing what was going on. Some fans around us recognized me, but they couldn't believe how quiet I was. Well, when the final out happened, I went totally bananas. I was crazy. And the fans said, "Hey, THAT'S the Kenny Wallace we know!"

Afterwards, I went down to the clubhouse where I expected to encounter the Cardinals' security guards, just about all of whom I know from being there in the past. But the post-season is run by Major League Baseball and it's a whole different set of people. And a guy—I think he had a corn cob up his ass—told me they weren't even letting family members in, so Kenny Wallace sure as hell wasn't going in.

So, I did what any resourceful fan would do—the second that guy turned his back I slipped into the foyer, where I saw one of the guards I did know. And after he and I embraced each other and jumped up and down like a couple of girls, he let me in the clubhouse.

High fives, pumping fists, just having a wonderful time being there, and I'll never forget it for a minute. It was incredible, and I have to thank Josh for the tickets or it would never have happened.

I live for racing. I live to race. But carving out a little time for my Cardinals reminds me that there's more to life, and along with my family, there's a reason Herman always looks so happy when you see me on television.

And you'll be seeing me on television for a while longer, probably still wearing my Cardinals jersey.

14

Smile, You're on Candid Camera

WHEN I WAS a kid I drove everybody around me freakin' nuts with my running commentaries.

"Hey, it's 72 degrees at 3:09," I'd boom out in my radio voice. "And now here's Conway Twitty and Loretta Lynn with your number one hit of the week!"

Shut up, Herman, somebody would holler.

So, I would change the "dial" and they'd be forced to listen to, "Ladies and gentlemen, Rusty Wallace is coming out of turn four, side-by-side with Richie Evans, and they're 202 miles an hour as they come to the stripe *with two laps to go!*"

I used to drive everybody crazy with my radio re-winds, including a "broadcast" of the fantastic race Rusty won over Richie Evans (#61) at Talladega. And they really were running 200 mph. *(Judy Wallace Collection)*

But, honestly—and I swear on Joe Buck's golden pipes—I never really thought anything about a radio or television career. It was just that I needed to focus my energy and I'd learned a lot by going up to the announcer's stand at Tri-City and Lake Hill Speedways. The announcer at the time was Davey Lee, a professional DJ for WIL radio in St. Louis. I got the biggest kick out of him sometimes putting the microphone to his Adam's apple when he was talking, and it came out the same as it did from his mouth!

I guess I absorbed more than I realized, although I haven't felt the need to repeat Davey's trick with the mike. I do know that many years of listening to Jack Buck and Mike Shannon call baseball games was a strong influence—not in terms of how I talk on-air because they were pretty sane in their approach—but in thinking about what's going on around me in a way that can be expressed to the listener. By the time, in 1994, that I was asked to try an on-air gig, I was used to the "voices" in my head guiding how I expressed myself.

That year I didn't have a Cup ride, and when Patti Wheeler (Humpy's daughter, who has been a real power in her own right with auto racing television development) called to ask if I would consider being a color commentator on TNN with Mike Joy and Buddy Baker, I decided it was a good way to keep my name in front of the car owners.

Before I started, I sought out Benny Parsons for advice. I still think no one has ever done a better job at it. And Benny, bless his heart, was patient and instructive.

The best advice he gave me was, "Remember that you have to talk about what's on the screen, not what you can see out the announcing booth window at the track."

Makes perfect sense. If you see something going on that's not on the screen and talk about it, you just frustrate the viewer. I'll bet every reader who's also watched a race has, at some time, yelled at the screen because the commentators have alerted you to a wreck or a pass or something of interest before the director switched to the camera that's following that. It's a guaranteed way, as a commentator, to get the behind-the-scenes people unhappy with you, too, because you just called attention to the fact that they aren't on top of what's happening.

It's not because they WANT to be a beat behind. It's because they're watching 43 drivers, the pit area and the grandstand, using a bunch of cameras and it would be just flat impossible to always anticipate what's going to happen in an unscripted sport where there's not a ball or something that's going to be the focus of everybody's attention. You may think you see a couple of guys rubbing together and one of them is going to end up in the fence, but most of the time stuff just happens. I'm always amazed when they catch as much as they do for replay, much less things that get caught live.

That early television effort was very well received. It was nice that so many racing fans came up to me and told me what a good job I was

One of the early jobs I had for SPEED was occasionally filling in on *Inside Nextel Cup.* This is (left to right) Alan Bestwick, me, my brother Mike, Johnny Benson and Mikey Waltrip. *(Jim Compton Photo)*

doing, but I have to admit that it was frustrating at times, too, mostly when people would say, "You ought to quit racing and do television full-time."

That's such a slap in the face to a racer. It's one of those things, you can think it but please don't say it. The love of my professional life is driving a race car. Announcing is like an affair—like I'm cheating on the driving.

If you don't understand that, it's okay. I know there's at least a half-dozen people in this world who totally get that. Their names are Kyle Petty, Buddy Baker, Darrell Waltrip, Wally Dallenbach, Ken Schrader, and Jimmy Spencer. Regardless of age, time since they last sat in a race car, accomplishments, and appreciation for what television has done for them, every one of them would hang up their microphone in a split second if Jack Roush called and said, "Hey, come drive one of my cars."

I mean, they wouldn't even have to think about it. It wouldn't matter how they did, either. Everybody wants to win, and we all have at some level or other, but it's just the seat time that matters. Driving a race car gives us something that nothing else in life can. Even families, who are more important than racing, still can't quite plug that hole in our hearts where racing wormed in and took over.

So, I went back to racing and accomplished a few things. But television coverage of NASCAR went wild a few years ago, with huge bidding wars for the rights, and the whole deal went critical mass. The stakes got a whole lot higher when FOX got in the picture.

And it meant something to me, too.

Are You Freakin' Nuts, Herman???

At times when she or someone else in the industry has needed a commentator, Patti Wheeler remembered me. She was one of the ground-breaking producers of auto racing on television, particularly cable coverage with racing news shows and documentaries. So, it's really Patti I have to thank when the telephone rang and it was Ed Goren, president and executive producer of FOX Sports.

He offered me a job, even though I was just 36 years old and still wanting to drive race cars. Ed pointed out that Howie Long was in his prime when he walked away from football to become one of the most famous commentators in all of sports—even more famous than he was as an All-Pro player.

It was a good point.

Mentioning that the job would pay $600,000 a year for 16 races, and that there would be additional opportunities to add to that wasn't bad either. (And I'll point out that I have no idea of what current color commentators make—it may be considerably more or less, but that is what I was originally offered.) Everybody has a price. I'll admit to you—with three girls to raise and potentially educate—we were in my ball park.

But you know the cliché where a little-bitty devil and an angel sit on opposite shoulders of a person who's trying to make an important decision? Well, I didn't have a devil and an angel, but there were two tiny Hermans riding around on me for a while.

"Hey, moron, you gotta take it," one said. "You may never get another chance to break into national television if you turn it down. You know you're pretty good at it, and it's not a growth industry. You have any idea of how many races you'll have to win to make that kind of money?"

"Dummy, your racing career isn't over," said the other. "There are still some opportunities out there, and you know how much you are just

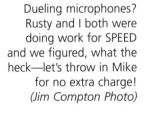

Dueling microphones? Rusty and I both were doing work for SPEED and we figured, what the heck—let's throw in Mike for no extra charge!
(*Jim Compton Photo*)

dying to win a single Cup race? If you do television at that level, they aren't going to want to let you off to drive."

Wally Dallenbach knows exactly what I'm talking about, and he took the TV job with NBC, but you can see it in his face. Wondering what he might have been able to do if he'd gone on racing a while longer.

If you're not Wally—or some other true race driver—you may wonder why it was even a toss-up. Let's face it—I hadn't forgotten what it was like to be Herman from Arnold, stealing empty soda pop bottles for spending change. I'd reached the point in life where racing was adding a few zeroes on that $10 I'd known as a kid, but I was nowhere near to the wealth of my oldest brother and several of my closest friends.

But, man, we're talking about getting behind a steering wheel versus a microphone. And it was such a huge decision that I grabbed my St. Louis pals Jerry Sifford and Bobby Mahoney and we went down to Springfield to talk to Larry Phillips.

Over lunch, I told Larry what the deal was. By this time, he was wracked with terminal cancer and suffering through treatment, but his mind was as sharp as ever.

"Well, you can't do that," he flatly declared. "You're a racer."

And the weight of the world lifted from my shoulders.

"Oh my God, thank you so much!" I told him, but he brushed aside my appreciation.

This was the first man I ever personally knew who made a living as a race driver, but he never got rich from it either. And facing his mortality, he wouldn't have changed anything. It took cancer to get him out of the race car, and nothing less. Certainly not a television gig.

I suspect I would have arrived at this decision anyway, but having Larry's blessing just put the stamp on it. And I still don't regret it one iota, even seeing how well Darrell Waltrip and Larry McReynolds have done at FOX. In fact, they're a gift to the racing community and I'm convinced it was meant to be this way.

And The Calendar Marched On . . .

A few years later, however, I was sitting in the airport at Chicago. In a hectic life, there's not a lot of time to sit and contemplate, and my days of driving the race-car hauler at 3 A.M. as thinking time are long past.

I owe my family, I thought. *I haven't done badly at all, and we won't starve this winter, but the prospects of getting and keeping a winning ride are slipping beyond my grasp because I'm getting older. So, what can I do?*

I can repair vacuum cleaners. I'm good at it, too. But I think Uncle Gary is tired of us dropping in and out of the shop. Dirt Devil isn't my calling, I decided.

I can drive a truck. I could probably get a CDL license pretty easily, but I went past 1,000,000 miles a while back, so I don't think that's my calling either.

I can fix vehicles. My dad is real proud of the fact that Rusty, Mike and I all are "fixers," instead of "parts changers." But that's not the answer either.

If I get a television job, however, I can keep my foot in the door in racing. I can transition into a career that I know I can do pretty well and not have to turn my back on racing either.

So, I got out the cell phone and called Ed Goren. And, wonder of wonders, he took the call. I told him what I was thinking—that it was time for me to take television seriously—and he not only listened, he was willing to work me into a deal.

As I was talking with him, my gut was falling to the floor because it meant that I was acknowledging that my NASCAR career was winding down with goals unmet. That was a bitter pill to swallow, even though I am always going to be very, very grateful to Ed and everybody at FOX and SPEED for all they've done.

Now, bear in mind that not everybody thought this was a good idea. My webmaster, Dale Johnson, thought the world might not be ready for large doses of Herman the German. And, yes, I have what's known as a pretty strong personality, but I was hurt that Dale felt that way.

"That's the deal," he pointed out. "You can get your feelings hurt a lot when you're a highly visible personality."

Well, I don't like people stomping on my feelings any more than anyone else does, but I can live with it. Like Mark Martin says about not winning a championship: "I'll still get up in the morning. I'm not going to curl up and die."

We started with a studio show, *NASCAR This Morning*, on Sunday SPEED, which is affiliated with FOX Sports. I liked it, and I got comfortable with the camera, too. But then some genius—and I truly mean that—figured out we needed to go to the track and feed off the crowd's enthusiasm.

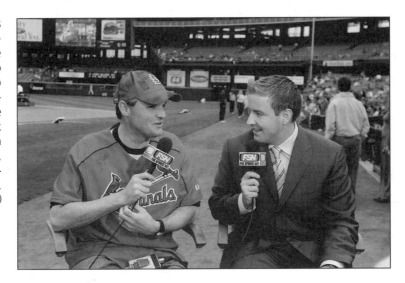

The folks at Fox Sports Midwest have done several documentary type shows on the Wallaces, so we're always glad to jump in and do a little commentary for them. I'm the only Wallace who can talk about the Cardinals with any authority, though, and here I am with announcer Dan McLaughlin. *(Jim Compton Photo)*

So then, before and after the races, SPEED has broadcast the wildest, woolliest, most fun racing shows ever. The whole team—in front of and behind the camera—have clicked. And in the process, we have grown to an average viewership of 3 million. For a little cable show, that's just incredible. If you're one of the viewers, may I say "thank you" for the support.

And keep watching, please.

Chemistry 101

Not everybody thought teaming up Jimmy Spencer and me was a good idea for *NASCAR RaceDay*. He's got a lot of ideas and I've got a lot of energy. I think there was some concern that we might overwhelm the mute button and take remotes across the country hostage. But I think there's several reasons why we have worked out so well.

One is John Roberts. What a great guy he is, and in an industry with monumental egos, John has his firmly in check. Beyond being the consummate pro, always prepared and able to control any situation, he's living out his life dream, too. There was a time not long ago that he wasn't even in the business, listening to races on Sunday afternoon while he cut the grass. So, he's just happy to be there, and I think that comes through.

Another positive is the behind-the-camera talent, starting with our director Chris "Muscles" Long. He is young, aggressive, and always coming up with ideas that really rock.

And, without a doubt, hiring Jimmy Spencer was truly inspired. Nobody messed with Mr. Excitement when he was on the race track, so they expected him to speak his mind. And, boy, does he. If he thinks something sucks, he pulls no punches, and you know it in exactly those terms.

In fact, all the decision-makers at SPEED have encouraged us to

Getting ready for the Cup pre-banquet telecast in New York: John Roberts, our producer Ted Laukitis, me, and Jimmy Spencer. *(Kenny Wallace Collection)*

Getting ready to go on-air, John, Jimmy and me. (Kenny Wallace Collection)

speak up. They're not looking for cheap shots with the sole purpose of muddying up the water and demanding attention, but we are not expected or told to toe the line either. To their credit, NASCAR never complains, even though I suspect there are times when they are biting their tongues. Drivers, car owners, sponsors, just about everybody associated with our racing, watch the shows and are willing participants, too.

Wendy Venturini and Bootie Barker have been added to the mix, and I think it's great. Both are well-prepared and bring totally different perspectives to what we do. That's critical to keeping the shows fresh and insightful.

Although the show is unscripted—*real* reality television, in fact—we actually plan what we do to a certain extent. We start with a conference call at 10 A.M. on Tuesdays with the producer, director and on-air people. We start throwing out ideas, and we are also asked about potential interviews. Sometimes the discussion degenerates into a laugh-fest, but, really, we get a lot done.

Then, at the track the day before the race I work with the crew in planning a little more. On race day we have a production meeting a couple of hours before we go on the air. We go through the entire show's timing guide and how we'll fill those few hours. For example, if I'm going to interview Mark Martin, they'll want to know something about what I'm going to ask. Maybe I plan to talk about turns three and four at this track, so production will go back and find some tape of Mark running through three and four. It's pretty cool, and it makes it look like we've got our act together, too.

But there's a tremendous amount of flexibility. I can change the questions I ask Mark if I feel like what I'm hearing during the interview needs to take us down another route. Or maybe something is happening that day in the garage area that changes the whole tone and focus of the broadcast. You just have to be able to jump in the saddle and ride in whatever direction it takes you.

I have no idea of what's going on that I'm trying to stoke the crowd, but it's *RaceDay* at Bristol in 2006. *(Kenny Wallace Collection)*

Then I settled down, so John Roberts, Jimmy Spencer and I try to do a thought-provoking show. *(Kenny Wallace Collection)*

This is possible, and it happens, because of the mutual respect our team has for one another. It's exactly the same thing that happens with racing teams. When everybody pulls together and appreciates each other's talents and what they bring to the party, you click, you probably win, and you certainly enjoy what you're doing.

Some announcers just have to be The One, and everybody on set is supposed to defer to them. That's not the case with John Roberts. He says what he needs to say, then defers to somebody else. And if Jimmy or I feel like we've gone on long enough about a topic, we bring the other into the discussion. Nobody hogs the camera, nobody even wants to, and that genuineness is one of our biggest assets.

Since we're not through when the broadcast switches over to the mega-networks, we're going to pay attention to the race itself. If I didn't make the race, first thing I have to do is deal with the depression that inevitably descends when the green flag falls, but it's a passing thing. I'll

Surprises

There's nothing like live television. Even with a five-second delay for the occasional *oops* word, there are times when stuff is happening that tests your professionalism.

For example, in October 2006, I was doing a live bit in Charlotte's Victory Lane, talking about how and why Kasey Kahne had won, when a girl walked up to the fence and took off her top.

Everybody freaked. The crew went wild, the fans went wilder, and it was chaos. But somehow, I kept talking about Kasey, and really I don't know how or why except that's what I was supposed to do.

I'd tell you her (missing) bra size, but Kim would kill me. I mean, I was the ultimate pro doing my job, but, hey, I'm not dead.

Early in the day prior to the race show, the whole gang poses for a photo together and then has a meeting to decide what we'll discuss on-air. *(Both photos: Kenny Wallace Collection)*

And, of course, we're always thoroughly serious. *(Kenny Wallace Collection)*

go over to the motorhome and watch the race on TV, have a bite to eat with Kim or my folks, talk with others in the compound and make some mental notes about what I'm seeing on the tube.

If, on the other hand, I've made the race, it makes for some pretty interesting discussions during *NASCAR Victory Lane* afterwards. John or Jimmy will ask what I saw from the track. Sometimes I've gotten a first-

The really great days are the ones when we have a good pre-race show, then I get to race, and we wrap it up at the end of the day with another good show. *(Kenny Wallace Collection)*

hand view of a particular action, but sometimes I don't have a clue what they're talking about because the deal occurred on the back stretch and I was over at the start-finish line when it went down. So, there's something to be said for being behind the wheel, but it's not critical to a good analysis. Understanding what you see through the windshield is great, but understanding what you see on the television screen is just as valuable, especially when you have the intelligence of John Roberts and the experience of Jimmy Spencer, adding their two cents.

Without a Picture

I also have my own radio show on KMOX, a 50,000-watt, clear channel radio station in St. Louis. Their line-up is pretty impressive, with lots of interesting shows, which is why it's not hard to figure out why they're Number One.

After the race, I've sweated off a few pounds and done wonders for my helmet-hair, so I pop into the SPEED trailer for a quick fix, then run to the set and greet some fans before we go back on-air for the post-race show. *(Kenny Wallace Collection)*

Pissing Off People

You simply cannot be a television commentator and never piss people off. I don't try to make anyone angry—I don't try to be controversial. I don't think it accomplishes anything positive, but on the other hand we've been coached by the powers at SPEED to be honest and forthright. They want John, Jimmy, Bootie, Wendy and me to speak our minds, and we've all taken that ball and run with it.

So when you do literally hundreds of unscripted hours on-air through a season, someplace along the line you're going to put your foot in it. For example, one day John Roberts made the observation that Tony Stewart was running very well (an understatement since Tony went on to win the championship that year), but why was another former champion, Bobby Labonte, struggling?

I said the first thing that popped into my brain. Usually, going with the spontaneous thought is not only honest, it tends to be accurate, too. But in this instance I maybe needed to have self-censored my choice of words. I said that Bobby's team wasn't as "smart" as Tony's. Even though I expanded on the thought and clarified what I meant, you get only about 30 seconds to say something complicated enough to require a half-hour to explain.

Bobby and his team weren't real happy with me for a while, and I totally understand. At least 99 percent of the people in the pit area watch the show, and you don't want to be shown up in any way in front of your peers.

But Bobby and I are good friends from way back so later on at a testing session he came up to me and said, "You were right. But it was just hard to hear."

And, really, I should have said it better because I wasn't dissing Bobby and his crew—I just wanted to make a point about how they weren't analyzing what was happening to them and then acting on that.

Jeez. Wish I'd said that at the time.

But they would probably still have been pissed, and I would still be using this example to explain how you can get it in the wringer without intending to.

I'm pumped, I'm ready—now let's just hope I don't piss off anybody. (Kenny Wallace Collection)

So, it was pretty cool when they asked me to host my own show. We're on from 7:00 P.M. to 8:00 P.M. on Friday nights, usually live. If NASCAR is racing on Friday night, we'll tape a couple of days earlier, and we're talking about possibly airing at another time so we can bring in more of the local racing element.

For a couple of years now I've had my own radio show on KMOX in St. Louis, a 50,000-watt, clear channel station. We're on the air for an hour every week and I get to interview a lot of heavy hitters in racing, but in this shot I'm the one being interviewed by the station's Ron Jacober. *(Kenny Wallace Collection)*

The show started with Mike Grimm, who had the concept and sold the station manager on the idea, but midway through 2006 Mike left the station for a good job in Minnesota. Greg Damon now does some local news and then they come to me. If I'm in St. Louis, I'm in the studio, but most Fridays I'm calling in from wherever we're racing. And there's two really great things that have come out of this experience: One, I get to invite some of NASCAR's heaviest hitters to be guests. Then I get to ask them the questions I would really like to ask—I have totally free rein to do what I want. Sometimes we are surprised by the response, and sometimes we break a little news on our show.

The other really cool aspect is that the show usually includes a call-in time. People listening in the 44 states where KMOX reaches call up and tell tales on me about when I was young, ask questions that I didn't think of for my guests, and generally I get to re-connect with fans one-on-one. That's something I really like.

It's gone so well that we're going to continue doing this, and I'm really happy. But there's still a surreal feel to it when I walk into the studio. You have to remember that when I was little Herman the German in Rolla and Arnold, I was listening to the mighty KMOX, and had anybody told me that someday I would have my own show with them, in spite of my young age I woulda asked what you were smoking.

With a Picture

I also have television to thank for introducing my entire family to racing fans. A little while back, Kim and the girls agreed to allow *NASCAR 360*, a cable show that politely invades a driver's life, to follow us around for a week. I think it was a good thing because in seeing us yelling at each other down the hallway, ironing clothes, doing all the things that normal people do every day, it de-mystified the world that NASCAR

Even though I've gotten very comfortable interviewing people, a big part of what I do as a NASCAR driver is being interviewed by other media. *(Jim Compton Photo)*

drivers live in. I'm sure that day-to-day for Jeff Gordon or Jimmie Johnson is different than what the average fan does, but many of us live and do things very much like the real-world fans. When they can identify with us, it creates a bond that's going to last.

Beyond that, my mug will be onscreen for a while longer. I'm early into a multi-year contract with SPEED that includes options for several years more. Rusty is going to be over on ABC/ESPN, too, so we just need to get Mike a show and then the Wallaces will take over your living room.

We're excited about doing the television, but that old cloud is still hanging over our heads, too. I will race as much as I can, but I can see how hard it's been for Rusty since hanging up his helmet. We were at New Hampshire in his first season as a retiree and he walked through the pits. "Shouldn't you have your driver's uniform on?" Jeff Gordon asked him, and Rusty said to me, "Dammit, Herman, I quit too soon. I could still beat three-quarters of these guys."

And he could.

I know that a little while back when I was at a reunion with a bunch of driver retirees—some of them getting up there in years, and I mean they had worn-out AARP cards—every single one of them still wanted to get in a race car.

I don't want to leave the wrong impression. I love doing the television and radio. I'm actually embarrassed to get paid for talking since basically it's what I'd say in a bar with my neighbors and pals, except I can't cuss. And, the support and encouragement I've gotten from the television folks from the very top on down has been nothing short of wonderful. It's a great group of people to be associated with.

Still, I'd give it up in the blink of an eye if I could drive Jeff Gordon's car for just one Sunday afternoon. And if that makes me an idiot in your eyes, go get the butterfly net, because I'd do it.

15

Define "Normal"

I'VE NOTICED THAT the words "normal" and "Kenny Wallace" don't always appear in the same sentence. But "normal" can become boring, and there are a lot of people who would give up their "normal" to trade places with me, so I feel very lucky, whatever word you want to attach to me.

I was going to tell you about a "normal" week in my life, until I realized there is no such thing. What happens fairly consistently is that I'm away from home five or six days a week, except for the months of December and January, when I can sometimes be found around the house three or four days at a time.

But as far as what I do, whether it's at home or on the road, my life varies so much it's impossible to set out a schedule. And interestingly, I find, my life is just continually getting more complicated. Having realized that it's time to expand beyond racing, I've become open to other opportunities, and that's what I'll tell you a little about here. A lot of the NASCAR drivers have schedules just as hectic, and some of them are doing similar activities so by telling you about my life, in a roundabout way I'm also telling you about other drivers' lives, too.

HELP!

There are things I do to make it possible to cram two weeks worth of work into one. Possibly the most important is having a business manager. Some drivers have several people on the payroll, but—having found myself unemployed a few times in my career—I resisted hiring anyone until recently. I just found it a horrible thought to have to tell someone I like, respect, and who's helped me, that I'm going to have to let them go because—well, hell—there's less to organize since I'm suddenly eligible to stand in line at the unemployment office. But I've got

My business manager, Allison Marshall, (on left), at Bristol in 2006 with Sherry Pollex, daughter of my then-Busch ride car owner Greg Pollex. *(Photo courtesy of Allison Marshall)*

so many irons in the fire now, especially with adding dirt-track racing, that I finally followed Kenny Schrader's advice and got help.

Allison Marshall is now my business manager. Not only does she make almost all my travel arrangements, she guides my schedule to help balance the need between work and play and private time, she talks to corporate people regarding their needs when I'm doing appearances, and she even makes sure that I get to drivers' meetings at the track on time. Considering how pulled I am in different directions at the track, she's got a tough job.

Even though we've worked together a fairly short time, I think it's a good fit. She is well-educated and well-spoken. Her father was a sprint car driver and she worked at the Texas Motor Speedway, so she really understands the racer's life. In fact, one day when I was talking about what happened to me in a Modified race, she finished my explanation by saying, "your tires sealed over."

Man. That's incredible. A lot of people inside racing don't even understand that, but Allison did so I knew then we were on to something.

Among her many duties is getting Kim and me where we need to go, and normally (there's that word again) we fly commercial planes. For the briefest of times when I drove for Andy Petree, I caved to the pressures and demands on my time, and I bought a plane. But a King Air 200 cost me $400,000 to run that year. There's definitely a convenience factor and hours saved by having your own plane, but you can fly JetBlue a hell of a lot of times for that much money. The ego thing of having your own plane just wasn't worth it. Yes, there are tax breaks that go with it, but in the end you can't come out ahead. If nothing else, when you sell the plane you end up giving Uncle Sam all that money back that you claimed on your return.

When we travel to and from the race tracks out of our home base near Charlotte, we are able to reserve seats on a Racing Logistics char-

For just a little while we owned our own plane, but there are so many good alternatives available these days that it just doesn't justify the $400,000 a year it cost. *(Kenny Wallace Collection)*

tered 757. These are nice-sized jets (so they don't react to turbulence as much as the small, personal planes do), and there's usually in-flight service, too. They also have larger, first-class type seats so we have both room and comfort. The cost is comparable to flying on a commercial carrier, but you get to board and de-plane at FBOs or away from the main gates at airports, significantly reducing the amount of time needed to travel, and they wait for you if the race runs late so you're not worried about trying to find another flight. This is a NASCAR-related deal that has really helped a lot of drivers, crew people and journalists reduce the hassle in getting to the races.

When I go to speaking engagements, Allison books me on regular flights, and I can't complain. First of all, I really like what I do, but I also don't have to travel around in my pick-up truck and sleep in rest stops. The only complaint, if I dare have one, is how much time is required.

What most people see is that you go in somewhere and you do a couple of hours for an appearance, whether it's simply signing autographs or giving speeches or doing a participation event. You might pick up a newspaper business section somewhere and read that so-and-so (a celebrity or athlete) gets—let's say—$10,000 for a two-hour deal, and think, wow—talk about raking it in! But, there's a whole lot more to it than just those two hours.

In addition to being away from family and home, these folks are investing in a lot more time than just the actual event. For example, let's say I just raced at Texas Motor Speedway, and even though I'd really like to go get a good night's sleep in my motorhome—or better yet, my bed at home—instead, I get on a plane and fly into San Francisco, getting to bed in a hotel room about 2 A.M. The wake-up call comes at 7 or 7:30 A.M., I maybe breakfast with people from the organization I'm visiting when, really, I could have used a couple more hours of sleep. But I have to keep on the move because I'm either going to ride with someone or use a rental car to drive out to Sears Point, another hour-and-a-half on the road.

Almost all public appearances involve autograph sessions, which is a good way to meet a lot of fans at once but a poor way to get to know anybody. Still, it's more tolerable with a friend like David Reutimann and family like Steve and Rusty. *(Jim Compton Photo)*

And sometimes you get asked to autograph some pretty interesting things—like a prosthetic leg. *(Jim Compton Photo)*

Then, I'll spend time talking with and entertaining people at a Bank of America fantasy camp. With any luck, another appearance has been piggy-backed on this one so I can cut out some travel time in the future. Whether I do one or several appearances, at some point I'm back at the airport looking at a five- or six-hour flight to Charlotte. Depending on the timing of flights, I may have to do another overnight before I can go home, and then I've gone from a couple of hours with my objective to a couple of days on the road.

Still seems like a good deal, *whatever* fee you get, doesn't it? Yeah, I totally agree, and that's why when I'm worn out and sitting at the airport, I just tip my head back, close my eyes and thank the Lord that my life has been interesting enough, and my personality unusual enough,

I have a few toys, including this 1963 Chevy truck, which is painted—ahem—purple. I just always wanted something from the year I was born. *(Kenny Wallace Collection)*

that people actually want me to come talk to them. Because I'm fully aware that the day will come when they won't—and I won't have to travel all over the country, but while I'm comfortably in my recliner at home, I also won't be earning anything for the retirement account.

Give Me the Microphone

Not long after I started doing speeches, former NASCAR champion and long-time television announcer Ned Jarrett asked if I'd ever taken a Dale Carnegie course.

I had no idea of what he was talking about.

No, I hadn't. Later, I found out that the company trains people in public speaking and how to not only be comfortable in front of people but also engaging at it. I guess being ignorant saved me the cost of the courses, and I know I'm lucky that the gift of gab seems to have come naturally.

These days I have several "accounts," meaning companies that have me come in and do pep talks for their employees fairly regularly. Or I visit hospitality tents at the race track. Or I do racing fantasy camps. Whatever a company needs. And since my television activities have increased, so have the number of companies who just call out of the blue and want to book me for a speech.

I'm going to let you in on a secret about that.

Sometimes, I get nervous.

Quit laughing.

Really, I do, because there are instances when I know that I'm going to be getting up in front of people who've never heard of Kenny Wallace, could care less about auto racing, think NASCAR is overrated, and came to the meeting only because their boss told them they had to. And I have to win them over.

Kim does a wonderful job of running my fan club—but sometimes she really wonders what I'm going to say next. *(Kenny Wallace Collection)*

Don't laugh—sometimes I get nervous before I speak to a group. But once I'm up there with a microphone, the nerves go away and normally I just have a blast. *(Kenny Wallace Collection)*

Or it's a group of very well-educated people—far, far beyond the Fox High-graduate Herman from Arnold. And maybe a few of them resent it that this goofball from a flyover state has earned more money than they can hope to. And I have to win them over.

Or there's people who wish I was a frequent race winner like Jeff Gordon or an icon like Dale Earnhardt Jr., instead of Kenny Wallace. Maybe they don't like the laugh. Maybe they think I talk too much on the TV shows. And I have to win them over.

So, what I do is tell myself, "Okay, Kenny, bottom-line: These are people who probably wear jeans every chance they can—just like you. And they want more time with their kids—just like you. And they probably have had a little wine to drink—just like you . . . *wish.*"

And when they put the microphone in my hand, it's like magic. The fear disappears, and—knock on wood—I've never had a gathering go bad on me. If they're less than thrilled to have me there, they laugh and applaud anyway. And hopefully go away feeling like it was worth their time.

And this is why I get invited to "speak" so often—a lot of people want to hear that damned laugh. *(All photos: Jim Compton Photos)*

Promotions

Every so often the phone rings and it's NASCAR, telling me they want me to do a personal appearance for them. As far as whether to do it or not, it's a no-brainer. You don't say "no."

That would be stupid on many different levels. Consider that without NASCAR and the huge marketing beast that's made it a household name and a sport to rival baseball and football for fans, we're just a bunch of hometown drivers trying to get attention. We need to never lose sight of the fact that every last one of us owes our place in the racing-world pecking order to NASCAR.

When you have a long-term relationship with a company in private industry, they may decide that beyond having you come in for speeches or similar events, they might want to use you in a promotion.

For example, KMOX radio did one in conjunc-tion with the Schnuck's grocery chain in the St. Louis area. The winner and his family spent an evening with me in the radio booth at the baseball park. They got to hang with Herman, but they also met Cardinals' radio announcer Mike Shannon.

I like, when I can, to do a little something extra for people, and in this case I got the chance. It turned out that it was a week in which Rusty was testing over at Gateway. So, I called him and asked him to come over.

The looks on that family's faces when the great Rusty Wallace walked into the booth was priceless! And when you get Rusty away from all the demands on him, he's a lot of fun to hang with, too.

I told him he couldn't drink any Miller Beer because this is a Budweiser-only stadium, but, to his credit, he stayed anyway.

When you're asked to do an appearance, whether it's with the media or in front of a group, you do it if NASCAR requests. (Jim Compton Photo)

A fan got to hang with me in the Cardinals' broadcast booth, but what you can't see is that my brother Rusty showed up and surprised the winner later on. (Jim Compton Photo)

Confession Is Good for the Soul?

I'm going to 'fess up here.

You know that I do commercials. Ever since Stacker 2 unleashed Herman on the world, I have ended up with at least a couple of commercials a year. But one I did in 2006 was an Academy Award-worthy job of acting on my part.

Here's the deal: I was tapped by SBG Board Games to work opposite Bobby Allison in an ad for their new NASCAR trivia game. So, after a race I flew to Montreal, Canada, and met up with Bobby and his wife Judy there, along with some people from the company, for a little socializing the night before.

Now, bear in mind that I come from the hometown of Anheuser-Busch, and that my brother has a long-time relationship with Miller Beer Company.

There's beer in my refrigerator.

But I'm not a big drinker. I've got too much going on all the time, I almost never drink for 24 hours before a race, and with my schedule, any plans to become an alcoholic are truly on hold. And over the years, even with my *out-there* personality, nobody's ever seen me get blitzed, even after the dirt races when time and opportunity present themselves.

But I got tanked that night. Not on purpose, I swear—it just happened. They just kept extending hospitality at every turn, and you don't want to be an Ugly American and turn them down. And while I normally don't blame other people for my shortcomings, may I just say—*those damned French-Canadians know how to party!* And I'm pointing fingers because they got the biggest kick out of my hangover the next day.

As we're going to the commercial shoot in a limo the following morning, Bobby and Judy tried not to sniggle and laugh when I made the driver stop the car so I could get out and take some deep gulps of air. And, between takes of the commercial, I had to go outside. I just prayed, *Dear Lord, let me get through this and I'll never drink again.*

At least not like that. I told Kim that's the sickest from alcohol I'd been since I was a totally stupid, under-age kid finding out I couldn't hold it nearly as well as I thought.

And one more thing about this commercial. I really, really hope you didn't notice this, but my hair was atrocious. I'm blowing the whistle on NASCAR Hair with this. You would be amazed at how many drivers, announcers, car owners, crew chiefs, and you-name-it, use hair-coloring products—and I'll be the first to step up and admit I'm in the group.

Hell, I'm 43 years old as this is written, and you tell me how many 40-ish guys you know who don't have gray hair—maybe quite a bit of gray. In a youth-obsessed sport like NASCAR Nextel Cup racing, it's one of the few things you have control over.

So, I'm *Just for Men Medium Brown*, if you're keeping track. The problem was that my daughter Brandy had purchased *Dark Brown*—and nobody noticed the box. And, if you go too dark, you just have to wash and wash and wash your hair to get rid of it, so when I went before the cameras in Montreal, not only was my head pounding inside *fool-fool, fool-fool,* like windshield wipers, but my hair looked like I was ready for the old-time, silent movies.

So, the next time you see that commercial, you'll know a little something about it that not everybody does.

And I wish I didn't.

My New Love

I've told you about loving baseball all my life, and loving Kim nearly all of it, but now there's a new player for my attention—dirt-track racing.

This is how critical I feel it is: I believe in my soul that I would never be a complete driver unless I ran dirt. I am running dirt-track races today because I need this to feel like a race driver.

My dirt career took a while to get started because I frankly didn't know where to start. *Buy a car,* you say, but if my asphalt start was retarded because I didn't race until I was in my 20s, here I was in my late 30s finally trying to get the horse before the cart. With guidance, I could hopefully cut down the learning curve a little, and believe me, having experience at Talladega will not help you master the fourth turn at I-55 Raceway.

Logically, the person to help is Dr. Dirt (Ken Schrader) but it took about two years of driving him crazy before Schrader finally gave in and plotted a dirt career for me. He got me hooked up with Dirt Works, a chassis-building company that's well known (and successful) in short track Modified racing.

At first, I sucked. I mean, I didn't wreck other people and I didn't tear up a lot on my car, but neither was I instantly fast and smooth. I spun out, and I *struggled* to get my car hooked up because it was all so foreign to me.

Not only my chosen brother but also my mentor—Dr. Dirt, Ken Schrader. *(Kenny Wallace Collection)*

Sliding on dirt can—in the right circumstances—be the fast way around, but honesty compels me to admit that I was too sideways at this point. I'm a dirt novice at Highland (IL) Speedway. I learned from this and every other mistake I've made so it was well worth it. *(Jim Compton Photo)*

And here was maybe the hardest part—I had to totally park my ego and put on blinders. Because when I went on the track, people would rush to the fence—not to see me race, but to see how bad I was going to wreck.

I had to endure a lot of embarrassment because I had one of the more public learning curves ever, and harassment because my old friends and acquaintances just couldn't quite contain themselves.

"Need some tie-rods tonight?" I'd hear, and I'm sure that guy was just teasing, but I'd grit my teeth and laugh along with him while wondering why he would think it was funny to put me down.

Fairly early in my dirt career, I went to I-55 and Schrader put me in his Late Model for the first time. There are a few differences between Modifieds and Late Models beyond the fact that the Mods don't have front fenders. The parts are a little less expensive and the cars are a little easier to work on. Steering is pretty quirky on a Mod, but that's good because if you can master the mod, then the bigger, heavier and more powerful Late Model becomes a lot easier to drive, too.

That night at Pevely, I asked Kenny, "If I don't get up to a transfer spot in the heat race, are you going to give me a promoter's provisional to run the A-Main feature?"

More than once, Kenny Schrader has allowed me to drive his Late Model, but I don't think he was wild about the idea at first. These days I have my own late model. *(Joyce Standridge Photo)*

Look carefully at my short-track helmet and you'll see all the pits in the paint scheme from rocks and crap that's been kicked up off the track by competitors' tires. The way to avoid this is to get out front and stay there. I'm working on that. *(Joyce Standridge Photo)*

He said no.

Okay, I thought, *this is a case of tough love.* He's right to want me to earn my way into the race, just like all the rest of the guys.

So, I went out there and ran my ass off. I was up over the dirt cushion, off the wall, and I didn't know where I needed to be on the track to be smooth enough and pass people. I missed the A-Main, and Kenny was true to his word—I didn't get to start it.

But I loved it. I loved every minute of wrestling that beast, and my own Modified beast, and banging wheels with all those other beasts. And, beyond being stubborn about learning to drive on dirt, I realized unbelievably fast how much this spoke to my soul. People were making fun of me, some telling me that I was just cruising for punishment, but you know what? I figured out that before it was all said and done, I'd get the last laugh in this deal.

Not everybody understands. Bear in mind that Kenny Schrader does a charity race at I-55 each summer, and Tony Stewart has begun a tradition at his Eldora Speedway in Ohio, too, where they bring in NASCAR stars to race. You can usually get guys to agree to come in—once. There's a handful that will come race any time they're asked, even though they are donating their time, because they just have so much fun. But there's a few who don't do it more than once because they're afraid of embarrassing themselves. Winning at Daytona or Bristol or Kansas does almost nothing to prepare you for controlling a dirt Modified through the turns. You get more knowledge from cutting doughnuts in an icy parking lot.

But I've had my ego slapped around by millionaire car owners and over-pressured crew chiefs and—most cuttingly—by fans on websites. If I never gave up after stuff like that, how am I going to react to not being able to do a clean slide job on Schrader at Pevely?

Damned right! I'm going to keep doing this until I can—and guess what? *Now, I can!*

I don't know exactly what the "last laugh" is, but I think there have been a few things that maybe point out I'm making progress. I'm at least to the "chuckle" stage.

Schrader sent his plane for me on Easter weekend 2006. I was running Busch at Nashville, and he had a special at his I-55 that night, but I got there so late that I had to tag onto the back of the B-Main race *(no favors to this point, remember).*

Before the race, Schrader came over and told me to shut off the motor, which I did. I flipped up my visor as Kenny squatted down by the car. "You gotta start at the back and I want you to be careful. Don't hurt yourself because I'm putting you in the A-Main, no matter where you finish."

"What?" I was startled. "How come you didn't put me in the A-Main a couple of years ago?"

"Because," he replied patiently, "at that time, you didn't know what you were doing."

Agreed, I winced silently. "So now you think I do?"

"Yeah," he nodded. "You do."

Other than my brothers and my dad, there's nobody else in the rac-

After a race at Schrader's I-55 on NASCAR Night of Stars, I'm demonstrating a slide job for Matt Kenseth, another born-on-asphalt driver just getting into the kicks of dirt racing. *(Joyce Standridge Photo)*

I'm not sure what kind of advice I was giving my nephew Steve but he humors me a lot. *(Jim Compton Photo)*

ing world whose opinion matters more to me, so you may infer from this conversation that I was walking on air. *Dr. Dirt thinks I'm doing okay.*

You know what? Having Kenny's stamp of approval made me feel better than I had at the race track for a long time. We all race for respect—or we should—and it made me very happy.

But it wasn't enough. I have to have self-respect, too. I can't just skate along, and while I wasn't going to do anything stupid—tear up myself or somebody else, if I could help it—I needed to prove Kenny's faith in me was right. So, from 12th starting spot, I raced my way through the field—didn't hit another soul—and *won* the thing! *I qualified for the A-Main on my own!*

The bonus was the ovation from the crowd. The same folks who'd shook their heads when I first tried dirt, who wondered if I had the *cojones* to stick it out, saw that my love for dirt was strong enough to overcome the odds, my own ignorance, and hang in there until I could actually control my car—and take it forward. The approval of the dirt-racing fans was overwhelming to me. There's been very few times in my racing career when I've felt better than I did when they handed me the checkered flag that night.

One of those few times came a few weeks later, again on dirt. I took my Modified over to K-C Raceway in Chillicothe, Ohio, and I won the A-Main. There were 92 cars on hand that night. I qualified fourth quick, finished third in the dash, and then won the feature.

I thought I'd won the Daytona 500.

When wins are hard to come by in a career, you find joy where you can. I've loved just about all of what's happened, no matter where I've finished, but it's all relative. As Dick Berggren has said in his magazine *Speedway Illustrated*, "It's damned hard to win a race at any track, anywhere in the country."

Amen.

From one of the greatest nights of my life—I out-ran 92 other drivers at Chillicothe, Ohio, for my first UMP Modified feature win. *(Kenny Wallace Collection)*

That's Jeff Kemp and Donnie Jumper in Victory Lane with me. I was walking on air and it's moments like this that keep you going through all the wrecks, blown engines and bad nights. Just ask any real racer. *(Kenny Wallace Collection)*

So, I had a beer, acted goofy for a little while, and savored the congratulations of my peers.

My peers.

Wow. I couldn't have considered myself in their category just a couple of years before, but now I really do consider myself a bonafide dirt track driver, and nothing in my career has been more satisfying. *As satisfying*, yes, *but more?* No, because I'm now competitive with guys who race for the passion of it, even though the glory is in a much smaller spotlight, and the purse won't put you on millionaire's row.

This is just fantastic, I thought as I drove down the road toward home afterwards. You can't beat the glow that goes with an A-Main feature win.

Until you remember that Schrader's won two or three hundred of these deals.

That brings you right back down to earth.

Hanging in the pits is one of the best parts of racing—you're with a bunch of like-minded people doing what you want to do and feel you have to do. *(Joyce Standridge Photo)*

16

Peering Into the (Cracked) Crystal Ball

CAN YOU HANDLE one more quote from Kenny Schrader? A lot of good stuff comes out of that guy. You may think he's just a funny dude, but, really, he's driven down the road a lot of miles, too, and he's spent some of that time reflecting on what happens. And it was Kenny who said, "This sport will tell you when it's time to leave."

He's right. It won't be a sportswriter, or an obnoxious, so-called fan, or even your own self. The sport will send you packing because either you can't do it anymore health-wise, or you're not as effective as a car owner needs, or there's somebody else more coveted than you are for the seat you occupy.

I'm very, very happy that I haven't reached that point yet.

I didn't write a book because I felt I had reached the end of my racing career. On the contrary, I'm just beginning to go good on the dirt, and that counts as "career" every bit as much as Cup and Busch racing, as far as I'm concerned. It won't make me rich, but it fulfills a significant need in me.

No, I wrote this book in part because I've had a lot happen over the past couple of decades—things that I think upcoming young racers could learn from. If I can inspire even one person of any age to not give up in the face of disappointment, then it will have been worth the many hours we spent putting this together. Racing fans, too. You don't have to be aiming for a racing career to want to understand what motivates us and what happens that doesn't make it onto the airwaves during the race.

Youngsters Building Careers

Auto racing is always in a state of transition as older drivers retire and younger ones come on the scene. There's always been a love of youth, but currently the Big Time particularly values those young faces to sell sponsors' products over older dudes' experience, even if it means wadded-up race cars.

So the perpetual questions about how to get into racing—meaning NASCAR Nextel Cup—are a little more intense than usual as people have to climb the ladder at a record pace. And, I have to answer honestly: I don't know.

I know how I got there. I know how Jeff Gordon got there. I know how Tony Stewart and Bobby Labonte got there. I have a pretty good idea of why Casey Atwood and Jason Leffler got there—and are gone already.

But, you know, it's all a matter of circumstances. The way to build a career is as individual as all the people who've done it—and haven't. And even though it means moving older guys out of the way, I'm glad that we're still seeing wide-eyed youngsters coming up and getting a shot.

When I get asked how to get into racing, it's always the dad who asks. Always. The kid just wants to race and trusts that it's going to happen, but Dad either understands that it's a huge commitment for the family—or he's got stars in his eyes and wants to live his life through the kid. I love meeting the former group and I really try to offer suggestions because I think they're looking for honest answers and guidance. That latter group have no idea of how transparent they are, either.

But here's the best advice I've ever heard: Just race. Just run anything and everything. Don't kid yourself that you need the best equipment; running mediocre or even bad stuff will make you more adaptive as a driver. As Kenny Schrader says, "Anybody can drive good stuff. It takes a real race driver to make the bad shit run."

Go into racing with your eyes wide open, watch all that goes on around you, and try to earn the older drivers' respect because they can help shorten your learning curve considerably if they take an interest in you. I know this first hand.

And don't think that running through people to get to the front is okay. A career is a long thing—or at least you hope it will be. It's far, far better to earn respect and affection for being a good guy than to be the winner everybody hates. Because when the history is written and memories are saved, that information will be included.

I remember Justin Allgaier in diapers—literally. Now he's one of the young kids who is driven by the need to race. Not so with my girls. That's my Brandy sitting on the Bandelero car we had for a little while, and you can see how she felt about the "pep" talk Dad has just given her. Mike's daughter Chrissy (behind Brandy) appears a little more willing to listen. (L: Joyce Standridge Photo; R: Kenny Wallace Collection)

NASCAR Racing

As this is written, I am driving the Furniture Row car in Nextel Cup, but not anything in the Busch Series. I had planned to run about 22 races in Busch in 2007, but Barney, the owner of the Cup car, asked—politely, but insistently—that I concentrate my efforts on just their car as they try to become more established on the highly competitive Cup circuit. The comparison he used was from his very successful furniture chain. "Kenny," he said, "everybody in my company specializes. For example, if you sell bedding, you don't go over and work in dining sets. You concentrate in one area so you can answer questions well. I'm afraid that if you try to do the combo, you are getting competing feedback from the cars."

I respectfully disagreed with him. I even pointed out that of the ten drivers in the 2006 Nextel Cup Chase, nine had also raced in Busch at least occasionally (and I'll bet the tenth—Jeff Gordon—ended up wishing he had because that feedback seems pretty valuable, at least as long as the cars are so similar). But Barney remained firm, and I respect his wishes.

However, don't ever write me off from Busch permanently. I was truly honored to be named the 2006 Most Popular Driver in BGN racing, for the third time in my career, so my ties are deep there.

I suspect the recent popularity in Busch comes not from on-track success as much as television exposure. I saw a change in how the fans

I was filling in for Kurt Busch in 2005 when I got to run side-by-side with Rusty during his very last Cup race. It was a special moment for both of us. *(Kenny Wallace Collection)*

reacted during driver introductions after Kim, the girls and I appeared on the cable show *NASCAR 360*. Seeing us as just normal, down-to-earth people gave fans the correct impression that we're a pretty accessible bunch. Fans, in general, act like they're running into an old friend when they meet me, and *I LOVE it*! If it seems like I'm interested in what they have to say, it's no act. I just find people fascinating. Everybody's got a story, and unless I'm late for an appearance or an appointment (I'm not going to be fined for being late to the drivers' meeting), I really like to hear what racing fans have to say.

I believe that NASCAR's run as the top dog in auto racing will continue long after I'm history, too. I worry—like just about everybody else—that it's gotten so big it's become the target for a lot of competing interests. Occasionally, I question a decision, but overall—and at least in part because there are so many people keeping track of what's going on—I feel that whenever a course correction is needed, it will happen.

I'm going to be fine when my NASCAR career ends, but I would like to see this huge company now worth billions of dollars, take a long hard look at the topic of retirement. I know there are a lot of people who look at racers as independent contractors and therefore responsible for themselves, and I know there are drivers who say, "Nobody puts a gun to our head to force us to drive," but it's about more than just the drivers.

Everybody who comes into this sport is driven by passion for it. And that sometimes blinds people to the years they spend doing this and not saving for the future. Every year that nothing goes into a retirement fund or a 401(k), or some kind of long-term savings, can push some people toward an old age of poverty. You can't buy groceries with only memories.

Guys like Jeff Gordon or Tony Stewart don't need the help. Or my brother Rusty, who tried to bring up the subject of crew members' retirement funds a few years ago but was met with resistance. And, I'm among those who won't need it either. After I was fired my from ride in 1993, my whole attitude toward money matured, so that upheaval in my life probably was a good thing because ever since I've been careful to save and invest instead of just spending.

But I think of other people who maybe didn't get out with as much. Like the Allison brothers, who were bricks in the wall that built NASCAR from a dusty little regional organization. Or Donnie Allison's son-in-law, Hut Stricklin, who was a journeyman driver for years but certainly didn't leave with a Brinks guard on each side of him.

What about Bud Moore? He was one of the greatest car owners in history, but he did it at a time when the purses and sponsorship were a drop in the bucket compared to today. The rich guys of today exist because of people like Bud, who built the giant.

And what about crew men? Some of the bigger teams have retirement plans, but there are a lot of guys pouring their hearts into racing without an eye on the distant goal.

It's hard to fault NASCAR in 90 percent of what they do, but I believe there's nothing wrong in sharing some of the wealth—not necessarily to ensure everybody leaves the sport rich, but to be sure that *60 Minutes* doesn't show up on their doorstep someday with tape of a former driver living in a cardboard box under the Interstate.

Remember? That was my biggest worry when I was not even 21 years old. I was afraid to marry Kim right away for fear of dragging her down to that level, too. And yet, ironically, that won't happen to me because of NASCAR.

Eating Dirt

I'm getting into Late Model racing more in 2007, maybe 15 or so races. I have driven Kenny Schrader's back-up car enough times to know that I'm going to love it, too. I'm going to run a C.J. Rayburn-built chassis, in part, because his cars are deceptively easy to dial in and get fast with.

That car, along with my Modified, will be sponsored by JEGS, one of the best parts-supply houses in the country. JEGS has long been associated with NHRA, particularly Pro Stock drag cars, but they provide equipment for the oval track crowd, too, and we think we can help them grow that side of the business.

A lot of people have asked what that will mean as far as the St. Louis Cardinals' sponsorship is concerned, and it will not change things with them. You see, the deal is not that they "sponsor" so much as we have a working agreement. If I had known how difficult it was going to be to make that happen—simply because we had to go through Major League Baseball for approval, rather than simply getting the Cardinals' okay—I might have thought twice. But, after I agreed to use some of their same suppliers for my collectibles, we got the deal together. And that's what it

These are the companies that help keep us on the race track. As long as I can continue to put together deals like this, I'll be rubbing wheels with Dr. Dirt. *(Joyce Standridge Photo)*

When we go to the short tracks, Kim either sets up a booth to sell collectibles or has her little mobile cart. And she has a great time talking with the fans, too. *(Joyce Standridge Photo)*

is—I have a license to use the Cardinals' logo on collectibles. They don't write me the big, fat check it's been rumored. Instead, Kim and her sister Kelly sell stuff from the Hermanator wagon at the tracks, and the money we make off that keeps us going.

We don't get rich. We don't even make a profit, but that's not the goal. We just want to go racing, and the stuff the girls sell allows us to buy parts and to hire Don Jumper to keep and maintain the car. Obviously, with my schedule, I can't do it, and having an old friend back in St. Louis (whose dad Ernie was a long-time car owner in the area, so the dirt knowledge is there) keeping things going for us just makes the whole deal a lot more fun.

I'm also going to jump into the track-owner arena in 2007. Schrader, along with long-time short-track promoter Bob Sargent and Dale Earnhardt Jr., own Paducah International Raceway in Kentucky. Schrader owns I-55 with his former sprint car owner Ray Marler and Ray's family. Tony Stewart bought Eldora Speedway in Ohio a few seasons ago. And

Kim and her sister Kelly in our collectibles booth. *(Joyce Standridge Photo)*

Kim and I were at Mighty Macon (IL) Speedway in 2006 for a race. In 2007, I am part owner of the track with several other drivers. *(Kenny Wallace Collection)*

now, Kenny, Tony, Bob and I have bought Macon Speedway in Macon, Illinois.

Mighty Macon, it's called, a little one-fifth-mile bullring built immediately after World War II and in continuous operation since. But, like a lot of small tracks, it's endured changes and challenges that threaten to end its 50-plus-year history. And we're a group who love racing's history.

We're not doing this totally as white hats riding to the rescue. We honestly believe we can make this a successful business or we wouldn't waste the time, but our group recognizes that if people in positions like ours don't do something, short-track racing may be doomed.

Now, let me be clear about this—I don't have illusions that I can rescue hobby racing. My ego isn't that big. But I want to be a force for good. I want to make sure that the guy who earns $45,000 a year isn't forced from racing because he can't afford the tractor-trailer to haul two complete cars worth $50,000 each to Mighty Macon and race for $1,000 to win. It's spending-out-of-control, and it's time we did something about it.

I don't doubt that it will take time. We may not even be successful, and whatever we do will be criticized based on whatever circumstances individuals are in, but we have to try.

We simply *have to try.*

This is the essence of being a race driver—you are hot, tired, the race didn't go quite like you wanted, but a little guy comes up and wants an autograph. And you don't think twice. *(Jim Compton Photo)*

And There's More to Life

I can't keep up with Schrader, and frankly, I don't even want to try. My race total in the coming years is going to be as high as I can make it, but I want to do some other things, too.

For starters, Kim and I are the force behind an annual cruise. I view it as a time to wind down and then start thinking about the coming year. I sort of see it as the dividing line between seasons.

It began as a deal with Rusty and Miller Brewing, but when they got out of it, I said, *"Hey! Wait a minute!* I wanna keep doing this!"

So, each December Kim and I (and often, our daughters, and a bunch of the rest of our extended family) board one of the Royal Caribbean ships and spend a week wandering around the sea. Through Simply Cruises in St. Louis, a pack of fans go with us, and we do more than shake a few hands and say "hi." I mean, I still get some head-clearing time to myself or with my lovely wife, but there's part of each day that we hang in the "office," a room that the cruise line sets aside where fans can mosey in and talk racing or whatever. We have drawings for prizes and a message board, too. Kim always ensures that there's a souvenir for everybody at dinner. It's always a great time.

I credit Kim for that. It's the same with our fan club. We have one of the most active in NASCAR, and that's because she and Brenda make sure it runs like clockwork. She also puts together one of the most fun events of the year in Loudon, and then again in Charlotte. It's a whole lot more than just a handshake and a photo op. We have a blast, and it's one of the few times of the year that I get to exercise my laugh—in overdrive—and I don't have to worry about who hears me or if they draw the wrong conclusion. Because, in this case, it's the right one—we are flat, having a ball!

During one of the cruises we had a photo taken of Kim and me with our parents. That's Charlie and Dee Poole on the left, and Judy and Russ on the right. *(Kenny Wallace Collection)*

This is Kim's favorite photo of the two of us, taken on one of the cruises. That smile can still knock me off my feet. *(Kenny Wallace Collection)*

I just had to share a photo of my girls (almost) grown up on the 2006 cruise. That's Brittany (who turned 16 a few days later), Brandy (18), and Brooke (20). No wonder I'm so proud. *(Kenny Wallace Collection)*

Charity work is also an important part of my life. I admire people like Jeff Gordon who have established a trust fund or a foundation to distribute support among various charities. Some foundations meet a singular, special need, too. Kyle and Pattie Petty may have been motivated to establish the Victory Junction Gang Camp as a memorial to their son, but it's beyond that. They're working on sainthood, at least in my book.

I have no single cause or charity. There are several that I'm interested in and donate time to helping, like the leukemia society because my uncle died from it. Autism is important, as is the Down Syndrome work done by the Pujols Foundation. But a particular interest that I've developed—thanks to AutoZone and the track at Memphis—is St. Jude's Hospital.

We have a very active fan club, thanks to Kim and her right-hand helper Brenda Hay. This is the office from which goodies are mailed, but also where we have a lot of memorabilia. This is part of the shop behind our house in North Carolina. *(Kenny Wallace Collection)*

Man, I go there and I see all these little guys who are jaundice yellow, or losing all their hair, or shriveling from diseases eating them up, and it rips my heart out. It makes me want to go straight to the bank and take out every dime I have, and give it to the hospital, *if it would just make a difference.*

Money matters, but so does time, especially if you are perceived as being "somebody." So I go, and being just a big kid myself, I get down on the floor with these kids. I don't care, I just have to hug them and love them. We have a good conversation—we act silly and play with toys—and I suspect I get far more out of it than they do.

And then I look up and I see the parents, often sitting by the bed, exhausted, their faces drawn in despair. And it's like a kick in the gut. I have three beautiful children who've never been really sick in their lives. How dare we take that for granted when these people are being devastated. Makes all those lost rides in NASCAR seem petty.

I had a lot of fun driving a Busch car sponsored by AutoZone, but what I hadn't expected from the relationship was an association with St. Jude's Hospital, which AutoZone supports as a charity of choice, and in which I've become very interested and involved. *(Phil Cavali Photo)*

We try to help other people as much as possible, whether it's just hanging with a little cancer survivor like Karson Barks, or going to a charity event with Dale Jarrett and Dale Earnhardt Sr. that was sponsored by Hasbro, or contributing a couple grand to a charity for Earl Baltes's last hat (complete with dirt on the brim). We know we've been blessed and we need to never forget that. *(L: Shari Stanfill Photo; C and R: Kenny Wallace Collection)*

The Finish Line

"Retirement" is relative. Once upon a time I thought Kim and I would get in the motorhome and just wander around the country when I quit racing. But, we're a real pair—neither one of us can just sit down and ride down the road. We both are busy—and wouldn't have it any other way. I will—hopefully—be more giving and thoughtful to Kim's needs at that point because she's more than earned it. I also hope and pray that our older years will be full of children and grandchildren, too. I can't imagine our lives without the extended family we have either. My father is battling cancer but doing well. But, as we found out when Kim's dad passed away in early 2007, sometimes you have to face the challenge of losing people you love. But when you have so many wonderful friends who are also like family, you know you'll meet the challenge.

For my 40th birthday, Kim got a lot of friends, family and fans to write letters to me, telling me what I meant to them—and then she compiled them into a book. It's the best gift I think I've ever received. *(Joyce Standridge Photo)*

We've made a bit of a progression during the 20 years we've lived in North Carolina. We started out in a single wide trailer when Brooke was tiny, then into a nice doublewide on property we bought, and finally we built our dream home (although the doublewide is still there—just in case things go bad somewhere along the line). We also have a condo in St. Louis, where we will probably retire someday. *(All photos: Kenny Wallace Collection)*

I suppose if you'd asked Herman the German years ago about reflecting on his life, that goofy kid would have blown you off. He was just trying to get on with things. But Inside Herman's World today, I recognize that the journey itself ought to be the goal. It's not like you work to some spot and then you stay frozen there. Like a permanent Victory Lane. Hell, no, they're chasing you out so they can clean up and get ready for next week's Victory Lane.

So, as we worked on this book, I caught myself re-visiting parts of my journey and realized how important it's all been. There were times when I felt wounded, but without those times, how would I have recognized how lucky and blessed I truly am? I mean, how can you know the highest of highs if you've never visited the lowest of lows? It's all relative.

I think this photo symbolizes the Wallace family's future in auto racing. My girls aren't going to drive, so I'm taking a pretty intense interest in Steve's career. This is how it's becoming for us as Steve moves to the forefront and Rusty is more in the background. *(Kenny Wallace Collection)*

And then there's the fact that you count blessings when you've got somebody to share it all with. Somebody once asked me, "Do you know why people marry?"

And, of course, being Herman from Arnold and pretty limited in my education to that point, I answered, "No, why do they?"

"So that person can witness your journey."

Well, my life has been like a heart monitor—up and down, up and down, and yet I wouldn't trade places with anybody in the world, if for no other reason than that Kim's been the person standing by with the paddles to zap me back to life. I would like to have tempered some of the pain, and I would like to have savored some of the triumphs a little more if I had only known how hard they would be to come by. I hope I am not done adding a few more achievements before we put the period on my life, but whatever happens, nobody can take away what's already happened.

And so I'd like to end this with something I recall my old friend, Dale Earnhardt Sr., once saying to me. I think I was blabbing away, telling him about all these plans I had and how I was going to do this or do that.

And Dale just shook his head and said, "Don't tell me what you're going to do. Tell me what you've done."

I do a bit of celebrating as Donnie Jumper, Jeff Kemp and Rich Steyh look on. This is how we started the 2007 racing season—in Victory Lane at Volusia County Speedway in Florida—and it's how we hope to spend a lot of time at the dirt tracks in the future. But even if we don't, you can count on lots of smiles and laughter from our team because there's nothing in the world more fun than goin' racin'! *(Dave Shank Photo)*

Index